RACISM AND EDUCATION

MODERN EDUCATIONAL THOUGHT
Series Editor: Professor Andy Hargreaves,
            Ontario Institute for Studies in Education

This important new series contains some of the very best of modern educational thought that will stimulate interest and controversy among teachers and educationalists alike.

It brings together writers of distinction and originality within educational studies who have made significant contributions to policy and practice. The writers are all scholars of international standing who are recognized authorities in their own particular field and who are still actively researching and advancing knowledge in that field.

The series represents some of their best and more distinctive writing as a set of provocative, interrelated essays addressing a specific theme of contemporary importance. A unique feature of the series is that each collection includes a critical introduction to the author's work written by another influential figure in the field.

Current titles:

Roger Dale: *The State and Education Policy*
Michael G. Fullan: *Successful School Improvement*
Jane Gaskell: *Gender Matters from School to Work*
Andy Hargreaves: *Curriculum and Assessment Reform*
Martyn Hammersley: *Classroom Ethnography*
Jean Ruddock: *Innovation and Change*
Barry Troyna: *Racism and Education*

Racism and Education
Research Perspectives

BARRY TROYNA

OPEN UNIVERSITY PRESS
Buckingham · Philadelphia

Open University Press
Celtic Court
22 Ballmoor
Buckingham
MK18 1XW

and
1900 Frost Road, Suite 101
Bristol, PA 19007, USA

First Published 1993

A catalogue record of this book is available from the British Library

0 335 15778 5 (Paperback)   0 335 15779 3 (Hardback)

A Library of Congress catalog number is available

Typeset by Inforum, Rowlands Castle, Hants
Printed in Great Britain by St Edmundsbury Press Ltd, Bury St Edmunds, Suffolk

Contents

Preface

So why, I've often been asked, have I committed my work to 'race'? Surely it's not an area in which white males should be involved; those who are, or have been, find themselves in a no-win situation. Researchers who 'dabble' in the area and then leave to explore other substantive issues are often accused of lacking commitment; those who stay are said to be opportunists and careerists. My answer to those critics is spelt out in some detail in Chapter 6 where, following Alvin Gouldner, Bruce Carrington and I argue that values, not factions, should be the pre-eminent concern in the conception, execution and dissemination of research.

A question which I'm rarely asked but which is equally tantalizing is: why education? After all, my experiences of school have always been less than gratifying. For the first three years, as a pupil at Tottenham Grammar School in North London, I experienced at first hand the offensive processes associated with rigidly streamed educational institutions. Following that, I found myself caught up in the disarray caused by the unplanned transition to comprehensive education: in this case, the 'unholy alliance' between the Grammar School and, sited three miles away, the all-male Secondary School. For the remaining time, at the 'Somerset Comprehensive School', I witnessed my (former Grammar School) teachers dismissing the value and contribution of the ex-Secondary School pupils and deprecating the onset of comprehensivization. They tried as hard as possible to retain the ethos, academic standards and regime associated with the Grammar School tradition. Routinely, they refused to confer status on the three things that I (and a number of my classmates) were good at: playing football (the Grammar School had cherished its rugby teams); playing truant; and when I was at school, wishing I was somewhere else, playing football! The result: four 0 levels, at the third time of asking, and two bare passes at A level.

It was little better as a student teacher. The marginal status accorded to student teachers by staff in teaching practice schools made life difficult. The problem was exacerbated by staff at the college. On the whole, progressive forms of History and English teaching were discouraged because they were at odds with 'what we do here'. I remember vividly, for example, being told that I couldn't write a critical appraisal of Paul Simon's lyrics for an assignment on contemporary poets because his work 'didn't fit the criterion'. In retrospect, it sounds trivial; at the time it spoke volumes about the archaic and anachronistic stance of the English Department. It was certainly too much for me to take and prompted my decision to leave the course and concentrate on History.

As a teacher in a comprehensive school I found the gap between rhetoric and reality difficult to tolerate. I accepted the post because of the school's ostensible commitment to community education. But that commitment was rarely adhered to by the senior management of the school. So, after numerous disagreements over the school's priorities, I left and began postgraduate research at the Centre for Mass Communications Research at Leicester University. I was determined, however, to return to teaching on the completion of my thesis and provide my students with more enlightened views on how to realize social justice principles in and through education.

Now, over 15 years later, as a senior lecturer in a university Department of Education and chair of governors at a community primary school in a multiracial area of Coventry, I find that what takes place in schools is heavily circumscribed by a range of 'regressive educational offensives', to use Stuart Hall's phrase (1983). It is dispiriting, to say the least, to witness the strains of teaching and learning in an underresourced, undervalued, often demonized educational system.

The intellectual journey which has accompanied this personal voyage has been neither smooth nor linear. I remember presenting a paper at the Centre for Race and Ethnic Studies at the University of Amsterdam in March 1987, where Professor Chris Mullard introduced me to the audience. He told the assembled group that my work had undergone a series of 'intellectual somersaults'. Perhaps he's not far off the mark. In the 1970s, as a (relatively) young postgraduate student interested in the cultural politics of black youth, I completed research on the relationship between reggae, Rastafari and black youth in Britain. At the time, I was completely seduced by the ideology of multicultural education and believed in the empowering potential of my research. I was involved heavily in the local branch of the National Association for Multiracial Education (NAME), and my position on the editorial committee of the NAME's journal, *Multiracial Education*, was testimony to those convictions.

By the 1980s, the misguided assumptions of my 'empowering' study of black youth had been laid bare by the Centre for Contemporary Cultural Studies in the book, *The Empire Strikes Back* (CCCS, 1982). It was a salutary experience. By then, however, I had become disillusioned with multicultural education and the erroneous base on which it had been erected. My research on local education authority (LEA) policies and school practices in multicultural education, based at the ESRC Research Unit on Ethnic Relations (later the Centre for Research in Ethnic Relations), confirmed the cynical and intellectually dubious properties of multiculturalism. Throughout the 1980s I committed most of my intellectual efforts to a critique of multicultural education, the understandings of 'black underachievement' which provided part of the *raison d'être* for this ideology, and committees such as the one headed by Lord Swann which continued to revere cultural pluralist ideals. But this iconoclastic approach (as my friend, Martyn Denscombe, once described it) did not blind me to some of the weaknesses in nascent antiracist approaches in education. Indeed, I was especially frustrated by their failure to engage with schools and colleges in predominantly white contexts. My brief period as Reader in Education at Sunderland Polytechnic in the mid to late 1980s provided the opportunity to develop theoretical and empirical work in this geographical setting.

It is my work in the 1980s and early 1990s which is highlighted in this volume. Although it focuses on the British context, it articulates with issues which transcend the national 'race' and education agenda. In this respect, I have gained enormously from researching and teaching in the United States, Australia, New Zealand, the Netherlands and Canada. Part 1 contains four chapters which cover my interrogation of national and local state policies on racial equality and the attempts to infuse these into the routine practices and procedures of schools. They consider the deracialization and racialization processes in the formulation of education policies and the various barriers to change operating in schools. They revise and update work which either explicitly or implicitly draws on my collaborations with Jenny Williams and Wendy Ball, during and after my tenure at the ESRC Research Unit. The following three chapters, which comprise Part 2 of the book, focus on methodological issues in the area of 'race' and education. Chapter 5 is a critical appraisal of research on young people and their attitudes towards their own and other ethnic groups. In Chapter 6, Bruce Carrington and I consider some of the ethical issues associated with research on race-related matters in education. In Chapter 7 I mount a defence of antiracist education against the critiques of, on the one hand, those who want to ensure that multicultural education remains in the ascendancy; and, on the other, writers on the Left who insist that antiracist education is in need of 'critical revision'.

I would not like my involvement in the maelstrom of 'race' and education to be seen as the efforts of a disinterested chronicler of trends and patterns. In the 1950s and 1960s, Tottenham in North London was a major area for the settlement of Afro-Caribbeans. I grew up with and went to school with black youths, and witnessed the racist abuse they experienced within and beyond the school gates. And as the son of Jewish parents, I witnessed and experienced similar forms of harassment, especially from the racist and antisemitic activities of the British Movement and National Front: the burning of synagogues, racist graffiti, physical and verbal abuse in and outside school, and so on.

So I'm not embarrassed by my long-standing involvement in this debate. On the contrary, it's a commitment I wish to continue. Among other things, it has brought me into contact with other activists and academics, some of whom have contributed to the research represented in this book. To acknowledge them all would be impossible. However, I'd like to thank Andy Hargreaves, the Series Editor, and John Skelton of the Open University Press for encouraging me to write this book. Thanks are also due to the following who, as co-authors of some of my published material, have given me as much as, if not more than they've received in return: Wendy Ball, Bruce Carrington, Ellis Cashmore, Andrew Dorn, Viv Edwards, Steve Farrow, Bill Gulam, Richard Hatcher, Libby Selman, Iram Siraj-Blatchford and Jenny Williams. I'm also indebted to my postgraduate students: Harbhajan Brar, Maud Blair, Paul Connolly, David Dodds, Anuradha Rakhit, Krutika Tanna and Carol Vincent, and to the support which I've received from my past and present heads of department: Robin Cohen, Jim Lynch, John Eggleston and John Rex. We've not always agreed, but they've respected my right to dissent.

The division between the personal and professional has always been a blur in my life. So I'd like to thank the following for keeping me going when life, work and Spurs' results (*especially*, Spurs' results) have got me down: John Blatchford, Bob Burgess, Martyn Denscombe, Charlene Dyer, David Halpin, Jim Harvey, Nigel Hutchinson, Grant Jarvie, Jayne Mills, David Milner, Claire Russ, Sandra Shipton, Pat Sikes, Chris Skelton, Kathy Sylva, Sally Tomlinson, Gajendra Verma and, of course, my dad who stands by me despite my inability to speak in RP! Thanks also to Fazal for writing the critical introduction to the book – the miles might keep us apart but, British Council willing, we will continue to exchange intellectual ideas and gossip.

I'd like to dedicate this book to my 'adopted' sons: Sam Kennard, James Lago and Joby Sikes – better, surely, than yet another present from the Spurs' shop! And to my own Three Ss: Sylvia (in fondest memory), Sam (with thanks) and Sally (with love).

Acknowledgements

I am grateful to the publishers and editors for permission to reproduce material from the following:

Chapter 1: D. Gill, B. Mayor and M. Blair (eds) (1992) *Racism and Education: Structures and Strategies*, pp. 63–91. London, Sage for the Open University.

Chapter 2: B. Troyna and J. Williams (1986) *Racism, Education and the State*, pp. 27–43. Beckenham, Croom Helm.

Chapter 3: 'Swann's song': The origins, ideology and implications of *Education for All. Journal of Education Policy*, 1(2), 1986, 171–82; Reform or deform? The 1988 Education Reform Act and racial equality in Britain. *New Community*, 16(3), 1990, 403–16.

Chapter 4: A. Green and S. Ball (eds) (1988) *Progress and Inequality in Comprehensive Education*, pp. 158–78. London, Routledge.

Chapter 5: Children, 'race' and racism: the limitations of research and policy. *British Journal of Educational Studies*, 39(4), 1991, 425–36.

Chapter 6: R. G. Burgess (ed.) (1989) *The Ethics of Educational Research*, pp. 205–33. Lewes, Falmer Press.

Critical Introduction: Researching Racism and Education

FAZAL RIZVI

Perhaps the most complex problem confronting anyone attempting to research racism in education is the problem of its identification and representation. It is increasingly clear that racism is an essentially contested concept, without any agreed meaning with which to identify its salience. Recent debates in Britain have demonstrated the wide gulf that exists between those who point to its pervasive presence in society and those who dismiss it as a problem manufactured by the Left for its own confused political ends. Thus, while social theorists like Mullard and Brandt argue that British society is inherently racist, philosophers like Flew and Scruton insist that racism is at most a minor problem, restricted to the aberrant antisocial behaviour of a small number of individuals.

In the USA, too, recent debates surrounding the beating by four Los Angeles policemen of a black motorist, Rodney King, have highlighted the contrasting ways in which the notion of racism may be interpreted. Central to these debates have been the questions of the extent to which the beating was racially motivated, and the ensuing trial racially structured. While the African-American community in East Los Angeles had little doubt about what had happened, many in middle America remained unconvinced. Indeed, the trial itself demonstrated competing definitions of racism at work, with the prosecution's case clearly based on showing how the beating represented an overtly racist act, while the defence lawyers argued that in engaging in the act of beating King, the four policemen were simply carrying out their duties. As much as anything else, the trial became a site of struggle over meaning.

Similar debates have also taken place in Australia. There has recently been considerable public outrage over a number of incidents which have focused attention on the police treatment of Aboriginal people. The Prime Minister, no less, has admitted that racism remains a major problem in the police force. The popular media has also been indignant. But both the Prime Minister and the media have assumed that the incidents are illustrative of a social pathology that defines only a small section of the Australian community. On the other side of this popular view are two contrasting interpretations. On the one hand, there are those who argue that this view understates the problem, and that racism actually continues to structure all aspects of social life in Australia, and is institutionally persistent. On the other hand, there are those who insist that racism has been 'in retreat' in Australia for most of this century, and that its overt institutionalized forms have all but disappeared.

It is clear, then, that while, in the late twentieth century, the term 'racism' is almost invariably used as a pejorative term, it remains one of the most contested notions in both the popular and sociological vocabularies. Debates over its meaning and relevance in explaining social relations involve such issues as what counts as 'racism'; how it is best represented; how its forms have changed; how generalizable are its forms; in sum, what is its nature and its scope. These are not simply terminological issues; rather, they are inherently practical. Much depends on them, in terms of both our interest in explaining racism's persistence and our interest in developing antiracist initiatives. These are, moreover, fundamentally political issues, concerned with questions of not only knowledge and power but also desire and hope. Their practical significance lies in the contribution they make to the organization of our social relations, since they structure the way we interpret the world and act upon it.

Much of recent social theory has helped us to see how it is impossible to research such social relations in a neutral or objective manner. Post-positivist theories of social science have demonstrated how traditional sociology's claim to provide an authoritative version of how things actually are cannot be sustained; and that, in ideological terms, the claim simply serves to support certain entrenched ruling interests. Traditional sociology works with the presumption of a number of dualisms: between the subject and the object; between the theoretical and the practical; between the normative and the descriptive; and, most significantly, between the knower and the known. Barry Troyna's work helps us to see how these dualisms are fundamentally misguided.

Troyna has shown how a detached 'objective' understanding of racism is impossible. To study racism involves 'seeing' the world in a particular manner, against the understanding the researcher has of its salience. The researcher cannot simply stand apart from the social and political relations that constitute the research process, and is inevitably implicated in the dynamics of racial structuring. In seeking knowledge about racism, the researcher enters into a relation with the object of knowledge. And as these relations change, then so might the way the researcher theorizes racism.

In this sense, the personal cannot be divorced from the research process. Fundamental to Troyna's mode of researching racism is the realization that we need to understand how our world is put together as a practical everyday matter and how our relations are shaped by the concrete conditions in which they are located. Racism resides in certain practices of representation that manifest themselves in various popular discourses, policies, particular actions and organizational arrangements. It is an attempt to understand these practices – the way they are organized, persist, change and are presented and rearticulated into more subtle forms – that is the central objective of Troyna's work.

The issue of the salience of racism in contemporary society is a highly complex one. Its exploration requires historical sensitivity as well as political commitment. To research racism is to investigate how various practices of representation are racially formed, and how it is possible to engage in different practices of representation. Indeed, my own personal history illustrates these processes.

A personal illustration

I first became interested in the issues of racism while teaching Mathematics in Manchester in the mid-1970s. The school in which I taught was a working-class school, with some 10 per cent of its students from minority ethnic backgrounds, mostly Afro-Caribbeans and Bengalis. During my two terms at the school, two incidents occurred that changed the way I looked at racism. The first related to the nickname I acquired almost within a week of being there – 'Super Paki'. It was the contradiction that this practice contained that confused me most. On the one hand, I was flattered by such obvious student affection, and the humour it embodied. On the other hand, however, I was deeply disturbed that I was called a 'Paki' when I was in fact born and brought up in India; that I was treated as a novelty in an educational system that should really have employed more minority teachers; and that my students could only understand their social relations with black people in Britain through such stereotypes.

The second incident was more frightening. One afternoon, I discovered one of the tyres of my car slashed with a Stanley knife. There was a note on the windscreen, saying simply, 'Paki Go Home'. Whoever had vandalized my car was not to know that for me home was not India, but in fact Australia. Prior to going to Manchester I had lived in Canberra, Australia, where my parents had taken me from India as a 16-year-old. The hegemonic understanding I had of the 'West' had meant that I had viewed the prospect of emigrating to Australia as an opportunity few of my friends had. After all, I was going to a country that signified, to middle-class colonial subjects such as myself, progress, both material and intellectual.

At that time Australia practised, more openly than now, a policy of forced assimilation. Only through assimilation into a homogeneous Australian nation, immigrants were told, could they expect to achieve the equality of opportunity that the country offered to all its citizens. As a middle-class boy, I accepted this ideology implicitly. Powerful incentives existed for me to assimilate into the dominant culture as quickly as possible in order to have a realistic chance of receiving its meritocratic rewards.

Of course, I knew that Australia still had a White Australia policy, and that its Aboriginal population was shabbily treated, and was not even given the vote until 1967. But, to me, these structural practices did not constitute 'racism'. I was happy enough to keep my nose clean, and not be distracted by issues that I felt affected only a very few Australians. I assumed racism to be an exceptional phenomenon which involved one individual being nasty to another on the grounds of their 'race'. Furthermore, the ideological view that Australian society was becoming progressively more enlightened and less racist played a crucial part in the way I conceptualized intercultural relations.

From a long way away in Manchester, I was able to 'see' these issues differently. And the two incidents and other experiences in the Manchester school simply served to shatter the enlightenment myths I had acquired in Australia. I now regarded issues of racism as not only relevant to the way I saw the world around me but also a crucial ingredient in the way social relations were structured in Australia.

This realization also had an impact on the way I interpreted the emerging rhetoric of multiculturalism in Australia. The official liberal discourses of multi-culturalism in the early 1980s involved a rejection of the idea of assimilation on moral as well as practical grounds. It was now acknowledged that, despite the myths of fairness and egalitarianism, minorities in Australia did not in fact enjoy the same opportunities as the dominant Anglo group, and that it was unreason-able to expect them to reject their cultural traditions. It was also maintained that cultural diversity was not necessarily a value inimical to the idea of a new socially cohesive nation, organized around the principles of cultural tolerance and social justice. However, amidst much celebration in Australia of the virtues of multiculturalism, I remained unconvinced that it was the policy panacea that many took it to be, that it could in fact be an effective instrument for tackling the problems of racism in Australia. And it was in researching the issues which my scepticism raised that I first came across the work of Troyna.

Multiculturalism as an educational policy

Much of Troyna's work investigates the policy processes surrounding the development, dissemination and legitimation of multicultural education. Throughout his writings, he has sought to demonstrate how the state is in-volved in managing the issues of 'race' relations, and how its policy initiatives have been contested and opposed at the local levels – in schools and in some LEAs. In approaching policy analysis in this way, Troyna has rejected the traditional view of policy analysis as a systematic study of the processes of decision-making as they relate to the issues of implementation and programme evaluation. Troyna's is a critical analytical approach concerned not so much with the search for ways of ensuring the efficient and effective delivery and implementation of policies as with the political dimensions of the policies themselves – of the issues of power and control.

Troyna is interested in examining the nature of the problems to which multiculturalism is supposed to be a solution. He seeks to understand how these problems are framed and how they are linked to the wider interests of the state. His approach to policy analysis is that of a social scientist interested in 'taking things apart'; in detecting 'the ambiguities and the multiplicity of contests, impacts, values and structures'; and in showing 'what might be the consequences of building alternative systems and maintaining existing ones' (Kogan, 1979, p. 8). Unlike the traditional approach to policy analysis which takes existing institutions and social and power relations for granted, Troyna's approach makes them problematic. This enables him not only to explore the dimensions of power inherent in 'racially explicit' policy but also to examine the way power may be exercised through inaction, inexplicitness and ambiguity.

In *Racism, Education and the State* (Troyna and Williams, 1986), Troyna seeks to show how the discourse of multiculturalism in Britain has been a fundamentally ideological one. The term 'multiculturalism' has become part of a slogan system, a rhetoric aimed at changing conventional patterns of interpretation. Troyna argues that the policy processes surrounding its construction and promotion cannot be adequately understood unless we also take into account the economic and social processes of the central state and the consequent forms which its local options assume. The struggle over the construction of the particular form which a policy might eventually take involves 'local political conflict which is set within limits defined primarily by the state but also by established professional and bureaucratic hierarchies' (Troyna and Williams, 1986, p. 6). The notions of contestation, resistance, compromise and settlement thus provide Troyna with the basic theoretical resources with which to analyse policy practices and changes within the framework of broader ideological shifts taking place in British society.

Troyna's critique of multiculturalism has a number of dimensions. As I have already noted, he has explored the ideological nature of its promotion by the state. It is a policy devised to contain the legitimate political and economic interests of black minorities in Britain. Significantly, the clearest support for multiculturalism has come on occasions when there has been unrest in the black communities, when minority voices have asserted themselves. Troyna has suggested that multiculturalism could be seen as an instrument designed to contain militancy, defuse social conflict and maintain social order and thus ensure the social conditions necessary for the accumulation of capital. Thus, as a liberal-welfare policy, multiculturalism remains trapped within the existing mainstream political structures which it does not challenge. And while it recognizes that black minorities in Britain are indeed systematically disadvantaged, the notion of equality with which it works is a minimalist one, concerned with equality of access of individuals to the dominant institutions, which, paradoxically, symbolize racial inequalities for many black people in the first place.

Furthermore, Troyna points to a fundamental conflict between this espousal of a commitment to equality and multiculturalism's other objective: the right of minorities to maintain their cultural identity. In documenting various practices of multiculturalism, Troyna has shown how this pluralist objective has become dominant in schools. This emphasis on 'saris, samosas and steel bands' has obscured the issues of disadvantage and structural inequalities which would seem to be much more crucial in any attempt to provide minorities access to power and improve their life chances.

Yet another dimension of Troyna's critique of multiculturalism relates to his contention that its logic assumes culture to be the primary category of social analysis. He argues that while it has to be acknowledged that people do conceive of themselves as belonging to certain groups, do describe certain types of situation and relation as ethnically or racially defined, it does not follow from this that social analysis must therefore be restricted to the interpretative categories they employ. Thus, for example, minority experiences in Britain are not confined to matters of lifestyle. They cannot therefore be entirely explicable in ethnic or racial terms. This is so because minorities also occupy a particular position in the class structure of British society and play an important part in the production and reproduction of economic relations. By divorcing issues of 'race' or ethnicity from issues of class, the policy of multiculturalism thus reifies ethnic identity, and obscures its social construction.

In contrast, Troyna highlights the dynamic nature of social relations, rejecting the view that 'race' is a primordial 'objective' category, resistant to change, and somehow autonomous, unrelated to issues of class, gender and other categories of social difference. 'Race', he insists, is a socially constructed ideological category, which has to be understood historically. The cultural traditions that multiculturalism celebrates are neither homogeneous nor static, especially when they become relocated through the processes of migration and come in contact with other cultures. As individuals and groups encounter new situations and confront new problems they not only form new networks but also theorize their traditions differently. In teaching about cultural experiences, it is therefore a mistake to assume uniformity in traditions, experiences and ways of relating. People approach social and cultural problems differently, and no a priori judgements are possible about the range of attitudes they might have or the problems which students from various backgrounds might regard as significant. Nor are teachers likely to encounter problems in the same way in dealing with particular students from groups believed to share common origins.

This anti-essentialism is consistent with the way Troyna theorizes racism, and its relation to education. In arguing that multiculturalism and antiracism represent two irreconcilable perspectives, Troyna (1987, p. 311) insists that they 'imply a very different view of the nature and processes of racism, which, in turn, prompts the development of different frameworks within which specific priorities for action are embedded'. It is this contrast that lies at the centre of Troyna's view of racism, and needs therefore to be described and examined in some detail.

Prejudice reduction and the individual

According to Troyna, while it is wrong to suggest that multiculturalism is a homogeneous discourse, its various expressions nevertheless seem to assume racism to be primarily a product of ignorance, perpetuated by negative attitudes and individual prejudices. This view of racism is, of course, not new. It can be found in the work of social psychologists of the 1950s, most notably, Adorno *et al.* (1950) and Allport (1954). And it continues to inform not only most of the media reports of racist incidents but also the policy work upon which the ideology of multiculturalism is based. Most programmes of multicultural education assume its validity implicitly.

Perhaps the best example of this tradition of thinking is James Lynch's influential book, with an apt title, *Prejudice Reduction and the Schools* (1987). It describes a variety of educational techniques aimed at 'prejudice reduction' in British schools and society. The analysis of racism upon which Lynch's liberal sentiments are based appears in a more official form in a number of government reports. The Swann Report (Department of Education and Science, 1985), for example, suggests that it is ignorance that breeds suspicion and intolerance, and that multicultural education is essential for achieving a society in which racism is no longer a barrier to educational and social advancement. Racism, Swann argues, cannot be rooted out unless we all have a more sympathetic understanding of other cultures.

Much of the policy work that has followed Swann has assumed a social psychological understanding of prejudice provided by such early writers as Adorno *et al.* (1950) and Allport (1954). Both of these influential works sought to locate racism in the characteristics of individuals, in personality traits and in particular attitudes. Allport argued, for example, that racism is best viewed to be a consequence of both tensions within the personality system and an individual's deliberate mistaken judgement. He suggested that people are racially prejudiced because they are either irrational or mistaken.

Racism is thus constituted as an individualized, exceptional phenomenon; it is an irrational, even pathological, response which originates in ignorance. This view implies that social structures or institutions cannot be racist, only individuals can. It suggests that where individuals are prejudiced, they must be trained to become more rational. As Henriques (1984, p. 62) puts it, this theory assumes that racism is restricted to a few 'rotten apples' in a basket that is basically sound. But to argue in this way is to presuppose a normative view of the sane, unprejudiced, rational individual who is ultimately the locus of his or her own judgements or capacities.

In recent years, the views of Adorno and Allport have been subjected to a number of criticisms, from both within and outside the disciplinary area of social psychology. Henriques (1984, p. 66) has shown that, for example, they both share a number of common assumptions. For example, both assume a belief in rationality as an ideal, and both stress the individual as the site where rationality breaks down. But significantly, both neglect the social world. Their orientation is thus based on a fundamental individual–social dualism, which 'posits a unitary individual or a rational intentional being as a point of origin, reducing the social to the intersubjective, and assuming that individual and society are commensurate as theoretical notions' (Henriques, 1984, p. 24). Such a dualism rests on a concept of the individual who is unitary and rational, abstracted from the structural aspects of social life. This cognitivist orientation therefore stresses the importance of research into the formation of attitudes as a way of understanding racist behaviour.

However such research not only invariably assumes a social–individual dualism, but also is predicated on the view that thought and action are two distinct psychological states. Both assumptions give rise to a number of theoretical and political problems. Theoretically, the view of racism they entail does not help us to explain how individuals come to develop the prejudices they have; nor does it explain how prejudices may be linked to the structural aspects of a society. And politically, such a view leads to programmes of educational intervention that are based on the assumptions that involve 'blaming the victim'.

Such an approach to antiracism is not only excessively psychologistic but also assumes a particular conception of rationality as an ideal, from which the racist individual is believed to deviate. Thus the notion of error is fundamental to the social psychological understanding of racism. According to Henriques (1984, p. 78), two major premises inform this view: 'The first is that individual errors can be contrasted with the correct perceptions and judgements of the scientist. The second assumption is that these errors are the result of the faulty workings of the cognitive mechanisms within the individual.' Henriques argues that underlying both these premises is the assumption that completely accurate representations of the world are possible. But recent history and philosophy of science have shown this assumption to be fundamentally mistaken, as it is now widely held that all observation is theory-dependent. Such an argument makes the popular social psychological account of racism inherently problematic.

Furthermore, such an account is predicated on a particular analysis of the notions of rationality and error which have themselves been shown by postcolonial writers such as Said (1985) and Bhabha (1990) to be Western artefacts. It thus presumes the essential superiority of a Western tradition of thinking about what counts as the sane, unprejudiced and rational individual. Indeed, antiracist approaches based on Eurocentric views of the individual and rationality may, paradoxically, themselves contribute to the very racism they are designed to combat.

Utilizing some of these and many other arguments, much of Troyna's work thus rejects the popular account of racism derived from early social psychological theories discussed above for not only its theoretical myopia but also its unacceptable political consequences. What Troyna has been able to demonstrate is that racism is not simply a function of the individual's subjective attempts at making sense of the world; rather, it is a manifestation of an ongoing collective process of group interaction, whereby the status and behaviour of minorities is defined and redefined with respect to the dominant group. Moreover, these definitions are not arbitrary, but are linked to various other modes of social production, such as those defined by gender and class relations.

Racism, then, is not a property of individuals; it describes, rather, a particular way in which social relations and practices are organized. Troyna insists that individuals are not remote from history and social structures, and expressions of racism cannot be adequately understood without reference to the issues of political and economic disadvantage or to the patterns of inequalities in society. Racism does not manifest itself only in the explicit attitudes or the use of deliberate emotive and inflammatory language, or even playground fights. More insidiously, it consists in what Hall (1980) has referred to as 'inferential racism', a more pervasive and subtle form that is based on taken-for-granted assumptions which often pass as commonsense. In *Racism in Children's Lives* (Troyna and Hatcher, 1992), Troyna shows how not all forms of racism rest on conscious intentions, but that many are located in mistakenly held stereotypes, negative patronizing attitudes and beliefs that hinder expectations and create misunderstanding. Moreover, racism, when located in policies and entrenched practices, goes beyond simple acts of discrimination such as direct abuse directed at one's background, but constitutes the very pattern of opportunities that people have.

Of course, such a conclusion may not be considered new. For many anti-racist educators have used the notion of 'institutional racism' to refer to those covert forms of racism which are structured into political and social institutions, arising not necessarily from the wilful acts of prejudiced individuals but as covert acts of indifference and omission. The notion of 'institutional racism' has also been used to suggest not only that racism refers to attitudes, beliefs and behaviours of individuals but that it can also refer to public discourses, policies and organizational structures. Structures can thus be said to incorporate racist assumptions and have racist consequences. A contrast is thus drawn between individual and institutional racism. It is important to note (something which some of his critics have not done) that Troyna's account of racism explicitly rejects the simplistic dichotomy this contrast suggests, which has often been used to explicate the main differences between multicultural and antiracist education.

Problems with the idea of institutional racism

On this issue, Troyna's view is consistent with Miles's (1989) observation that the idea of institutional racism involves a 'conceptual inflation'. The term 'institutional racism' was first developed in the USA by Carmichael and Hamilton (1968) in their book, *Black Power*. They defined institutional racism as 'the predication of decisions and policies on considerations of race for the purpose of subordinating a racial group and maintaining control over that group' (p. 3). They distinguished between overt and individualized racism, on the one hand, and covert and institutional racism, on the other. Individualized racism, they suggested, resided in the explicit actions of the individual, while institutional racism referred to those actions and inactions which maintain black people in a disadvantaged position and which rely 'on the active and pervasive operation of anti-black policies, ideologies and practices' (p. 5).

Carmichael and Hamilton's analysis has proved to be highly influential. According to Miles (1989), most writers who have used the notion of institutional racism have emphasized a number of common themes. First, the notion of institutional racism highlights the idea that the defence of a system from which advantage is derived is based on a pattern of racial differentiation.

Racism is thus viewed as a structural relationship based on the subordination of one group by another. A position is racist when it defends, protects or enhances social organizations that are based on racial inequalities. Second, it suggests that the concept of racism is a generalized one, referring to all beliefs, actions, processes and practices which lead to, or sustain, discrimination against and the subordination of minority ethnic groups. Third, it involves a rejection of the social psychological view that insists that intentionality or motivation are necessary measures of the presence or absence of racism. Fourth, it implies that the idea of racism necessarily involves reference to dominant and subordinate groups. Social formation is thus assumed to be constituted by the presence of homogeneous groups which have hierarchical relationships with each other.

These themes can be found in the analyses of racism of a number of recent writers. Pettman and Chambers (1986, p. 7), for example, contend that

> institutional racism refers to a pattern of distribution of social goods, including power, which regularly and systematically advantages some ethnic and racial groups and disadvantages others. It operates through key institutions: organised social arrangements through which social goods and services are distributed.

These social arrangements include such institutions as the judiciary, the parliament, the public bureaucracy and, of course, the school. The structure of the school, it is argued, is based on certain normative definitions of what knowledge is valuable, what is good pedagogy and how the students are best assessed and rewarded. The reward system of the school is thus seen as a powerful determinant of people's life chances. The appeal of the idea of institutional racism is obvious. Its existence in both Britain and Australia can be demonstrated by pointing to a large corpus of data which shows a clear pattern of disadvantage correlating with 'racial' or 'ethnic' origin. For example, Afro-Caribbeans in Britain and Aboriginal people in Australia have the highest infant mortality rate, the worst health profile, the lowest educational outcome, and so on. Women from ethnic minorities have also been shown to be a disadvantaged group. What these data indicate are the structural operations of societies in which individual life chances are determined by one's 'racial' or 'ethnic' origin.

In recent years, many critics of multicultural education have widely used the notion of institutional racism to suggest that more radical educational responses to racism are required. They have rightly argued that the limited programmes in multicultural education which stress the celebration of lifestyles will not have any great capacity for achieving the goals of cultural tolerance and intercultural understanding until they acknowledge the structural causes of racial inequality. It should be noted, however, that the critics are not suggesting that certain programmes of multicultural education may not be helpful in some specific cases; rather, their argument is that multiculturalism overstates the capacity of schools to transform society. As de Lepervanche (1984, p. 194) points out, 'education *per se* will not lead to the removal of prejudice and discrimination or to the institution of equal opportunity'. If racism is a product of broader institutional conditions, then we cannot expect to challenge it adequately by simply encouraging cultural tolerance in classrooms. Racism cannot be tackled adequately unless we also attend to the broader social and economic factors that help to produce it in the first place; that is, unless we change the nature of the institutions in which racism is practised.

Troyna has been one of the leading critics of multiculturalism in Britain who has underlined the importance of structural issues. However, in doing so, he has also asked a number of fundamental questions about the theoretical status of the notion of institutional racism, and the part its recognition might play in contributing to genuine educational and social change. He has suggested that the notion of institutional racism has become oversimplified – a slogan that is now dislocated from the political context in which it was constructed and had significance. It has lost any specific explanatory power, and therefore becomes unhelpful in the construction of realizable antiracist educational policies and practices.

The term 'institutional racism' was used by black radical theorists in the USA to emphasize the manner in which the state was 'racialized' (Omi and Winant 1986). It was designed variously to show how the social psychological model of racism was insufficient for an adequate understanding of the forms and scope of racism in the USA; to stress that inequalities in urban settings were perpetuated through the interconnecting relationships of several institutional sites such as housing, schools and the labour market; and to counter the prevailing pluralist theory of the state as the neutral arbiter of competing interests which had trapped antiracist reform within the existing framework of political processes.

However, Troyna has suggested that the current usage of the concept is abstracted from this historical meaning. It has generally come to be used to refer to the functions and mechanisms of a single institution, such as the school. So, the term has been reduced to denoting a direct and causal relationship between one form of inequality (such as educational underachievement) and one institution (such as the school). It has been used to delineate one particular aspect of inequality which is then said to derive from the routine institutional mechanisms operated by people who may or may not be racially prejudiced.

A number of other problems with this generalized understanding of institutional racism have also been identified by Miles (1989). Miles has suggested that the concept has now become inseparable from a theory of stratification that is both simplistic and misguided because it assumes or ascribes primary significance to race and/or ethnicity. From the perspective of both the Marxist and Weberian traditions, Miles has argued, this overlooks the importance of class divisions and conflict in society. It sidesteps the complexity of the issue of the distribution of members of the same group to different class positions. Consequently, the simplistic definition of racism as prejudice plus power, upon which the notion of institutional racism trades, ignores class and gender divisions, and the differential access to power within both the dominant and subordinate groups. This is a serious problem because there is now considerable evidence to demonstrate that black people in Britain do not, if indeed they ever did, constitute a homogeneous group, occupying a common economic position which is subordinate to every member of the dominant group. To talk of the 'dominant group' is, moreover, to overlook the complexity of contradictory and interlocking ways in which its members belong to that group. Thus, as Miles (1989) contends, what is collective disadvantage is not necessarily an individual disadvantage, or at least not in the same way; and similarly, the determinants of a collective disadvantage are not necessarily the determinants of individual disadvantage.

Miles (1989) has identified another serious problem with the notion of institutional racism: by defining racism as the consequence of what the dominant group does, the distinctions between belief and action and between intentionality and unintentionality are obscured. The interrelation between belief and action in specific cases, he has suggested, is more complex, since beliefs may not be accompanied by appropriate action or give rise to appropriate action; and actions may not occur in ways which are consistent with beliefs. Furthermore, the sloganized use of the notion of institutional racism does not adequately explain how institutional racism determines behaviour and consequences.

Insufficient attention to these complexities results in attention being diverted away from the often contradictory interplay of the determinants of disadvantage and exclusion. There are clearly many different forms and determinants of disadvantage, and to claim that all disadvantages can be shown to be the consequences of institutional racism is to overlook the fact that there are a large number of actions and processes that take place in institutions which play different roles for different people of the same background.

While the view of racism as a phenomenon constituted by individuals and the view of racism as institutionally constituted are radically different in most respects, it is indeed paradoxical that they are both located within the framework of the same fundamental individual–social dualism. However, if we reject the individual–social dualism then both accounts of racism can be shown to be equally problematic, as indeed can the view that suggests individual and institutional racism simply describe two different levels at which racism operates. The talk of levels is basically misguided because it is impossible to describe institutions which are not historically constructed and defined by some individuals. Nor is it possible to imagine discursive discourses or practices in which individuals engage having any significance outside their institutional meanings.

Representations and practices of racism

What is notable about Troyna's work is that it seeks to avoid the errors not only of this dualism but also of essentialism. His recent writings, in particular, demonstrate his conviction that no universal characterization of the nature of racism is possible, and that representations and practices are continually changing, being challenged, interrupted and reconstructed. He thus emphasizes the historical specificity of racism. His view is thus consistent with Stuart Hall's (1986, p. 23) contention that while there are no doubt certain general features to racism, what is 'more significant are the ways in which these general features are modified, and transformed by the historical specificity of the contexts and environments in which they become active'.

Racism then is a pre-eminently sociohistorical concept. This is so because a discourse 'inherited' from the past is often reconstituted and rearticulated if it is to be used to make sense of the world in its new context. Racial categories and meaning are given concrete form by the specific social relations which they express and the historical context in which they are embedded. But such rearticulation is never uniform or complete. Much of the debate about what counts as racism in the events I described in the beginning of this Introduction can thus be explained in terms of the various conflicting constructions of 'the Other' (Miles, 1989) and differing conceptualizations of the social world which the protagonists have.

In Troyna's discussion of these views, the concept of 'racialization' is central, though his use of the concept is radically different to the way the early advocates of institutional racism used it. Its scope is not universal but historically and contextually specific. Drawing heavily on Reeves (1983), Troyna suggests that the term 'racialization' refers to the complex processes through which racial designations are established. Thus, policies, practices and institutions can be said to be racialized if they are predicated on an assumption of racial differentiation, either biological or cultural. It should be noted, however, that not all practices of racialization are racist, since racialization may be directed towards eliminating racism through the identification of racial inequalities, though most practices of racialization are evaluatively negative, imposing a hierarchical ordering on groups of people.

Of course, practices of racialization are not homogeneous or static. They are continually changing, often through the processes of resistance and contestation as people attempt to understand their world differently. On occasions, people seek to construct new patterns of social relations, while in other circumstances, particular practices persist, often through the use of new code words and new ideological forms that obscure discriminatory behaviour.

It is because no single form of racialization is universal that we cannot define racism essentially. Even the visible colour difference that is so often assumed to represent the essence of racist ideology is socially constructed and can and has changed over time. As Cohen (1988, p. 14) points out,

> racist discourses have never confined themselves just to body images. Names and modes of address, states of mind and living conditions, clothes and customs, every kind of social behaviour and cultural practice have been pressed into service to signify this or that racial essence.

Particular practices of racialization thus represent distinctive modalities of racism, with their own history and structure of meaning. It might be argued, however, that while they have quite distinct patterns of historical development, in a structural sense, all instances of racism involve marginalization and exclusion. While this is clearly true, it is also important to note that mechanisms of marginalization and exclusion vary considerably, and have a historically specific form. They may involve physical violence, political repression, psychological abuse, harassment, paternalism, inequalities of access and treatment, legislated inequalities and so on, but *not in the same way*.

Thus, it is indeed appropriate to identify, as writers such as Gilroy (1987a) have, the emergence of new expressions of racism which avoid being recognized as racism because they are able to mask themselves behind the discourses of nationhood, patriotism and nationalism. 'New' racism, as Gordon and Klug (1986) have called it, takes a necessary distance from crude ideas of biological inferiority and superiority and seeks to present an image of a nation which is characterized by an alleged unified cultural community. It ties ideas of national culture and social cohesion in a homogeneous form, an ethnic essence, in which minority cultures are regarded as alien. Such a practice of racialization is an ideological construction concerned not with absolute notions of racial superiority, but with the threat that some communities are supposed to pose to the social cohesion and racial harmony of Britain. This was the basis of the racism upon which Enoch Powell formulated his arguments concerning 'excessive' levels of black immigration to Britain. And while Powell's views are now regarded as extreme, other coded racialized inferences that suggest that the mixing of people who are phenotypically and culturally different causes social division are widely held not only in Britain but also in many other countries. In Australia, for example, Asians are often regarded as unassimilable because it is often asserted that the cultural and physical differences between 'them' and 'us' are such that they do not 'belong here'.

While in political terms, such racialized views are considered unacceptable, they do seem nevertheless to tap into some of the assimilationist sentiments that continue to define 'common sense' in Australia. This common sense is essentially informed by a theory of human nature which holds that human beings supposedly have a most deep-seated desire, a biological instinct, to prefer the company of 'their own kind'. Moreover, the theory suggests that it is 'natural' for people to be hostile to other groups, and thus protect their territory from 'aliens'. Jim Walker's ethnography of a boys' high school shows claims of territoriality in the talk of 'us' and 'them' to be common. As Walker (1988, p. 47) observes:

> our overwhelming impression was that the traditional ASC working class in the locality regarded certain areas, and in the global sense whole of Stockham, as really 'ours', even if as a result of decisions made by others of another class in other places, they were invaded by unwanted outsiders and aliens – wogs, chows and coons.

In a parallel manner, Troyna's *Racism in Children's Lives* (Troyna and Hatcher 1992) reports similar racist views in the schools he researched in Britain.

Troyna's research also supports the findings of Billig (1988), who has indicated that new forms of racism are contradictory and often trade on their supposed 'reasonableness'. As Billig (1988) has pointed out, while the proponents of new racism are broadly committed to the Enlightenment project of an 'unprejudiced' society, they are nevertheless able to accommodate ideological beliefs that are based on racist assumptions. He has suggested that it is necessary to understand modern racist discourse in its rhetorical context, in which opposition to racism is often stated in a preliminary clause that is then followed by an expression of an overtly racist view. This rhetorical device is most evident in such phrases as 'I am not prejudiced but . . .' and 'some of my best friends are Asians but . . .'.

Billig's contention that racist ideologies are often contradictory is helpful in explaining how it is possible for some programmes of antiracism, including most versions of multiculturalism, to be predicated in fact on racist assumptions, or have racist consequences. It is also helpful in explaining how it is possible for the victims of racism to be mystified by the very racist ideologies that imprison them, and willingly consent to continue to participate in the discourses and structures that define them.

Researching racism and education

What is evident, then, is that racism is an ideology which is continually changing, being challenged, interrupted and reconstructed, and which often appears in contradictory forms. As such, its reproduction in schools, and elsewhere, can be expected to be complex, multifaceted and historically specific. As Miles (1989, p. 132) has argued, we must avoid any assumption of simple, historical duplication, because 'ideologies are never only received but are also constructed and reconstructed by people responding to their material and cultural circumstances in order to comprehend, represent and act in relation to those circumstances'. If this is so, then specific forms of racism can be expected to change, and inherited racist discourses are likely to be reconstituted. New circumstances are likely to lead to new formulations of racism. This also means that an expression of racism in media, textbooks, policies and in schools, is not necessarily going to be the same as its reception.

Such conclusions raise a number of important but complex issues for those interested in researching racism and education, and for constructing programmes of antiracist education. For if racism in different social locations is constructed in ways that are often contradictory, and if people interpret and work with racist representations differently, then how might we study its expressions?

Troyna has insisted that any sound strategy for researching racism must involve studying its expressions in its concrete material context. Accordingly, much of Troyna's research on topics as diverse as the media and racism, extremist organizations, racist incidents in schools, teachers and racism, children's representations of racism, implications of the 1988 Educational Reform Act for antiracist initiatives and, more generally, processes of policy development and implementation, seeks to examine the particular historically constituted expressions of racism at concrete levels. Methodologically, such research has involved detailed ethnographic work that cannot be divorced from the advocacy role that a commitment to antiracism must clearly entail.

The anti-essentialism that characterizes Troyna's work has shown that racism cannot be researched in a way that is divorced from an investigation of the broader social relations which might exist in the school, for racism is likely to articulate with a variety of other factors in such a way as to render its distinctive delineation impossible. Racism, Troyna has repeatedly argued, often articulates with other ideological discourses, and with other forms of exclusion and oppression, often in ways that are contradictory.

Teachers, too, occupy positions in relation to racism which are often contradictory. Those who are engaged in tackling racism in their schools and communities are often acutely aware of their complicity in such discriminatory practices as grading according to norms that rest on assimilationist assumptions. But there is no way of devising an educational structure that is free of all contradictions. In a sense, a central objective of antiracism should be to confront them squarely, so that strategic educative work can take place in the limited political space that is now available to teachers. There is, then, a pragmatic dimension to Troyna's view of the possibilities of antiracism. Thus, in *Education, Racism and Reform* (Troyna and Carrington, 1990), Troyna considers what room for manoeuvre there might be for an antiracist education in a political context that is dominated by the New Right, and the systematic attack it has mounted on the capacity of local authorities to support equal opportunity initiatives. It may be that in such a context only a defensive struggle will be possible.

From all that has been said in this Introduction, it should be clear that racism is a difficult issue to research, not only because its forms are continually changing but also because it requires the kind of political commitment that very few scholars are able to sustain over a long period of time. The struggle against racism often appears fruitless, especially in the face of a 'conservative restoration' (Shor, 1986) that has characterized British politics throughout the 1980s. Throughout this period, many of the gains made by black people have dissipated under a sustained Thatcherite attack on social democratic reforms. Expressions of racism have become more complex within a context of postmodern times in which there has been a general crisis of authority. The modern state can no longer be trusted to work for liberal-democratic reforms. However, a fundamental contradiction now exists between the need to use the agencies of the state to work towards antiracist reforms, on the one hand, and the realization that the state inherently serves racist interests, on the other.

It is in the context of these theoretical and political challenges that Troyna's work should be located. It should be seen as issuing these challenges, as well as responding to them. In this way, Troyna's work does not represent a static and uniform set of ideas, as some of his critics have assumed, but a politically informed intervention in the academic arena. Troyna has thus written extensively about the ethics and politics of research into racism – about the reasons for doing research and who should do this research. He has argued against the popular view which has been referred to by Gilroy (1987b) as 'cultural insiderism'. We are all implicated in the practices and processes of racism, and to assume that only particular people can research racism is simply absurd. As Troyna has argued, it is a commitment not to a particular group but to a set of values, that should guide research into racism.

Bibliography

Adorno, T.W., Frenkel-Brunswik, E., Levinson, D. and Sanford, R.N. (1950) *The Authoritarian Personality*. New York, Basic Books.

Allport, G. (1954) *The Nature of Prejudice*. Reading, MA, Addison-Wesley.

Bhabha, H. (1990) Interrogating identity: the postcolonial prerogative. In D. Goldberg (ed.), *Anatomy of Racism*, pp. 183–209. Minneapolis, University of Minnesota Press.

Billig, M. (1988) Prejudice and tolerance. In M. Billig, S. Condor, D. Edwards *et al.* (eds), *Ideological Dilemmas*. London, Sage.

Carmichael, S. and Hamilton, C.V. (1968) *Black Power: The Politics of Liberation In America*. London, Jonathan Cape.

Cohen, P. (1988) The perversions of inheritance: studies in the making of multi-racist Britain. In P. Cohen and H. Bains, *Multi-racist Britain*. London, Macmillan.

de Lepervanche, M. (1984) Migrants and ethnic groups. In S. Encel and L. Bryson (eds), *Australian Society* (4th edn). Melbourne, Longman-Cheshire.

Department of Education and Science (1985) *Education for All* (Swann Report). London, HMSO.

Gilroy, P. (1987a) *There Ain't Black in the Union Jack*. London, Hutchinson.

Gilroy, P. (1987b) *Problems in Anti-racist Strategy*. London, Runnymede Trust.

Gordon, P. and Klug, F. (1986) *New Right – New Racism*, London, Searchlight.

Hall, S. (1980) Teaching race. *Multiracial Education*. 9(1), 3–13.

Hall, S. (1986) Gramsci's relevance to the analysis of racism and ethnicity. *Journal of Communication Studies*, 10(2), 5–27.

Henriques, J. (1984) Social psychology and the politics of racism. In J. Henriques, W. Holloway, C. Urwin *et al.* (eds), *Changing the Subject: Psychology, Social Regulation and Subjectivity*, pp. 60–89. London, Methuen.

Kogan, M. (1979) Different frameworks for educational policy-making and analysis. *Educational Analysis*, 1(2), 5–14.

Lynch, J. (1987) *Prejudice Reduction and the Schools*. London, Cassell.

Miles, R. (1989) *Racism*. London, Routledge.

Omi, M. and Winant, H. (1986) *Racial Formation in the United States*. Boston, Routledge and Kegan Paul.

Pettman, J. and Chambers, B. (1986) *Anti-racism: A Handbook for Adult Educators*. Canberra, AGPS.

Reeves, F. (1983) *British Racial Discourse*. Cambridge, Cambridge University Press.

Said, E. (1985) *Orientalism*. London, Penguin.

Shor, I. (1986) *Culture Wars*. London, Routledge.

Troyna, B. (1987) Beyond multiculturalism: towards the enactment of anti-racist education in policy, provision and pedagogy. *Oxford Review of Education*, 13(3), 307–20.

Troyna, B. and Carrington, B. (1990) *Education, Racism and Reform*. London, Routledge.

Troyna, B. and Hatcher, R. (1992) *Racism in Children's Lives*. London, Routledge.

Troyna, B. and Williams, J. (1986) *Racism, Education and the State*. London, Croom Helm.

Walker, J. (1988) *Louts and Legends*. Sydney, Allen and Unwin.

PART 1

The Racialization of Education Policy

1 From Deracialization to Racialization: Race-related Policies in Education

In this opening chapter I want to analyse the policies of local education authorities (LEAs) on race-related matters in the 1980s. In Chapter 2 I will extend the
analysis by exploring in greater depth the predisposing features of the multicultural education policies developed in the Inner London Education Authority (ILEA) and Manchester in the late 1970s and early 1980s. In broad terms,
my argument is that during the 1980s the decentralized education system in
England and Wales provided a permissive context for the development of local
policies in response to local problems. At the same time, it is important in this
analysis not to lose sight of the fact that the nature and orientation of these
policies and the sociopolitical context in which they emerged, were delimited
by national state policies. This is not meant to imply an overdetermined model
of local policy-making. It is simply to argue that they were, and continue to be,
subject to various extraneous influences. For this reason, the arenas in which
local policies are framed may be viewed as 'sites of struggle'. As Henry Giroux
has argued, in all social formations there is room for self-creation, mediation
and resistance. As a result, 'there is a substantial difference between the existence of various structural and ideological modes of domination and their
structural unfolding and effects' (Giroux, 1984, p. 259). On this view, then, the
state is not conceived as uniform but as a complex set of institutions which, in
the words of Sophie Watson (1990, p. 19), 'cannot be assumed to act as a
coherent or uncontradictory beast' (see also Grace, 1987, p. 196).

I want to begin by mapping out the different ways in which policy-making
has been conceptualized in the social science literature. From there I will focus
on the ways in which LEA policy-making on race-related matters has been
conceived since the 1960s. In the third part of the chapter I will appraise the
various rationales used to underpin the respective 'racial forms of education'
between the 1960s and 1980s, arguing that these are inadequate and misleading. Finally, I will show that the differences between multicultural and
antiracist paradigms of educational reform, as represented in LEA policy documents, were more apparent than real.

The social science project

According to the cover blurb, *The Social Sciences in Educational Studies*, edited by Anthony Hartnett (1982), was intended to act as a 'comprehensive source book for students and others interested in education and in the social sciences'. In this respect Michael Parkinson's review of the existing literature on politics and policy-making in education was especially revealing. His main contention was that 'social scientists in Britain have paid relatively little attention to the process of educational policy-making' (Parkinson, 1982, p. 114). Parkinson (1982, p. 115) reckoned that one of the main reasons for this sorry state of affairs was that 'much of public education is actually provided by local government and study of this field has, until recently, been relatively impoverished'.

Four years later, Roger Dale (1986) provided a more nuanced appraisal of the material on policy-making in education. In his view, studies crystallized around three main 'projects'. The social administration project was concerned to improve not just efficiency but also social conditions and was directed towards potential policy problems. Following Mishra (1977), Dale considered empiricism – the concentration on 'facts' rather than theories – as one of the distinguishing features of this project. The policy analysis project limited its scope to maximizing the effective and efficient delivery of policy. Its origins are to be found in the United States and centred on a determination to discover why there might be a shortfall between the stated aims of policy and their impact. Finally, the social science project, the most underdeveloped in the literature, geared itself to finding out how things are and how they came to be that way. In contrast to the first two models, it was not primarily concerned with the implementation of policy. In many ways, Wenger's (1987) analysis augments Dale's typology. In her view, the discontinuities between the social science project and the social administration and policy analysis projects transcend all aspects of the research process, 'from the abstract fundamentals of basic value orientations to the pragmatics of the form of the publication of findings' (Wenger, 1987, p. 201).

Dale's conception of the social science project is compatible with what Stuart Hall has defined as the distinguishing characteristics of social science; that is, to deconstruct the obvious, to show 'people that the things they immediately feel to be "just like that" aren't quite "just like that" ' (Hall, 1980, p. 6).

'Racial forms of education'

In his address to the National Association for Multiracial Education (NAME) in 1984 Chris Mullard presented what some have seen as a seminal contribution to an understanding of the relationship between the educational system and race-related matters. Mullard (1984, p. 14) argued that 'racial forms of education' had progressed through a number of distinctive phases since the 1960s: 'immigrant', 'multiracial', 'multicultural' and 'antiracist'. More recently, Cole (1989, p. 6) synthesized these into three categories: monocultural, multicultural and antiracist. While these help to describe and periodize changes, they provide little understanding either of the dynamics of change or the ideological imperatives of each form.

Greater explanatory power could be found in the writings of Street-Porter (1978) and in earlier work by Mullard (1982). Alongside my own analysis in this period (Troyna, 1982), they drew on concepts from the sociology of race relations and specified ideological and policy responses in terms of assimilation, integration and cultural pluralism. What did these typifications denote? In blunt terms, assimilation refers to the process of becoming similar. However, as a number of sociologists have noted, it is necessary to refine this definition, especially when it is applied to 'race' and ethnic relations. As Banton (1988, p. 26) reminds us: 'Members of a group who differentiate themselves in one respect (as, say, Sikhs wear turbans) may assimilate in another (like language use)'. Nevertheless, while the nature of change might be provisional, the direction is both predictable and non-negotiable. For black people in Britain it is a one-way process. As I argued with Ellis Cashmore, in this asymmetrical power relationship acquisition involves loss. This is exemplified by the following outbursts, separated by 25 years, but united by the racist convictions which characterize the assimilationist ideology. First, George Partiger (former MP for Southall) in 1964:

> I feel that Sikh parents should encourage their children to give up their turbans, their religion and their dietary laws. If they refuse to integrate then we must be tough. They must be told that they would be the first to go if there was unemployment and it should be a condition of being given National Assistance that the immigrants go to English classes.
>
> (cited in Troyna, 1982, p. 129)

Consider the lexicon: 'we', 'they', 'tough', 'told', 'condition'. The imperative is clear: 'they' must become indistinguishable from 'us', or else. And, in the 1980s, during the controversy surrounding the publication of Salman Rushdie's *The Satanic Verses*, politicians and journalists invoked similar arguments in response to those fundamentalist Muslims who called for the banning of the book. BE BRITISH, HURD TELLS IMMIGRANTS, screamed the front-page headline of the *Daily Mail* in its report of the former Home Secretary's speech to Muslim organizations in Britain in 1989. George Gale, allegedly the 'voice of common sense', informed the readership of the same newspaper that there was 'No room for aliens'; he continued:

> we must do nothing through legislation or the use of public money to preserve alien cultures and religions. Likewise, they must seek to be assimilated . . . They have chosen to dwell amongst us. In Rome, do as the Romans do.
>
> (*Daily Mail*, 3 March 1989)

Monocultural education

When expressed in the discourse of education, assimilationist ideas in the 1960s prompted the development of monocultural education. The aim was to encourage 'them' to be like 'us'. Monocultural education, then, centred on the suppression and deprecation of ethnic, linguistic and cultural differences. In formal policy terms, it assumed two main expressions. The first was the setting up of language centres to provide teaching of English as a second language (ESL) to those children (mainly of South Asian origin) whose first language, or 'mother tongue' as it is commonly termed, was not English. These centres were often located beyond the school site and non-English-speaking pupils were removed from mainstream lessons and their friends for ESL purposes. Assimilationist arguments also gave rise (and spurious legitimacy) to the policy of dispersal, or 'bussing'. This emerged in response to complaints from white parents in Southall, West London, that the presence of a 'large' number of non-English-speaking pupils in the classroom distracted teachers from the learning needs of white pupils and, therefore, inhibited their educational progress. Although bussing was never adopted as official Department of Education and Science (DES) policy, the DES recommended to LEAs that it should be applied when the proportion of immigrant pupils in any one school exceeded 30 per cent. Of course, the DES did not base its support for bussing on explicitly racist grounds. On the contrary, it justified its stance by appealing to the 'contact hypothesis' – the belief that racial prejudice and discrimination are dispelled by the everyday interaction of whites and blacks (for a critique of this theory, see Hewstone and Brown, 1986; Troyna and Hatcher, 1992). The rhetoric failed to conceal the reality, however. Bussing exemplified the differential power relations between white and black citizens in Britain – a relationship which monocultural education underscored. After all, if the development of better ethnic relations was the main concern of the DES, then why did the DES only recommend the dispersal of black children?

Multicultural education

We will see in Chapter 3 that assimilation and its expression through the discourse of monocultural education has been revitalized in the framing and implementation of the 1988 Education Reform Act (ERA). Faith in its initial incarnation began to wane, however, in the late 1960s. For some writers, such as Rex (1987), this was the logical outcome from Roy Jenkins's insistence in 1966 that integration should be given priority as a social and political goal in the formulation of race relations policy. For Jenkins, then Home Secretary, integration constituted not 'a flattening process of assimilation' but 'equal opportunity accompanied by cultural diversity, in an atmosphere of mutual tolerance'. On its own, however, Jenkins's exhortatory statement had little strategic value to commend it to educationists. It was in the articulation of the statement with two emerging and not entirely separate trends in education, that it assumed credibility on the educational landscape.

Milner's (1975) work on black children's negative self-identify and its allegedly causal links with their academic 'underachievement' was crucial here. It prompted some educationists to reconsider the efficacy of monoculturalism in the light of the education system's commitment to equality of opportunity and meritocratic principles – the cornerstones of the 1944 Education Act. Equally significant was the emergent resistance of black parents to the racist impulses of schooling, and the incipient growth of the black voluntary school movement (Carter, 1986; Chevannes and Reeves, 1987). These provided an equally potent challenge to the credibility of these principles. By 1975 these criticisms reached a crescendo and were given institutional backing in Lord Bullock's report, *A Language for Life*: 'No child', according to the Bullock committee, 'should be expected to cast off the language and culture of the home as he [*sic*] crosses the school threshold' (DES, 1975). And, prefiguring the DES (1977) Green paper, *Education in Schools: A Consultative Document*, Bullock and his colleagues recommended the integration of ethnic, cultural and linguistic diversity into the curriculum. The convergence of these influences resulted in an increasing number of 'accredited sources' on the educational terrain casting a critical eye over monoculturalism. Its successor: a fusion of integrationist and cultural pluralist ideas. By the mid-1970s, multicultural education had risen like a phoenix out of the ashes of monocultural education.

Educationists often find themselves out on a definitional limb in their efforts to specify the uniquely distinctive features of multiculturalism as a conception of educational reform. At the same time, it has retained a range of seductive, if empirically questionable, properties. Brian Bullivant's (1981) study of multicultural education in six countries in the 1970s enabled him to distil three key assumptions of this orthodoxy.

(1) That by learning about his [*sic*] cultural and ethnic 'roots' an ethnic [*sic*] child will improve his educational achievement;
(2) The closely related claim that learning about his culture, its traditions and so on will improve equality of opportunity;
(3) That learning about other cultures will reduce children's prejudice and discrimination towards those from different cultural and ethnic backgrounds.

(Bullivant, 1981, p. 236)

It is not difficult to see why these propositions are attractive to teachers and policy-makers. All three seem to articulate closely with the principle of equality of opportunity which, I pointed out earlier, is the ostensible goal of education in Britain. The first two also appeal to a common-sense belief in the power of child-centred approaches to enhance the educability of pupils, and to the role of educational qualifications in determining the occupational life chances of pupils, irrespective of their class, gender or ethnic backgrounds. Bullivant's third proposition, the contact hypothesis, is also attractive because it rests on the grounds that a pupil's school experiences are sufficient, in themselves, to counteract the divisive racist influences which she or he may encounter outside the school gates. It resonates, therefore, with the widely held belief that education can compensate for society. Finally, it will be noticed that all three propositions centre on curriculum change; it follows, therefore, that teachers assume responsibility for change. Policy-makers, on the other hand, are absolved from the role of initiating the systemic and institutional reforms necessary to mitigate racial inequalities in education.

Antiracist education

The assertion that 'multicultural education is synonymous with good practices in education' (Duncan, 1986, p. 39) soon became the clarion call of those who championed this educational orthodoxy. But it was not long before the allegedly emancipatory powers of this programme of reform came under heavy fire from those committed to antiracist perspectives. It is sufficient to point out here that, in contrast to multiculturalism, antiracism, which assumed the ascendancy briefly in the mid-late 1980s, rejects the view which sees racism primarily as an individual problem. Nor do antiracists endorse the voyeuristic imperatives of multiculturalism in which 'they' rather than 'us' become the subject of scrutiny. The iconography of multiculturalism is the three Ss: saris, samosas and steel bands (Troyna, 1983). Its imperative is to ensure that people understand each other's culture; its conviction, that in a context of cultural understanding racial conflict would 'be unnecessary and would wither away' (Macdonald *et al.*, 1989, p. 344).

From an antiracist perspective, however, racism is seen to reside 'squarely in the policies, structures and beliefs of everyday life' (Thomas, 1984, p. 2). The concerns of antiracists go beyond providing information to white children on the expressive and historical features of ethnic minority cultures in efforts to dispel racial prejudice. Their starting point is a recognition of the significance of power relations associated with 'race', sex and class; their rationale, that these must be exposed and challenged in a programmatic strategy of education. The antiracist paradigm, therefore, centralizes the need to provide the appropriate organizational, pedagogical and curricular context which enables children to scrutinize the manner in which racism rationalizes and helps to maintain injustices and the differential power accorded particular class, ethnic and gender groups in society (see Chapter 7 for an elucidation of this perspective). Of course, how far this conception of antiracism was integrated into policies which adopted this nomenclature is a question I will address later in the chapter. Before that I want to look more closely at the analytical tools used to explain the shifts in ideology and policy in this field of enquiry.

Analysing 'racial forms of education'

The analytical framework erected around the concepts, assimilation, integration and cultural pluralism provided a helpful, but by no means complete, picture of the dynamics of race-related policy initiatives in education. Certainly, it went beyond the largely descriptive and atheoretical accounts which had previously dominated discussions in this area. But there were weaknesses. It implied, for instance, that each stage was unique, constituted an independent conception of the relationship between black pupils and the state and, perhaps most worryingly, that each 'form' was an improvement over its predecessor(s). Both Mullard (1982) and I (Troyna, 1982) argued against this view, preferring to see multicultural education as the most liberal variant of the assimilationist perspective. Differences, we contended, were in degree, not kind. Despite this caveat, multicultural education continued to be presented in grandiose terms – a radical change from assimilationist ideas, incorporating the main educational agenda of antiracists (Leicester, 1989) and rejecting its more invidious, 'political, confrontational, accusatory and guilt-inducing' features (Lynch, 1987, p. x). Phil Cohen went even further in his call for a reconciliation between multicultural and antiracist education. He asserted that at every level of the education system there are those 'who have come to realise that the polarisation between anti-racist and multi-cultural positions had become sterile and self-destructive' (Cohen, 1988, p. 4; see also Short, 1991).

But the linear progression of 'racial frames of education' and the allegedly distinctive positions occupied within the framework suffered not only from certain untenable assumptions but also from delusions of grandeur. An alternative could be found in Kirp's (1979) study, *Doing Good by Doing Little*, the first major empirical investigation of the framing of educational policies around race-related matters in Britain.

Kirp argued that until the late 1970s these policies could be theorized in terms of their 'racial inexplicitness', a term which denoted both description and evaluation. He asserted that it usefully distinguished the British approach from the one in the United States. In the USA 'race' had figured prominently on the educational policy-making agenda at least since 1954 when the Supreme Court ruled that segregated schools were unconstitutional. Since then, attempts to mitigate the impact of racial inequality in education have been a major concern of policy-makers. As Kirp argued in his later book, *Just Schools*, 'racial fairness and educational equity' have been 'tightly linked' in policy formation (Kirp, 1982, pp. 32–3). In contrast to this explicit concern with 'race' in the USA, policy-makers in Britain had stayed firmly on the road of 'racial inexplicitness'. For Kirp, this was a preferable route to follow. 'In the usual instance', he wrote, 'inexplicitness implies doing nothing concerning race. The term may also mean doing good by stealth' (Kirp, 1979, p. 2). And later in the book Kirp elaborated on this evaluation. Doing good by doing little derived from his conviction that 'one helps non-whites by *not* favouring them explicitly. The benefits to minorities from such an approach are thought to be real if invisible – or better, real because invisible' (Kirp, 1979, p. 61; emphasis in original). To sustain his argument, Kirp referred to bussing as the single exception to racial inexplicitness in policy formation in Britain. The furore this caused, according to Kirp, demonstrated the veracity of his thesis that policies should be structured around racially inexplicit concepts and issues: cultural and material deprivation, educational disadvantage, the inner city, and so on.

If Kirp's thesis is empirically correct, then we might have expected the black communities to be satisfied with the racially inexplicit policies which prevailed under these banners. They were not. Nor did the rise of multicultural education in the 1970s and early 1980s assuage their discontent, despite its apparent emphasis on racially explicit issues. This was because what has concerned Britain's black citizens, their children and the antiracist movement in general are not the changes implied in the racially inexplicit–explicit couplet but what precisely educational policy has been explicit *about* in its understanding of race-related issues. As I noted earlier, despite the differences in emphasis, neither monocultural nor multicultural education shone the spotlight on racism. Nor did it consider in detail its corrosive effects on the educational experiences of black children. Simply put, racism did not figure as a basis for policy intervention. It was therefore necessary to reformulate the question about racial explicitness and ask: how and why policy-makers in the 1960s, 1970s and early 1980s succeeded in marginalizing issues of racism in the development of policy interventions. To address this question we need to apply a new set of analytical tools.

Racially inexplicit or deracialized?

Central to a reconstituted approach to understanding the evolution of 'racial forms of education' is the term 'racialization'. According to Robert Miles, this is a concept which has emerged in analysis in the 1970s to refer to a political and ideological process by which particular populations are identified by direct or indirect reference to their real or imagined phenotypical characteristics in such a way as to suggest that the population can only be understood as a supposed biological unity (Miles, 1988, p. 246). Miles is interested in mapping out an historical account of the economic, political and ideological conjunctures when this process has occurred (Miles, 1988; 1989). Along with others interested in this issue (for example, Hall *et al.*, 1978; van Dijk, 1991), he points to politicians, the media and the police as crucial agents through which such ideological developments take place. Miles goes on to argue that racialization processes are, with few exceptions, propelled by racist assumptions and propositions. They are, explicitly or otherwise, premised on an imposed ordering of groups – some better or worse, superior or inferior than others. Now, in these 'enlightened' times, such conceptions are only rarely derived from classical or 'scientific racism'. As Michael Billig *et al.* (1988) have shown, these interpretations of 'the way things are' are expressed in various forms and through a range of proxy concepts: ethnicity, culture, nationality, heritage, language and 'way of life' (see also Troyna, 1988; Rutherford, 1990). In Barker's (1981) words this discourse constitutes the 'new racism'.

So how might the education system reflect and contribute to this racialization process? To secure a tighter purchase on this matter, I want to use the analytical tools developed by Reeves (1983) in his book, *British Racial Discourse*. His analysis of the racialization process is especially incisive because he goes beyond the simple either–or dichotomy implied in most discussions on this theme.

Reeves argues that racial evaluations in political discourse may be overt or covert; what is more, they are geared towards either benign or racist goals. For example, the process of 'discursive deracialization' typifies a scenario in which 'persons speak purposively to their audiences about racial matters, while avoiding the overt deployment of racial descriptions, evaluations and prescriptions'

(Reeves, 1983, p. 4). This *covert* use of racial evaluations serves important political purposes, writes Reeves (1983, p. 4), because it is often capable of 'justifying racial discrimination by providing other non-racist criteria for the differential treatment of a group distinguished by its racial characteristics'. Britain's immigration laws of 1962, 1965, 1968, 1971 and 1981 are good examples of 'discoursive deracialization'.

The immigration laws were aimed progressively towards a racially selective mode of immigration control, though none was framed or justified in such explicit ways. In most political discourse non-racist criteria – including over-crowding, an additional strain on scarce resources, loss of British cultural iden-tity, and so on – were invoked to justify the introduction of increasingly more stringent immigration laws (Cashmore and Troyna, 1990). Deracialization is also the staple diet of the New Right's political discourse. Contributors to *The Salisbury Review*, a leading organ of the New Right, frame their concerns in deracialized language. In eschewing the blunt terminology of 'scientific racism' and couching their arguments in the discourse of the 'new racism', they erect a façade of respectability. In the process, they distance their arguments from the overtly racist invective of, say, the National Front. On the educational terrain there have been a number of cases in which racist imperatives have been reconstituted into the lexicon of culture to justify, say, the withdrawal of white children from ethnically mixed schools, the resistance to teaching in and through the main community languages of some black children, and the main-tenance of Eurocentric conceptions of the curriculum and religious priorities of the school (Oldman, 1987).

'Discoursive racialization' denotes the explicit use of racial categorization and evaluation. This may be directed towards avowedly racist aims when it figures in theories of fascism or scientific racism. Alternatively, it may assume benign forms. In this latter context, discoursive racialization 'reflects a growing awareness of and indignation at racial injustice. Racial evaluation and prescrip-tion is directed at refuting racialism and eliminating racialist practices' (Reeves, 1983, p. 175). Examples of this include the support for ethnic monitoring by the Commission for Racial Equality and some local authorities. Here, the aim is to identify racial inequalities in the distribution of resources in the housing and labour markets. In short, it is seen as a means to an end: racial equality and justice.

This form of 'benign racialization' also summarizes the focus of antiracist debates. Because these debates have made explicit reference to perceived racial differences and centralize these in subsequent policy initiatives, they could, in other contexts, be regarded as racist. But because they represent a means to an end – to mitigate racial inequalities and discrimination by first making their presence visible – such a characterization would be misplaced.

The distinction between *discoursive deracialization* and *benign racialization* allows us to tease out the continuities and discontinuities within and between the changing 'racial forms of education' in Britain. In addition, it provides a more sensitive lens through which to identify and interpret the muddled and contra-dictory ways in which key concepts such as 'race', ethnicity, culture, identity and

deprivation have been presented and related. Not only does it provide a correc-
tive to the linear process of policy development implied by the assimilation–
integration–cultural pluralism model, it also releases us from the conceptual
straitjacket imposed by Kirp's racially inexplicit–explicit framework.

It would seem appropriate to designate the 'racial forms of education' in the
1960s and 1970s as exemplars of a deracialized discourse. By obscuring the
realities of racism in the educational system, both monocultural and multicultural education helped to sustain the ideological façade of equality of opportunity. In Chapter 2, I will examine more carefully the way in which two
LEAs, the Inner London Education Authority and Manchester, operationalized
a deracialized conception of educational policy. Here, I want to spend some
time charting the move away from deracialized educational policy frameworks
and identify some of the most potent influences in this trend.

Towards the racialization of education policy

I noted earlier that some theorists and practitioners have remained stubbornly
committed to multicultural conceptions of educational reform despite the dubious empirical, theoretical and political grounds on which it is erected (Bullivant, 1981; Troyna 1987; see also Chapter 7). Even its most enthusiastic
custodians, however, would find it difficult to disagree with Williams's (1981,
p. 221) claim that: 'Very few theories can have suffered so short an optimistic
phase' as multicultural education.

As the 1980s wore on, an increasing number of LEAs, schools and colleges
eschewed what was fast becoming a discredited ideological and policy stance.
LEAs in a variety of political, demographic and material circumstances began to
introduce policy initiatives which gave prominence to a new explanatory concept in the British context: institutional racism. Not surprisingly, this highly
controversial conception of racism attracted hostile criticism from those on the
Right, who preferred to endorse what Henriques (1984) has declared as the
'rotten apple theory of racism' – namely, that there are racists in Britain and laws
to combat their discriminatory behaviour should be enforced; but that there is
nothing inherently or institutionally racist about the structure of the society and
accusations along these lines should be summarily discarded. The concept of
institutional racism has also attracted criticism from the Left. The main thrust of
this criticism has been to do with the elasticity and lack of precision implied in
the application of this all-embracing term (see Williams, 1986; Miles, 1989).

There is insufficient space to elaborate on these critiques here (but see
Chapter 7). However, it should be noted that in Britain institutional racism was
used to attack theories which blame victims for their oppression; theories, in
other words which resolve around deficit or pathological conceptions of racially oppressed groups. Institutional racism also influenced the nature of interventionist social and educational policies aimed at eradicating those practices
which help to generate and perpetuate racial inequalities. In the 1980s antiracism emerged as a summarizing variable for a range of ameliorative measures

related to education, institutional and otherwise. This shift towards the racialization of education policy occurred in a number of local authorities (Ball and Solomos, 1990) and seems to have derived from four principal sources.

Pressure groups

I noted earlier how the black communities in Britain had voiced their discontent at the role of education in the persistent 'underachievement' of their children and the racist deprecation of their cultural and ethnic backgrounds. In Chapter 2 I will look more closely at this issue. But it is important to point out here that their indictments of the British education system could not be wished away. Their demands for fundamental change were expressed in various ways: in organizations such as the Black Parents Movement; in the publication of pamphlets, including Bernard Coard's highly influential *How the West Indian Child Is Made Educationally Subnormal in the British School System* (1971); and through their support for black pupils' determination to show their discontent at the way they are treated, including, for example the strike witnessed at Tulse Hill School in South London (Dhondy, 1982). During the 1980s, these calls for action were expressed more vociferously and with great fervour. The growth of the black voluntary school movement, the publication of research pointing to enduring inequalities in the achievement levels of black and white children, threats of secession and boycotts and the forging of alliances between black groups and various local and national antiracist organizations helped to effect a shift in the thinking and provision of LEAs in different parts of Britain.

Events in Berkshire in the early 1980s provide a clear example of this process. Some local communities had been concerned about changes in the procedures governing the allocation of pupils to secondary schools. They were worried that this would have a detrimental impact on the opportunities available for black children. As a direct result of a campaign organized by an alliance of black and white activists, the LEA zoning scheme became the subject of a formal investigation by the Commission for Racial Equality. It also led to the Authority reappraising its routine modes of understanding and responding to issues of racial equality (del Tufo *et al.*, 1982).

'Policy entrepreneurs'

Historically, criticisms by parents, especially black and working-class parents, about the educational opportunities offered to their children have rarely prompted major policy appraisals and change. They are likely to be 'heard' only in circumstances where it is in the interests of local councillors and/or professional officers to respond positively. So why did these 'voices' begin to effect change in the 1980s? According to Young and Connelly (1981), the answer lies in the active role assumed by 'policy entrepreneurs'. That is, 'officers and councillors who were committed to change and who could make skilful use of such pressure from the community or from central agencies as were to hand' (Young and Connelly, 1981, p. 164). This is an attractive interpretation of the

origins and dynamics of newly conceived policy goals in local government. But
the emphasis on the campaigning activities of certain individuals as an explanation for the change towards the racialization of policy agendas also strikes me as
naive and little more than a truism. It also begs a couple of important questions.
What events, both locally and nationally, encouraged these individuals' commitment to change? And, what was the nature of the 'race policy environment', to use Saggar's (1991) phrase, operating in the specific locales? Did this
facilitate the move towards racialization? The 'policy entrepreneurs' thesis
provides an individualized interpretation of change. Because it dislocates those
individuals from broader structural and sociopolitical influences it fails to operate as an explanatory concept. In the following chapter I will expose more fully
the limitations of the 'policy entrepreneurs' thesis when I trace the development of policy in the ILEA and Manchester.

The work of Ben-Tovim *et al.* (1986), Saggar (1991) and Sivanandan (1983)
provides a more sophisticated sociological understanding of the changing nature
of local race-equality initiatives in the 1980s. They link the change with the
ascendancy in the 1980s of certain sections of the Labour Party in the local state.
According to this account, these councillors saw as part of their constituency a
range of 'disadvantaged' groups to whom they could offer access to resources in
return for votes. But it is clear that some local Labour parties were more responsive than others. These tended to be controlling areas which contain relatively
large black communities with voting strength in certain wards. Most were in
areas where one political party traditionally does not enjoy a clear majority at
elections; either there is a fairly regular change in political control (as in Birmingham) or a 'hung' council (as in Berkshire and Leicestershire).

Furthermore, while the Labour Party members generally took responsibility
for the initiation of the racialized policy, the document tended to emerge
publicly as a bipartisan stance, accepted and continued if and when the Conservative Party assumed local political control. But we should not oversimplify
and generalize these trends. In Liverpool, for example, a particular variety of
leftism meant that in the early 1980s the controlling Labour group interpreted
antiracism in a way which stemmed from a specific form of class analysis of
society. In Sheffield, where the Labour Party has generally been in power,
antiracist policies were a recent phenomenon in the 1980s, and only after 1982
did they figure on the policy agenda.

In general, then, the racialization of policies in local settings was stimulated
largely by a need to attract black electoral support and to incorporate the
communities into day-to-day political activities. With the continuing concentration of black citizens among the ranks of the poor, unemployed and
poorly housed electorate (Bradshaw, 1990), their support becomes increasingly
more important to those local and national politicians who wish to fight the
effects of the restructuring of capital through monetarist policies. Put another
way, local authorities, including their education departments, became one of
the key arenas for resistance against that political ideology known in the 1980s
(and beyond) as Thatcherism (see also Ball and Solomos, 1990; Butcher *et al.*,
1990). The geographical and residential concentration of those who have

suffered most under Thatcherite policies seems to provide at least part of the explanation for the local emergence of racialized policies which contrasted sharply with the multicultural concerns that continued to prevail in an over-whelming majority of LEAs in this period.

Professional and bureaucratic groups

Like their locally elected counterparts, professional education officers are vulnerable to complaints from parents that the education system is failing a sizeable number of pupils. Such criticisms are likely to evoke a more positive response if teacher and school competence rather than service provision *per se* constitutes the focus of complaint. In this context, where teachers are said to hold either 'unadmitted' racist attitudes and expectations or retain Anglocentric and out-moded syllabuses, administrators have been able, until recently, to use Section 11 moneys to provide in-service training and curriculum support services. This tactical approach corresponds with Wellman's (1977) claim that whites are adept at understanding racism in ways which do not implicate themselves in either its causes or remedies.

At the same time it is also true that some teachers and their professional organizations have played leading roles in the advocacy of antiracist policies. Neither the National Union of Teachers nor the Assistant Masters and Mistresses Association circumvented the issue of racism in its policy statements (AMMA, 1987; NUT, 1989). Alongside them, campaigning groups such as NAME, the All London Teachers Against Racism and Fascism (ALTARF), the Campaign Against Racism in Education (CARE) and the Antiracist Teacher Education Network (ARTEN) have campaigned in favour of schools' publishing racialized policies. In some cases, these have precipitated action from hitherto recalcitrant LEAs.

Despite these grassroots activities, it is clearly the case that calls for action, however rational or justified, do not gain credence or stimulate activity automatically. The racialization of local policies in the 1980s also has to be located in a broader framework which recognizes the articulation of educational imperatives with sociopolitical concerns.

Black youth and the 1981 'riots'

Even the most cursory glance at the interpretations adduced for the disturbances in Brixton, Toxteth, Moss Side and elsewhere in 1981 would reveal that the education system was exhorted to assume pivotal status in preventing their recurrence. In his report on the disorders in Brixton, for instance, Scarman (1981) highlighted the responsibility of schools to provide 'suitable educational . . . opportunities' for black pupils. They were also called upon to produce more skilled young workers and contribute to the development of more harmonious race relations. After the disturbances in Tottenham and Handsworth in 1985, Scarman reaffirmed this view: 'the real causes of the trouble', he told the *Sunday Times* (12 January 1986), 'are bad housing, jobs and education. Education above all'. Since 1981, in particular, a growing number of LEAs have responded to Scarman's recommendations by producing explicit policies affirming a commitment to multicultural and, to a lesser extent, anti-racist goals. Indeed, the trend accelerated after the disturbances in 1985.

Nineteen eighty-one was also the year in which the Parliamentary Home Affairs Committee on Race Relations and Immigration recommended that schools examine their formal and 'hidden' curriculum to ensure that they provided the means to combat racism and promote equality of opportunity. It warned that a 'failure to act, now the facts are generally known, will cause widespread disappointment and ultimately unrest among the ethnic minority groups of our society' (House of Commons, 1981, p. 106). The growth of youth unemployment, particularly among black youngsters, the acceptance of Rastafari by some black youths, and the manufacture of a 'moral panic' around the issue of mugging contributed to the perception of young blacks as a 'social time bomb', ready to rebel and tear apart the social fabric. The ways in which the state interprets these events are more likely to lead to control measures such as law and order campaigns and extra policing, on the one hand (see Cashmore and McLaughlin, 1991), and particular sorts of post-school employment schemes, on the other. However, they can also provide a setting within which radical policies may find space and legitimacy.

Looking back on the 1980s, it is possible to see both of these competing trajectories in the framing of social and educational policy. I have already noted a growing acknowledgement, especially in the local state, of the pervasiveness, even institutionalization of racism, as opposed to 'rotten apple' theories. Even outside the local state it was possible to discern this trend in, for instance, the interim report of the government's inquiry into the education of ethnic minority children (DES, 1981), under the stewardship of Anthony Rampton. This specified racism as a significant factor in accounting for 'black educational underachievement' (see Chapter 3). Yet the same period saw the intensification of discriminatory immigration legislation undermining further the citizenship status of Britain's black communities (Gordon, 1985). In a context of concern and repression, law and order and integration rhetoric, the state's contrivance of 'aliens' and 'citizens' and so on, the education system is delegated responsibility for dealing with a range of insoluble problems.

Central and local state relations

During the 1980s successive Secretaries of State for Education (Mark Carlisle, Keith Joseph and Kenneth Baker) and their respective ministers spoke convincingly about the need to eradicate racial discrimination in education. And their successors, John MacGregor, Kenneth Clark and John Patten, have continued to do so. Their interventions, however, have been firmly embedded in the discourse of the 'rotten apple' theory of racism. In this regard, neither they nor the DES played a role in the development of racialized conceptions of education policy. However, neither did they intervene in a formal or obstructive way to the development of antiracist policies at the level of the local state. How can this disinterest be explained, given the state's concern and alarm after the urban disturbances of 1981 and 1985?

Implicitly, at least, the argument goes something like this. The urban disturbances were confined to relatively few cities; black pressure groups and radicals operate within certain localities; black youth unemployment is geographically concentrated areas. *Ergo* antiracism is an issue for the inner cities and must be developed, if at all, by LEAs in those geographical areas. Needless to say, the devastation of these areas which has given rise to these problems derives largely from more broadly based economic and social crises and the way in which the national state has responded. However, the discourse of 'social problems' keeps this broader setting off the political agenda. In the relatively decentralized education system which prevailed between 1944 and the passing of the 1988 Education Reform Act, LEAs were provided, implicitly or otherwise, with the opportunity to develop local policies in response to perceived local problems. Teachers and schools may be reformed; antiracism may be introduced in local state arenas, but the national state can continue to adopt the stance of 'benign neglect' and disinterest – expressing concern while delegating responsibility in accordance with the perceived distribution of roles inferred from the 1944 Education Act. What was invoked in this scenario, then, was the inviolability of the 1944 Act and the institutional powerlessness of the central state allegedly enshrined in this legislation. As Dorn and Troyna (1982) have argued, however, this was a policy of expedience. It was not a demonstration of an unswerving commitment to legislative principles, as the intervention of the central state in other areas of education (such as vocational education and the curriculum) clearly shows.

But the most important point to be made here is not claims of institutional powerlessness, or otherwise; nor is structural decentralization the key issue. It is that the racialization of LEA policies took place in a context profoundly influenced by national state policies. The rise in (black) youth unemployment, the contraction of local services and facilities, increasing emphasis on 'national needs' and 'accountability' and the associated demands for more rigorous 'training' constitute some obvious examples. To reiterate an earlier argument, it is the national state which provides the social, economic and ideological contexts in which local educationists have to respond.

We can now see why it is useful to see LEAs as 'sites of struggle'. It is on this stage that attempts to reconcile political pressures, parental demands, teacher and pupil activities and administrative inertia are acted out. But these struggles take shape and form in response to material and ideological contexts which themselves are moulded by national and international developments over which local actors have no control.

A critical appraisal of racialized education policies

The development of 'racial forms of education' in Britain has parallels with the move towards multicultural education in the United States. In challenging some other interpretations of this trend (for example, Banks, 1981), Olneck (1990) suggests that the differences in the USA are rhetorical rather than substantive. He argues that the form of multicultural education which emerged in the USA in the 1970s and 1980s differed little, in either its ideology or symbolism, from the discredited intercultural education orthodoxy of the 1940s.

It is tempting, if provocative, to argue a similar point in relation to the move from multicultural to antiracist education in Britain in the 1980s. I want to sustain this argument by scrutinizing the policy statements of seven LEAs (Brent, Berkshire, Sheffield, Manchester, ILEA, Haringey and Bradford). Each had ostensibly completed the journey from deracialization to racialized education policies by the mid-1980s. However, I want to suggest that this process resulted in little more than putting old wine in new bottles. Wittingly or otherwise, ideological sleights of hand in the presentation of these policies resulted in obscuring rather than clarifying the nature of racism in education and the specific processes which generate racial inequality. These key issues were hidden behind a version of racism which rests on certain discursive themes, or what Edelman (1964) typifies as 'condensation symbols'. According to Edelman, condensation symbols have a specific political purpose: to create symbolic stereotypes and metaphors which reassure supporters that their interests have been taken into account. But these symbols have a contradictory meaning so that the proposed solutions to perceived problems might also be contradictory, or ambiguously related to the way in which proponents and supporters initially viewed the issue.

There are some commentators, however, who are impatient with textual analysis of policy documents. They assert that it is at best a limited, at worst a misplaced, exercise. From this perspective, textual analysis is seen as providing only a partial glimpse into how policy-makers intend to use their policies to mobilize action along desired routes. Moreover, focused attention on the conceptual and semantic (im)precision of documents is said to ignore the hostile political context in which policy-makers have to function and within which their policies originate and seek to establish legitimacy.

Richardson (1983) argued from this standpoint. He played a leading part in the formulation and diffusion of Berkshire's 1983 policy initiative, *Education for Equality*, and later assumed a similar role in the London Borough of Brent. He suggested that the main aims of policies were: to provide institutional support for isolated teachers already working along antiracist lines, and to facilitate the process through which racial inequality would be established as a lens through which routine matters of educational provision would be viewed in discussions at LEA level. Policies *were* worth the paper they were written on, insisted Richardson, because they represented 'a petard by which an LEA consciously and deliberately seeks to be hoisted'. It is a view which corresponds closely with Kogan's (1975, p. 65) characterization of policies as 'statements of intent'.

Despite Richardson's reservations about this approach to policy statements, I want to insist that, for the policy sociologist involved in the 'social science project', textual analysis is a legitimate venture. These policy statements reflect deep-rooted values and project ideal versions of society (see Grace, 1984; Ball,

1990). As Dale (1986, p. 64) points out, the domain of the 'social science project' is to be found in the interrogation of 'the appropriateness and framing of the problems and questions'. He goes on to say that by adopting this perspective, 'we can begin to refine the questions we ask of, and the problems we set policy-makers – by seeking to identify which problems are amenable to solution at which level, and in which area of policy-making' (1986, p. 64). It is imperative, then, that we deconstruct the versions of reality enshrined in policies and explicate the values which underpin and guide them. In this way we are able to identify precisely whose versions of an 'ideal society' they represent. If we find obfuscation or ambiguity in their conceptual make-up this needs to be illuminated. Otherwise, the policies are susceptible to mis-interpretation or worse, appropriation, hijacking and subversion by those who are indifferent, even opposed, to their concerns.

Four condensation symbols characterized the racialized, or antiracist, education policies of LEAs in the 1980s: plural society; justice; equality; and racism. I want to spend some time looking critically at their deployment in the seven LEA policy statements.

Plural society

'Plural society' assumes both normative and substantive status in policy state-ments. Repeatedly, these distinctive ideological positions are conflated so that the term is used both in descriptive and prescriptive senses: we *are* a plural society; we must aim to *become* a truly pluralist society. The difference between what society is and should be is neatly blurred. This construction allows policy-makers to create what Bullivant (1981, p. 228) designates as 'specious models of society'. Consider the following assertion found in the first of Brent's 1983 booklets, *Education for a Multicultural Democracy*:

> The Council is committed to a fundamental and significant change to a multicultural education based on a concept of cultural pluralism. The recognition that all people and cultures are inherently equal must be a constant from which all educational practice will develop.
>
> (London Borough of Brent, 1983, p. 15)

A similar piece of ideological chicanery can be found in Haringey's claim that the Authority comprises 'a multiracial, multicultural society and the council will continue to foster good relations between all sections of the community . . . cultural diversity has enriched, not weakened British society' (London Borough of Haringey, 1978, p. 6). And, finally, the Sheffield multicultural support group asserts that: 'Schools need to recognise the growing need to prepare *all* their youngsters for life as citizens in a just, humane, multicultural democracy' (Sheffield, 1982). In none of these passages is it possible to dis-tinguish between appraisals of society as it is currently constituted and wishful thinking about what society might become.

The political symbolism behind these assertions denotes a harmonious society where divisions based on perceived racial differences are no more or less

significant than cultural divisions. In effect, policy-makers promote the view
that cultural and racial differences are synonymous. They give spurious legitimacy to the view that the subordination of black people in Britain is due as
much to their cultural distinctiveness as to the fact that they are designated
racially inferior. The merger of 'race' with culture is precisely what Macdonald
et al. (1989) identified earlier in this chapter as one of the fundamental flaws in
multicultural education. The political significance of this strategy is that it
enables debate to switch from an outline of existing divisions, conflicts, discrimination and inequalities which derive from racism, to an ideal towards
which we might all strive. There is no clear analysis of how the two might be
related. What is absent from these policies is a more stipulative definition of the
role of the education system in the perpetuation and reproduction of racial
inequalities and what part it might play in the development of a genuinely
plural society – a society, that is, in which horizontal not vertical differentiation
prevails.

Justice

In policy documents, 'justice' embraces a wide range of citizenship rights: from
the right not to be physically or verbally abused on the grounds of one's
perceived racial origins, to the more ambiguous right to have one's history and
culture recognized in a respectful and non-tokenistic way in the routines of
educational institutions. But when the concept is deconstructed, its ambiguities
and contradictions, generally concealed in everyday discourse, are laid bare. For
instance, because Britain is an unequal society, stratified by 'race', class and
gender, it follows logically that an essential part of natural justice demands an
acknowledgement of what might be acceptable and unacceptable inequalities
under a meritocratic system.

On the basis of Berkshire's document, racial inequalities are designated
as unacceptable in so far as black students are overrepresented in low-status
positions in school and society. Thus:

> There will be perfect racial justice in Britain if and when the practices,
> procedures and customs determining the allocation of resources do not
> discriminate, directly or indirectly, against ethnic minority people and
> when these practices are on the contrary fair to all.
>
> (Berkshire Education Authority, 1983, p. 5)

It continues:

> There will be racial justice in education, it follows, if and when the factors
> determining successful learning in schools do not discriminate, directly or
> indirectly, against ethnic minority children.
>
> (Berkshire Education Authority, 1983, p. 5)

But this mystifies rather than clarifies the position. By privileging a concern
with the eradication of racial inequality it implies, probably unwittingly, that
other structurally derived inequalities in education are acceptable. It also

projects an overdetermined model of schooling. How? First, by ignoring the complex articulation of 'race' with gender and class in non-school contexts. Second, by suggesting, as a corollary, that schools have the means, in and of themselves, to obviate racial inequalities. As McCarthy (1990) has shown, there is an intersecting and relational impact of class, 'race' and gender in the production and reproduction of educational inequality which is both inconsistent and contradictory (see also Chapter 7). The concealment of these complex processes within Berkshire's conception of justice leads to distortion and obfuscation. To use Gilroy's (1990) term, it legitimates 'a coat of paint theory of racism' in which racial inequality is conceived and addressed in ways which dislocate it from the broader social, political and historical processes in society which have institutionalized unequal power. Berkshire's policy-makers would have been taking a more propitious route if they had differentiated economic, political, social and educational injustices and proceeded to show the specific role of schools in perpetuating different forms of injustice.

Equality

Equality, in the context of policy statements, is generally a shorthand term for equality of outcome. It legitimates the liberal concern with ensuring that equality of opportunity derives from a set of conditions under which 'the proportion of people from different social, economic or ethnic categories at all levels and in all types of education [is] more or less the same as the proportion of these people in the population at large' (Halsey, 1972, p. 8). In the discourse of race relations this interpretation is linked to the realization of a colour-blind meritocracy. This approximates to what Green (1988) characterizes as the 'competitive' understanding of equality of opportunity. 'Equality under this understanding', argues Green (1988, p. 6), 'consists in equal competition for scarce resources'. By deferring to this idealistic view of equality, policy-makers distance themselves from alternative interpretations, especially those which champion forms of affirmative action or positive discrimination, necessary, of course, to counteract the deeply embedded nature of inequalities in British society.

Equality means sameness in this context. As the following passage from Berkshire's policy indicates, it is the liberal rather than radical version of equal opportunities which prevails – a scenario in which the establishment of 'fair procedures' is seen as sufficient (see Troyna, 1987, for further discussion):

> No, the statement is not recommending positive discrimination. That is, it does not envisage that membership of an ethnic minority could ever be a reason, in itself, for treating one individual more favourably than another.
> (Berkshire Education Authority, 1983, p. 3)

This prompts the question, why not? After all, the most common argument for antiracist education is that policies and practices need to be developed to counteract processes whereby membership of an ethnic minority group has historically and currently ensured that some individuals are treated less favourably than others. The logical outcome of this position is that affirmative action policies *do* have a legitimate, even essential, part to play in the framing and enactment of antiracist education programmes.

Racism

As a condensation symbol, racism is often used as a synonym for institutional racism. It is intended to convey how far racist assumptions and ways of doing things have been naturalized into established attitudes, procedural norms and social patterns. However, if the divisive properties of racism were to be accorded significance in policy documents, this would raise uncomfortable political issues. It would demand a radical critique of society and the role it assigns to education in the production, strengthening and reproduction of inequalities. In other words, it would raise serious questions about the selective and allocative function of schools. Not surprisingly, this is discarded as a viable policy option. So how do policy-makers avoid this dilemma?

Racism is conceived expressly in terms of immorality and ignorance, rather than oppression and exploitation, and is invested with individualized not structural properties. The outcome? Policies which focus on changing white attitudes towards minority ethnic cultures. As a result, in-service training and racism awareness courses figure prominently on the menu of LEA antiracist initiatives. 'Reformed' teachers are then expected to influence positively their pupils' racial attitudes. ILEA (1983, p. 17) quoted favourably the following passage from the NUT's (1983) *Combating Racialism in Schools*:

> Only by adopting such a positive stance (that is, valuing the cultures and achievements of ethnic minority pupils) and by using opportunities to replace ignorance with factual information about other cultures and the reasons for immigration to this country, will teachers show that they are effectively anti-racialist.

It is reasoned, then, that racism can be dislodged simply through a presentation of 'the truth' – a factual, undistorted and objective view of the world. This perspective, of course, is an axiom of multicultural education.

Putting to one side the theoretical and political objections to this oversimplified, some might say caricatured and essentialized conception of antiracist education (which I critique more thoroughly in Chapter 7), this conception of racism raises other, equally problematic issues. If racism is seen as an integral part of a system which has privileged white people, then what incentive is there for white people to immerse themselves in antiracist programmes? What would they gain – economically, politically or psychologically – from disturbing a system which has served them so well? An answer to these questions is found in Berkshire's (1983, p. 6) *General Policy*: 'Racism is against the long-term interest of all, since it is bound to lead eventually to social unrest'. Antiracism is therefore seen as a pre-emptory strike; an appeal to white people willingly to concede some of their privileges now, in order to prevent those privileges being forcibly removed in the future.

The passage from Berkshire's document illuminates another dimension of policy-makers' understanding of racism. It is seen primarily as a white problem. But antiracism is also situated (at least implicitly) in a framework of 'special needs'. Black pupils (and their parents) are said to be presenting problems to the education system through their allegedly poor academic performance, disruptive behaviour, demands for voluntary community schools and recognition of their culture in the mainstream curriculum, and insistence on other political concessions. These are presented as examples of their 'special needs' which require 'special treatment' in the form of certain refinements to the education system. What is implied is that, in the absence of these concessions, the ideals of political and social cohesion, stability and harmony are unlikely to be achieved.

The continuities between this ostensibly racialized position on education and seemingly discredited (and discarded) multicultural approaches are obvious. The strategy comprises the re-education of whites for the sake of harmony and for demonstrating cultural justice to black people. Antiracism can be diverted away from a concern with material inequalities towards the removal of barriers which prevent the full flowering of ethnic and cultural identities and individual social mobility.

Conclusion

Earlier in this chapter I criticized writers such as Mal Leicester, Phil Cohen, Geoffrey Short and James Lynch who asserted that the distinction between multicultural and antiracist education was illusory and that the debate about the relative worth of these paradigms of change was 'sterile' (Cohen, 1988). On the basis of an exploration of the condensation symbols in racialized LEA policy statements it might be difficult to disagree with their assessment, even if their characterization of the theoretical positionings of these respective paradigms leaves something to be desired. The radical departure of racialized policies from deracialized understandings of the relationship between black pupils and the education system is more apparent than real. Racialized policies in the mid-1980s were, on the whole, pretentious – promising more than they could deliver. The conception of antiracist education which they embraced tended to retain and reproduce many of the theoretical weaknesses and ideological perspectives more commonly associated with multicultural education.

This failure stemmed from the reluctance of policy-makers to cohere 'race', class and gender inequalities into a more broadly conceived programme, alongside their inattention to specifying more precisely the ways in which the education system contributes to the legitimation and reproduction of racism. The analysis also reveals how far the conception of antiracism projected in these policy statements corresponds with understandings of racial discrimination circulating in the national state. In both discourses, racism is disarticulated from other forms of inequality and injustice and distilled into individualized forms. Both the national and local state collude in constituting 'race' and racism as superficial features of society; aberrations, rather than integral to our under-

standing of the way society functions. This is why Gilroy refers to this positioning as 'the coat of paint theory of racism'; he argues:

> This is not in fact, a single theory but an approach sees racism on the
> outside of social and political life – sometimes the unwanted blemish is
> the neo-fascists, sometimes it is immigration laws, other times it is the
> absence of equal opportunities – yet racism is always located on the
> surface of other things. It is an unfortunate excrescence on a democratic
> polity which is essentially sound, and it follows from this that with the
> right ideological tools and political elbow grease, racism can be dealt with
> once and for all leaving the basic structures and relations of British econ-
> omy and society essentially unchanged.
>
> (Gilroy, 1990, p. 195)

In all, then, the racialized education policies of the 1980s amounted to little
more than an exercise in left-wing gesture politics. Despite the move towards
racialization, antiracist education policies, like the more radical multicultural
policies, contrived a version of reality in which racism was seen as independent
of and not integral to the way society is organized, structured and legitimated.

2 'Benevolent Neo-colonialism'? Local Case Studies of Deracialized Education Policy

In this chapter I want to present two case studies which document the origins and legitimation of multicultural education in two LEAs in the 1980s. This will not be an entirely descriptive account. The imperatives of the 'social science project' demand a more critical appraisal of this development and an exploration of the social, structural and historical factors which help to structure, maybe even distort, the process of policy-making and implementation.

Crucially, the story I will tell, of how and why ILEA and Manchester adopted deracialized policies in this period, ends up with a picture which is profoundly different from that which exists in the early 1990s. To start with, the ILEA no longer exists. By the end of the 1980s it had developed a coherent, cohesive and high-profile policy stance on racial, class and gender equality. Despite its many theoretical flaws and the enduring discrepancy between rhetoric and practice, the ILEA policy package on equal opportunities 'symbolised for the Right everything it hated about education' (Jones, 1989, p. 151). The Conservative Party's discourse of derision towards the equal opportunities initiatives of LEAs prompted the abolition of the ILEA in April 1990 as part of the 1988 ERA restructuring of the educational system (see Chapter 3). Since then, responsibility for education in inner London has been devolved to individual London boroughs. Reynolds (1991, p. 75) argues that by singling out the ILEA,

> the [Conservative] Government was able to discredit other attempts at 'equal opportunities' initiatives in other Local Education Authorities. The attack on the ILEA became the 'raison d'être' for similar attacks on educational philosophies and techniques committed to developing anti-racist and anti-sexist approaches.

In place of the ILEA the boroughs show a fragmented, hesitant and ambiguous commitment to racial equality, as can be seen from their Development Plans, issued in 1989 (see Table 1).

This strategic deployment of the totalizing fallacy by the Conservative administration also helped to provide a legitimating gloss for the anti-egalitarian

Table 1 Inner London Borough plans for Antiracist/Multi-ethnic Education

	Camden	Greenwich	Hackney	Hammersmith	Islington	Kensington and Chelsea	Lambeth	Lewisham	Southwark	Tower Hamlets	Wandsworth	Westminster
Acknowledges obligations under 1976 Race Relations Act	yes	yes	yes	no	no	yes	yes	yes	yes	yes	yes	yes
Acknowledges Swann or Eggleston reports	no	yes	no	no	no	no	no	yes	no	no	yes	no
Backs Anti-racist teaching	no	yes	no	yes	no	no	yes	no	no	no	no	yes
Will provide 2nd language support	yes	yes	yes	yes	yes	yes	yes	yes	yes	yes	yes	yes
Will provide INSET on race and ethnicity	no	yes	no	no	yes	no	yes	no	yes	no	yes	no
Proposes a Multi-ethnic Inspectorate	yes	no	no	no	yes	no	no	yes	yes	yes	no	no
Outlines Section 11 plans	yes	yes	yes	yes	yes	yes	yes	yes	yes	yes	yes	yes
Acknowledges work of Supplementary schools	no	yes	yes	yes	no	no	no	no	yes	yes	yes	no
Recognizes imbalance of Black children suspended and expelled	yes	yes	no	yes	no	no	yes	no	yes	no	no	no
Policy on the appointment of Black teaching staff	yes	yes	yes	yes	yes	no	yes	yes	yes	yes	no	no
Offers statistics on Black school population	no	yes	yes	yes	no	no	yes	yes	yes	no	yes	no
Proposes ethnic monitoring	no	no	yes	no	no	no	no	yes	yes	yes	no	no

Source: London Voluntary Service Unit/Afro–Caribbean Community Development Unit (1989): *The 1988 Education Reform Act and Its Impact on London's Black Communities*, p. 5.

thrust of the ERA. In the event, it paved the way for the rise of what Kate Myers calls 'equiphobia' – that is, 'an irrational hatred and fear of anything to do with equal opportunities' (Myers, 1990, p. 295).

Equiphobia transcends geographical and political boundaries and is a discernible feature in the educational priorities established in and acted upon in Manchester, the other case-study LEA. Again, by the late 1980s, this LEA had adopted a more politicized and racialized policy to tackle racist and sexist forms of inequality in education (see Ball et al., 1990). This was underpinned by a series of initiatives designed to ensure the translation of policy commitments into practice. By the early 1990s, this commitment had receded; this was partly due to financial expedience associated with a declining budget and the onset of prescriptive funding for in-service education (Harland, 1985; Knight, 1987), partly also because of the perceived political benefits deriving from deference to the Conservative educational agenda and the 'New Realism' of the Labour Party.

I will elaborate on many of these issues in the next chapter when I consider the state's articulation with racial equality concerns in the late 1980s. Here, I want to revisit the late 1970s and early 1980s – a historical moment in which the seeds of deracialized policies began to flower in the ideology of multiculturalism. Let me begin, however, by considering the efficacy of case-study research as a means of understanding the concerns and priorities of this particular historical moment.

Case-study research

Case studies, according to Wilson (1979), have 'certain basic generic properties'. First, they are particularistic, describing events in a specific situation. Second, they are holistic, exploring the multifaceted features of the situation through interrogation of a range of salient variables. Third, they are longitudinal and therefore dynamic; they trace developments over a length of time and chart their continuities and discontinuities. Finally, they are based on qualitative rather than quantitative research methods.

Not all writers agree that these properties essentially define case-study research, however. Elliott (1990), for instance, argues that 'these qualities are not generic in the sense that they are defining characteristics of all case study research'. He goes on to say: 'The only common characteristic I can think of which covers all the case studies I have read is their focus on particular situations and events' (Elliott, 1990, p. 47). Helen Simons agrees. In her view, the unique feature of case-study research is the focus on a single setting as the unit under investigation. In education, this may be a classroom, cohort of students, peer group, institution or system (Simons, 1989, p. 116). Simons is insistent that case-study research does not imply a commitment to qualitative research or the necessary privileging of one form of data collection over others.

The issues of typicality and generalizability also pose problems for researchers focusing on single cases. It is possible to conceive of solutions to these problems, however. As both Elliott (1990) and Bryman (1988) point out, the external validity of case studies derives mainly from their *usefulness as projective models* for others in exploring their own unique situations' (Elliott, 1990, p. 59; emphasis in original). Bryman elaborates this argument and suggests that case-study researchers should not necessarily conceive of their unit of analysis as if it were a sample of one drawn from a much wider universe of such cases. The issue, Bryman (1988, p. 90) suggests, 'should be couched in terms of the generalizability of cases to theoretical propositions rather than to populations or universes'.

'Race' and local politics

It is tempting to assume on a priori grounds, that national patterns and trends in race-related matters in education in the 1960s, 1970s and early to mid-1980s, were reproduced perfectly in the thinking and practices of LEAs throughout Britain. However, because of the vagaries of local politics and the structural decentralization of the education system in the period 1944–88, such an assumption is unwarranted. As I argued in Chapter 1, LEAs are more appropriately seen as 'sites of struggle' where local professional officers, elected members and teachers retain some influence over what goes on in their local educational institutions.

The local response to DES support for bussing in the 1960s and early 1970s provides a good example of the discretionary powers enjoyed by LEAs, particularly before the introduction of the 1988 ERA. As the DES (1971, p. 18) noted, the impact of its 1965 circular on this issue had been patchy, to say the least: 'Some [LEAs] have adopted a policy of dispersing immigrant children, but the majority have not, either because it was impracticable or because they did not agree with it'.

In the context of decentralization and the variable influence of those commissioning and facilitating factors operating in local milieux, identified in Chapter 1, differences in LEA thinking and provision were to be expected. But this is using only the broadest brush strokes. To paint a clearer picture it is important to select, for detailed analysis, cases which provide a specific focus for the integration of theory with empirical data. But why the ILEA and Manchester?

There are good pragmatic grounds for this selection. In the late 1960s, and particularly during the 1970s, a number of LEAs in a range of circumstances had drafted documents on race relations. On the whole, these tended to be position papers confined to specific issues such as English as a second language (ESL) or bussing. Of course, it is possible to infer general educational and race-related principles from these documents. Even so, they were, generally speaking, specific guidance or advisory notes in response to immediate contingencies. The policy statements produced by the ILEA in 1977 and Manchester in 1978, were of an entirely different status. These were affirmations of the ideology of multicultural education which had the support of their respective Education Committees and were intended to be circulated to and acted upon by all LEA employees. Those officers and elected members who formulated these policies conceived of them as change agents. Their aim was to provide a reconstituted conceptual framework for curricular, organizational and pedagogic procedures. How far they achieved these aims is not a question I want to address here (but see Troyna, 1984a; Troyna and Ball, 1987). The point I want to stress is that they assumed a qualitatively different status from other race-related documents produced at this time either within or beyond the two LEAs.

The ILEA and Manchester policies also attract attention because they became exemplary models for other LEAs. Neither the concerns they addressed nor the solutions they proposed were exceptional. They operationalized particular interpretations of cultural pluralism in response to locally perceived and interpreted problems through which racial issues impinged on local politics and educational institutions. In this sense, they are concrete examples of a de-racialized policy discourse despite differences in the process of policy-making and underpinning conceptions of multicultural education. What is more, they typified the uncritical acceptance of what I identified in Chapter 1 as the key assumptions of multicultural education.

Conceptions of multicultural education

In an attempt to insert greater conceptual and analytical precision into the debate about multicultural education, Margaret Gibson (1976) disaggregated the various approaches developed in the name of this genre. This exercise threw up five ideal types of which two, 'benevolent multiculturalism' and 'cultural understanding', are of particular relevance here.

The conditions which give rise to the 'benevolent multiculturalism' model, writes Gibson (1976, p. 7), are 'the continuing academic failure of students from a certain minority ethnic group whose school performance continues to lag behind national norms'. In accounting for these differences in performance, 'benevolent multiculturalists' reject cultural and genetic deficit models and focus on the development of educational programmes which aim to increase compatibility between the home and school culture. The target population for these reformist programmes is the particular group of pupils designated as 'underachievers'. The strategy is the provision of a culturally relevant curriculum and teaching aids; the goal, to achieve equality of outcomes.

The 'benevolent multiculturalist' perspective resonates with two of the key assumptions which give multicultural education (spurious) legitimacy: that a child from an ethnic minority background will achieve greater academic success if her or his cultural background is acknowledged in the school; and that this approach enhances equality of opportunity.

In contrast to the particularistic concerns of 'benevolent multiculturalism', the 'cultural understanding' approach is universalistic in orientation. It is an inclusive conception of multiculturalism, intended to implicate all pupils in the process of reappraisal and change. Thus, it links in with the third of Bullivant's (1981) key assumptions: that learning about other cultures will dislodge (white) children's racial prejudice and discrimination.

The analytical and conceptual distinctions drawn by Gibson help to sharpen the following discussion about the way multicultural education was interpreted in the ILEA and Manchester. I will argue that the 'benevolent multicultural-ism' approach was adopted in the former, while the path taken in Manchester approximated to the 'cultural understanding' perspective. But systematizing the approaches is only part of the story. It is also important to tease out the reasons why policy-makers embarked on the route of multicultural education and, having chosen to do so, why they privileged a particular version of this genre. To answer these questions we need to reconstruct the local events and de-velopments which impacted on the consciousness of local policy-makers in the two LEAs and prompted them to disavow previous and alternative educational principles in favour of multicultural education.

'Benevolent multiculturalism' in the ILEA

London has always been one of the main settlement areas for migrants to Britain, a pattern which continued with the arrival of migrants from British colonies and ex-colonies in the Caribbean and South Asia after the Second World War. Townsend and Brittan (1972) reported that of the 270,745 pupils defined by the DES (1971) as 'immigrant', slightly over half attended schools in London. Despite this history, the ILEA did little to encourage its teaching and administrative staff to take ethnic and cultural diversity – never mind racism – into account in appraising the appropriateness of their practices and procedures. As a local Community Relations Council officer noted: 'Before the 1977 policy it was a case of nondiscrimination, that we treat everybody equally. We are all God's children, that kind of approach' (personal communication). In the mid-1970s, the Afro-American educationist, Raymond Giles (1977, p. 96), reached the same conclusion on the basis of his discussions with local head-teachers and their staff.

> Many heads and teachers did not favour multiracial approaches to educa-tion, nor did they feel that children should be seen or treated any dif-ferently because of race or colour. Many schools with this philosophy were in favour of cultural assimilation as an educational goal.

An essential feature of cultural assimilation was language provision for pupils whose first language (or 'mother tongue') was not English. In this respect, the ILEA assiduously followed national conceptions of the educational system's responsibilities in a multicultural society. It provided first-stage ESL tuition to pupils of South Asian origin, although those of Afro-Caribbean origin were omitted from the programme. The aim was simply to provide non-English pupils with functional competence in English, a service which would facilitate their adaptation to the British educational system and, at the same time, help to secure its meritocratic credibility. As I argued in Chapter 1, the prime impera-tive of assimilation is to provide the means by which 'they' become as near as possible like 'us'.

Monocultural education in the ILEA received tacit support from Eric Briault, its Education Officer between 1971 and 1977. In his influential document, *An Education Service for the Whole Community* (Briault, 1973) he maintained that 'any future provision' must be based 'on the existence of a multiracial society'. Despite this laudable rhetoric, the discourse of the document failed to reveal any programmatic strategy for promoting cultural diversity or tackling racism at a personal, institutional or systemic level. On the contrary, the following extract from the document suggests that assimilation was uppermost in his mind if educational provision was not to be distorted by the ethnically mixed nature of the local school population: 'Recent immigrants present difficulties of language, insufficient education before arrival and problems of settling into a strange urban way of life. Their different outlook and background constitute a special challenge to teachers' (Briault, 1973, p. 19). The corollary, of course, was that the 'problem' was seen as transitory. The discontinuities in immigrant children's educational experiences would, with the help of the school, disappear with the passage of time. From this vantage point, all that was required was the provision of traditional teaching materials and curriculum practices augmented by an ESL programme and time.

This assimilationist ideology was also reflected in the way the ILEA delegated responsibility for race-related matters within the inspectorate. Between 1966 and 1974, the Inspector for the Socially and Culturally Deprived assumed this responsibility within a more general brief. It was not until 1974 that an Inspector for Community Relations was appointed – a decision inspired as much by political as by educational motives. It was expected initially that he would 'look at the issues related to black kids at school and work on the question of liaison consultation with communities'. The rationale for the establishment of the post and his appointment? 'Being crude', he told me, 'I suspect [they] can also be seen as a concern over lack of achievement and problems of behaviour'. These were issues which were beginning to compel the time and attention of officers and councillors in the ILEA and played a significant part in the eventual publication of the 1977 *Multi-Ethnic Education* policy statement.

During the late 1960s, the ILEA's Research and Statistics (R and S) branch initiated a longitudinal study of a cohort of pupils born in London between 1959 and 1960. They were tested on their reading attainment on four occasions in their school career, the first in 1968 when they were 8+ years old. Seven years later, the former director of the R and S branch, Alan Little, reported on the combined results of the 1968 literary survey and a related project which had looked at a range of other abilities. One of his four main conclusions was that:

The relatively poor performance of minority pupils is across the curriculum (passive and active vocabulary, verbal reasoning, reading, English, mathematics and study skills) although some differences can be found in certain parts of the curriculum. Finally, under-privileged white children perform at a higher level than West Indian settlers and this appears to be true of pupils before and in the early years of their primary education.

(Little, 1975, p. 68)

This apparent trend towards the 'educational underachievement' of black pupils, especially those of Afro-Caribbean origin, had another dimension which had first been brought to light in an internal ILEA report in 1966. This revealed that while only 13.2 per cent of the Authority's pupil population were 'immigrants', those of Afro-Caribbean background comprised 23.3 per cent of those in the ILEA's schools for the educationally sub-normal (ESN). These data assumed an even more insidious complexion when, in 1967, an ILEA survey reported that teachers in ESN schools reckoned that many of these black children had been misclassified. Tomlinson (1981, p. 75) remarked that in the teachers' view, 'a misplacement was four times more likely in the case of immigrant children and that the methods and processes of attainment were the major reasons for this misplacement'.

It was not only in inner London that disquiet about the racist maltreatment of black pupils and their tendency to 'underachieve' had been aroused. Since the late 1960s, the nearby outer London Borough of Haringey had become the 'symbol of resistance' (Carter, 1986, p. 83) to racism in education. The issues of bussing, banding and disproportionately high number of pupils of Afro-Caribbean origin in ESN schools constituted the most visible concerns around which antiracist campaigns were organized. Of particular significance were the activities of the North London West Indian Association (NLWIA), part of a network of groups affiliated to an umbrella organization, the West Indian Standing Conference. In Haringey, the NLWIA played a major role in mobilizing black parents to contest local policies and practices which discriminated against their children. However, as Trevor Carter, a black educationist and activist in this period recalls, many black parents were initially reluctant to accept their children's claims that racism assumed a significant role in their educational experience. 'To begin with', he writes, parents were 'baffled' by their children's poor performance in school. Initially, 'our lack of knowledge about the education system and our defensive unwillingness to believe that racism was to blame, tempted us to think that something might indeed be wrong with us or our children' (Carter, 1986, pp. 83–4).

Adherence to this pathological conception of failure originated from, and was cultivated by, white educationists politicians operating within the general *Zeitgeist*. But it was effectively nullified in 1971. That year saw the publication of Bernard Coard's *How the West Indian Child Is Made Educationally Subnormal in the British School System*, which I mentioned briefly in Chapter 1. It is impossible to exaggerate the significance of this pamphlet. As Hassan and Beese (1982, p. 28) record,

> the response to the pamphlet was fantastic. 10,000 copies were sold. Coard spoke up and down the country. There was enormous press, TV and radio coverage, including the international press. Supplementary schools were formed in all the major cities with large black populations. It was clear that this was an issue which black communities throughout England were aware of and were mobilising to do something about. No

one had to go and organise them around the issue in order to convince them that they should do something.

So how did administrators and politicians in the ILEA respond to this mounting tide of criticism?

The 1973 document, *An Education Service for the Whole Community*, is testimony to the fact that the ILEA did nothing publicly to assuage these anxieties and protests. Rather, it retained a commitment to a community-orientated education service in which social disadvantage, not racism, was established as the predicate on which policy, resource allocation and practice would be based. Indeed, the interpretation of the data from the R and S group's longitudinal literacy study did little to disturb the conviction that any (educational) problems experienced by black pupils derived largely from their newness in British schools.

But this complacency and optimism was not shared universally. As I mentioned in Chapter 1, government concern over black youths, within and outside school, escalated into a 'moral panic' during the 1970s. The imperative, according to government thinking at this time, was for schools to enrich the experiences of black youth and pre-empt the drift into criminal – or, to be more accurate, 'criminalized' – activities. The Community Relations Commission (CRC) agreed. A number of schools, according to the CRC (1974, p. 27), had 'not adjusted to the needs of West Indian pupils, but were carrying on as if nothing had changed from when all pupils were indigenous and white'.

Quite apart from this, data generated by the latter phases of the ILEA's survey demonstrated that the educational problems experienced by black youth were not diminishing with the rapidity or inevitability that Briault and his colleagues had anticipated. On the contrary, what was discerned was a process of attrition, especially in the comparative attainment levels of pupils of Afro-Caribbean origin (Mabey, 1981).

How could these be interpreted? The researchers concluded that neither full education in Britain nor 'social deprivation' (measured by a range of indicators) were sufficient to account for the widening gap between the attainment levels of pupils of Afro-Caribbean origin and their counterparts from other ethnic backgrounds. The most plausible, if controversial explanation seemed to lie within the schools – teacher attitudes and expectations about black pupils.

The R and S group's tentative endorsement of this interpretation vindicated the decision of an increasing number of black parents and community groups in inner London (and elsewhere) to send their children to voluntary community – or supplementary – schools. This was to provide the skills denied them in state-funded education. Although it was neither a new nor uniquely Afro-Caribbean initiative, the development of voluntary community schools in this period assumed an extra urgency and necessity. In fact, the black voluntary community school movement gained momentum in the 1970s as a direct result of various related developments: the refusal of the Race Relations Board in 1970 to designate as 'an unlawful act' the disproportionately high placement of children of Afro-Caribbean origin in ESN schools; the typification of these pupils as 'underachievers' and 'uneducable'; their relative failure in 16+ examinations; and their subsequent representation among the ranks of the unemployed. As Nel Clark, founder of the Dachwyng Saturday School in South London, argued: 'A community cannot be passive and allow a racist education system to disadvantage our children. We need to do something' (Clark, 1982, p. 123).

It is only against this broader historical and political backcloth that the ILEA's decision to affirm multicultural education in 1977 can fully be understood. The move towards separatism, precipitated largely by the black community's determination to ensure that their children were not additionally constrained in their search for work by their lack of formal credentials, constituted the main catalytic force here. Why? Because it challenged the credibility and stability of inner London's educational provision. It also threatened to undermine the ILEA's responsibility under the 1944 Education Act to provide a common and inclusive education for all pupils. From a black and antiracist perspective, the ILEA could have been accused of encouraging, rather than taking steps to avert, the incipient 'racial crisis' forewarned by central government reports. By adhering to an assimilationist, monocultural perspective the ILEA not only strengthened the anxieties and concerns of the black communities but also allowed a large mass of relatively poorly qualified and frustrated school leavers on to the streets who felt that they had been given a raw deal in the schools.

The role of the new Education Officer and his colleagues was clear, and in this context their visit to New York city in 1976 assumed major significance. It provided a graphic insight into the social and political unrest which could be caused by the reactions of frustrated and angry pupils and their older counterparts. This was testified in the high rates of indiscipline and truancy. For the ILEA visitors 'race' became the focus through which an imminent crisis was perceived. If its enactment in the schools and on the streets of inner London was to be averted, local education policy-makers needed to reconstitute the framework in which practices were located.

On this view, the ILEA's policy initiative on multicultural education was reactive: it did not stem from pedagogical foresight; nor did it represent policy-makers' unshakeable belief in the efficacy of multiculturalism as an informing premise of educational provision. It was a coping strategy, no more or less: a change in direction which had been provoked by compelling political and social concerns. As the Education Officer of the ILEA put it, assimilationism is 'attractive [and] contains much that is valuable'. In his view it was 'to be modified only with great reluctance'. But the stability of the ILEA's education service depended on a reformulated approach and the eventual policy document, *Multi-ethnic Education*, published in November 1977, aimed to establish a new set of ground rules based on an effort to 'reconcile the opposed notions of assimilation and separatism'. The compromise which emerged suggested a set of principles which had implications for all ILEA pupils:

the essential duty of the Authority continues to be to ensure that all people within its area benefit from the widest possible range of educational opportunities that can be provided. Unequivocally the commitment is to all. Just as there must be no second class citizens, so there must be no second class educational opportunities.

(1977, p. 1, para. 1)

Yet, this championing of universalism sat uneasily with the following paragraph in the document. This revealed the ILEA's sharply focused concern with pupils of Afro-Caribbean origin. In the context of the specific behavioural and academic problems which the ILEA associated with these pupils there is no other way the passage could be interpreted:

The Authority has done much to meet the needs of its changing population but despite these efforts and the individual successes achieved, there is some evidence that disproportionate numbers of people from ethnic minority groups are low achievers in terms of educational standards, have low expectations and aspirations, and lack confidence in the education system which itself appears not to take advantage of the vitality and richness to be derived from a multi-cultural society.

(1977, p. 1. para. 2)

The type of provisions recommended in the policy also suggested that the ILEA's avowed commitment to meet the needs of 'the wide range of minority ethnic groups' was more apparent than real. With the exception of language provision for non-English speaking pupils in local schools, the educational needs of other minority ethnic groups were largely ignored. Even pupils of Turkish-Cypriot origin whose reading attainment levels, according to the ILEA literacy survey, also deteriorated as they passed through their primary and secondary school careers, failed to attract the attention of policy-makers. This restricted focus is only explicable in terms of my earlier analysis – a position corroborated by the insistence in the policy that those in the ILEA were determined to contribute to 'a society *that is cohesive not uniform* [where] cultures are respected, differences recognized and individual identities are secure' (1977, p. 4, para. 1; emphasis added). To reiterate an earlier point, it was the problems associated with pupils of Afro-Caribbean origin which were perceived as the most potent threat to social cohesion in inner London.

A noticeable 'silence' in the policy surrounds the issue of racism. Policy-makers failed to explore its relationship either to the relatively poor performance of pupils of Afro-Caribbean origin or to the anxieties and frustrations of their parents. The policy addressed race-related matters in so far as it was precipitated by and directed towards pupils of Afro-Caribbean background. But it was embedded in a conceptual framework underpinned by ideas of cultural pluralism. As a result it deflected attention away from the corrosive and pervasive aspects of racism in education. Without wishing to promote a conspiratorial view of these developments, the policy does suggest a model of 'benevolent multiculturalism', originating from a deliberate political manoeuvre.

An alternative and more generous explanation for the absence of an anti-racist perspective from the policy would develop along the following lines.

With the 1976 Race Relations Act on the statute book the ILEA did not need to declare publicly its abhorrence of racism in education. As one elected member put it to me: 'we regarded it as unnecessary to say that we were in favour of not breaking the law'. Furthermore, antiracist conceptions of education were not in the ascendancy in the late 1970s. 'If you remember back to 1977', an ILEA inspector remarked, 'people weren't talking about racism, it wasn't generally being discussed' (personal communication). Both these explanations fly in the face of the facts, however. To begin with, the black communities in inner London gave priority to antiracism in their list of demands to the ILEA. And the ILEA/CRC consultative committees provided the conduit through which this demand was channelled to the Authority. The failure of policy-makers to respond simply widened the gap between them and the local black communities. As one black member of the consultative committee said: 'The policy has gone right the way down the wrong alley and the main reason is because people didn't recognise racism in an institutional sense as something that would affect even the most well-meaning efforts' (personal communication).

The commitment to multicultural rather than antiracist education was also based on grounds of political pragmatism: the determination to achieve bipartisan support. According to one elected member, the objective was to 'get everybody behind' the policy. It was not challenged precisely because it was 'prepared with such a lot of care' (personal communication). On this view it is also possible to understand why the issue of mother tongue was ignored in the policy. In stark contrast to cultural pluralist ideals – easily accommodated within the ILEA's conception of equality of opportunity – mother-tongue provision 'smacked of separatism' and had the potential to arouse opposition. The goal of 'social cohesion' could not be realized, or so the argument went, if the nascent separatist movement was allowed to develop with impunity.

To sum up: by promoting cultural pluralism, based on the model of 'benevolent multiculturalism', ILEA policy-makers hoped to win the consent of the black communities and restore their confidence in a system which had been seen to fail their children. The political goal of social cohesion was translated into the educational goal of securing equality of opportunity for all pupils in inner London schools.

'Cultural understanding' in Manchester

In the 1960s and 1970s, at least, race-related matters in education assumed a less conflictual status and a lower profile than, say, in inner London. Neither the apparent trend towards black 'educational underachievement' nor moves towards separate provision constituted such a severe or obvious threat to local state schools. This is not to suggest that the educational performance of black pupils was on a par with that of their white colleagues. Rather, in the absence of any longitudinal statistical profile of performance along ethnic lines, nobody was sure of the pattern in Manchester.

At least that was the situation until the publication of an influential study, *Beyond Underachievement* (Driver, 1980) by the Commission for Racial Equality. Although he did not focus exclusively on relative performance levels of black and white pupils in Manchester, one of the sample schools in Driver's study was an inner-city, multiethnic school in the Authority. Despite the controversial nature of his data, and the interpretative framework in which he embedded his findings, Driver's study did not give educational policy-makers in Manchester particular cause for concern.

In fact, as I suggested earlier, the origins of Manchester's policy on multi-cultural education, derived from other sources, linked more closely to the characteristics of what Gibson typifies as the 'cultural understanding' model of multiculturalism. The key assumptions of this model are that

> schools should be oriented toward the cultural enrichment of *all* students, that multicultural education programs will provide such enrichment by fostering understanding and acceptance of cultural differences and that these programs will in turn decrease racism and prejudice and increase social justice.
>
> (Gibson 1976, p. 9; emphasis added)

This demanded a universalistic approach to multiculturalism, contrasting with the particularistic concerns of policy-makers in the ILEA. The title of Manchester's policy, *Education for a Multicultural Society*, the rationale for its formulation, and the organizational and administrative arrangements which stemmed from it give clues about the orientation favoured in this Authority. Like London, the city of Manchester has experienced a long history of white and black migrant settlement. According to the 1971 census, the New Commonwealth (i.e. black) population in Manchester numbered 17,290 and consisted mainly of migrants who had arrived from the Caribbean, especially Jamaica, and South Asia. By 1978, this number had increased to 50,000 (and to 7.6 percent of the city's population by the mid-1980s). However, according to a former Chief Education Officer (CEO) of Manchester these communities were confined to 'inner-city areas with housing and amenity problems . . . designated educational priority areas'. (1974, p. 1)

The rise in the number of black citizens was obviously reflected in city schools. In 1970 black students comprised 5.7 per cent of the total school population; by 1973 this had risen to 6.3 per cent and, in 1978, to 11 per cent. Given the skewed distribution of the residential pattern it was not surprising to find that black pupils were concentrated in a relatively small number of schools. In 1978, 55 schools (out of the then total of 312) comprised 10 per cent or more black students and 45 schools included 33 per cent or more on their rolls.

Administrators in Manchester LEA saw little need to depart from what had been their traditional organizational or pedagogic response to white migrant children. Therefore they rejected the idea of dispersal and proposals to establish reception centres for (black) non-English speaking pupils. The CEO characterized the LEA's approach like this:

> The traditional view is that Manchester has always been a welcoming community to all manner of people from all manner of cultures. It has a proud record of taking in many of the Eastern European refugees from oppression, particularly Jews. It has a very proud Ukrainian community and some Polish people. So there is no difference in the measures needed and the response needed for the settling of those who have come from Asia and the West Indies. They will be welcomed for what they are; there is no need to do anything special for them . . .

He continued by reiterating the *ad hoc* stance taken by the LEA in the 1960s and 1970s:

> The Education Committee and Officers believed that the right thing was to go to the school appropriate to where you lived and if that resulted in a concentration of children which were assumed to present a problem to this school, to tackle them there with resources into the school but not to put them in specific reception centres.

> (personal communication)

In practical terms, the local policy departed from centrally prescribed advice. Its ideological underpinnings, however, were the same: assimilationist, with a considerable emphasis on language provision to smooth out the discontinuities between the private and public domains of the black communities. Indeed, the policy bore many of the hallmarks of compensatory education both in terms of the basis for differential funding to schools (and the purposes to which funding was put) and in the allocation of responsibilities in the LEA's administration. The Curriculum Development Leader who had responsibility for race-related issues worked under the direction of the Senior Stage Inspector for Special Needs. And when, in 1976, the Education Committee appointed an Inspector for Special Education, the successful candidate realized only after he had been appointed that he would be responsible for race-related matters. This despite his own admission that he was not 'competent to take on the issue'. Clearly, the tendency was to subsume the issue under the broader label of disadvantage and deprivation and to equate the needs of black pupils with those of their white, working-class counterparts.

Margaret Gibson writes that the 'cultural understanding' approach emerged in the USA mainly through the efforts of various ethnic groups determined to ensure that schools 'became more sensitive to cultural differences and modify school curricula to reflect more accurately their concerns' (Gibson, 1976, p. 9). There are clear parallels here with the demands of the black communities in Manchester in this period. For instance, black voluntary groups such as the West Indian Organisations Co-Ordinating Committee (WICC), set up in the city in the late 1960s, voiced concern at the way in which the LEA had routinely conflated black and white working-class needs. This reductionist approach ignored the fact that, as a member of the WICC put it, 'over and above the disadvantages of the working class are the problems of racism and discrimination'.

The failure of the Authority to recognize the specificity of racial inequality in education prompted the WICC to demand greater use of Section 11 funds explicitly for the purpose of bringing extra staff into ethnically mixed schools. This type of intervention was not endorsed by all local black community groups, however. In contrast to the particularistic stance, others favoured the development of an inclusive policy of reform – a policy, that is, aimed at the elimination of racist attitudes and practices and the abolition of monocultural and ethnocentric versions of the school curriculum. On this view, the site of change would be the white majority, not the ethnic minority cultures.

But these demands fell on deaf ears until 1977–8. Then events in Manchester and beyond stirred policy-makers into action. What first caught their eye was the perceived electoral growth of the National Front and a rise in its agitational activities. These included marches in Manchester in 1977. Nor did the launching of the party's youth wing, Young National Front, go unnoticed. This was accompanied by the distribution of inflammatory racist literature around schools throughout Britain. Early in 1978, Mrs Thatcher made her infamous claim on a television current affairs programme that Britain was being 'swamped' by black immigrants. The precise impact of these events on the routine climate of schools is difficult to gauge. However, they played a leading role in precipitating a reappraisal and subsequent reorientation of the Authority's stance on race-related matters. The articulation between the school and broader sociopolitical developments was heavily stressed by the CEO in his report to the Policy and Estimates Sub-Committee in March 1978. Part of the pressure to reconstitute the LEA's policy position, he insisted,

> is undoubtedly coming from the recent revival of activity from the National Front. Its importance is underlined by the national political debate about immigration policies. To date Manchester schools have reported only one incident involving National Front activities close to school entrances and the Committee made public immediately their strong support for those teachers who firmly resisted attempts to distribute literature to pupils on school property . . . It has to be acknowledged that the nature of parts of the current national debate and events beyond the scope of the education service are not at present helping schools to evolve good multicultural teaching.

Two significant issues are encapsulated here. First, the recognition that educational initiatives, however well intentioned, could be impaired, if not entirely vitiated, by wider social and political trends. Paraphrasing the ILEA approach, for the moment, we could say that while Manchester's CEO was determined not to provide 'second class educational opportunities', nevertheless he recognized that 'parts of the national debate and events beyond the scope of the education service' might still help to construct differential citizenship rights. Second, the CEO admitted to the harmful role which the National Front played in circulating racist materials. Of course, this was only a circumscribed concern with racism, but it was a concern nevertheless.

The main purpose of the 1978 report was to set in motion a process of consultation between the LEA, local black community groups and individual schools. Out of this would emerge a reconstituted policy. But what was the nature of this consultation?

In his analysis of the consultation process in 'Milltown', David Gibson (1987) devised a typology of consultation meetings. Retracing the development of the consultative procedure in Manchester in this period suggests that it approximates to what David Gibson describes as the 'control model' in which:

> Meetings are called by officers with the purpose of increasing their information and understanding. There is no benefit to the black groups and the information gathered by officers can be used to check out reactions of the representatives and to inform officers so that they do not need to give concessions when it is not essential'.
>
> (Gibson 1987, p. 82)

In Manchester it was LEA policy-makers who set the agenda for discussion. Among the substantive issues identified were: 'inadvertent discrimination'; the suitability of attainment tests; the treatment of West Indian pupils; multicultural education in 'all-white' schools; and ground rules for the appointment and deployment of Section 11 staff. It was hoped that consultation on these matters would allow the LEA to put flesh on the bones of its commitment to 'ensure the continued development of multicultural education throughout the city' – a commitment spelt out by the chairperson of the Education Committee in the 1978 document.

The consultation procedure took two years to complete. As a result, in June 1980 the CEO presented his 'multicultural package' of three documents to the Education Committee. The first two documents simply rehearsed the scope and nature of existing provision. The third included recommendations for action and a reformulated approach based on a 'clear and unequivocal' commitment to cultural pluralism. It encouraged all local schools to 'adopt a pluralist approach and to actively seek ways to use the minority cultures of our community'. Its aims were to develop 'good relations on the basis of mutual respect for different cultures'. The establishment of an Ethnic Studies Unit in the city would help expedite this goal.

This exemplified all the constituent features of Margaret Gibson's 'cultural understanding' model, particularly since it represented a shift away from the concerns addressed in 1978. Then, it will be recalled, *racism* was seen to threaten the security of black pupils and what was implied was the need for an antiracist stance. By 1980, however, this had been displaced by a concern with ignorance about 'cultural minorities' as the main obstacle to 'good relations'. The favoured strategy was to provide all (white) pupils with more information on these cultures – an approach which links firmly with one of Brian Bullivant's key assumptions about multicultural education – namely, that 'learning about other cultures will reduce children's (and adults') prejudice and discrimination towards those from different cultural and ethnic backgrounds' (Bullivant,

1981, p. 236). This deracialized position was condemned in the following terms by a member of the local Black Parents' Association:

> It might make some people happier; it might give some teachers a sense of being liberal and genuinely concerned about making English education less ethnocentric. It does not seek to address the political culture of the inner city, the local multiracial community . . . It begins to deal with culture and aspects of ethnic life without looking at where education fits in with the class set up.
>
> (Personal communication)

The line of reasoning in Manchester's policy assumed a direct and causal link between lifestyles and life chances. But it failed to interrogate those wider social and structural realities which circumscribe the life chances of black pupils. Nor is there much evidence to support the efficacy of the 'cultural understanding' model in combating racism (Amir, 1969; Reicher, 1986). In the words of Chris Mullard (1982), this deracialized understanding of change is based on 'wishful thinking'.

Conclusion

The policies developed by the ILEA in 1977 and by Manchester Education Committee three years later, represented logical enactments of theories about multiculturalism which were stimulated by local concerns. Consequently, they were based on different assumptions, developed along different paths, and were geared towards different target pupil populations. But there were also continuities and consistencies in the way they approached this issue. First, to reinforce a point I made in Chapter 1, both LEAs exploited the 'space' available within the decentralized system which operated in England and Wales between 1944 and 1988. Second, this 'space' was exploited, not because of policy-makers' entrenched commitment to the ideology of multicultural education, but because they saw the need to respond to particular sociopolitical pressures which had the potential to disrupt the nature and credibility of their educational provision. Third, the reformulated approaches were aimed at reducing conflict and minimizing tension between groups designated as racially different. Both LEAs wanted to encourage harmony and social cohesion through educationally based interventions. However, the experiences of these groups were reconceptualized within the multicultural policy paradigm in ways which privileged cultural rather than racial considerations. Following on from this, both policies centred on the ethnic and cultural backgrounds and lifestyles of black pupils rather than on the wider political culture in which the pupils' life chances were more fundamentally influenced. This three Ss interpretation of cultural pluralism – saris, samosas and steel bands – subordinated political realities to cultural artefacts. In both inner London and Manchester the three Ss constituted a reformist strategy which was intended to operate sufficiently as a panacea for more fundamental and intractable social injustices.

Finally, these two case-study analyses of how policies emerged, and the shape they assumed, provide classic examples of deracialization. While responsive to certain demands that they should encourage and legitimate more inclusive curricula (that is, in acknowledging in part the histories, cultures and experiences of minority ethnic groups), this was secured at the expense of interrogating how dominant configurations of power privileged certain cultures over others. Neither LEA centralized an antiracist ideology as an organizing variable for its future educational provision. In this sense, then, the policies were informed by what Henry Giroux terms 'a benevolent form of neo-colonialism' – that is, an ideological positioning that 'refuses to hold up to critical scrutiny its own complicity in producing and maintaining specific injustices, practices and forms of oppression that deeply inscribe its legacy and heritage' (Giroux, 1991, p. 506). Political exigencies clearly played a role in this as policy-makers in inner London and Manchester were concerned to ensure that their policies should attract and retain bipartisan support. It was necessary, then, to avoid contentious issues. However, this deference to political opponents within the respective County Halls led to a strengthening of their hegemonic hold over decision- and policy-making and, as a corollary, the marginalization, even denunciation, of black community demands. As a result, perceptions and understandings of the issue were culture-, not 'race'-bound.

In the next chapter, I will show that this focus was retained and reinforced in two major educational documents of the late 1980s. The first, *Education for All* (DES, 1985), has been viewed as 'probably the most important document to emerge within the discourse of race and education' in Britain (Brandt, 1987, pp. 61–2). It has also transcended national boundaries as a landmark for pluralist education (Verma, 1989). The second, the 1988 Education Reform Act, changed significantly the educational landscape in Britain. In this process it has reinvigorated monoculturalism as an educational orthodoxy.

3 The 'Liberal Moment': From Swann to the 1988 Education Reform Act

In its editorial of 15 March 1985, *The Times* greeted the publication of *Education for All* (DES, 1985) as 'the strangest dog's breakfast ever to emerge from HMSO'. But even this inelegant epithet was mild compared to what had appeared six months earlier in the columns of the *Daily Telegraph* and, more especially, the *Daily Mail*. Based on carefully orchestrated leaks about what would be recommended in the report, both newspapers set about creating the impression that Lord Swann and his committee were about to suggest radical changes to the content and structure of the English education system. Changes along multicultural lines would encourage a 'white backlash', according to the *Telegraph*. Less restrained and more offensive was Mary Kenny's article for the *Daily Mail* (3 September, 1984). Headlined RACE MADNESS, Kenny castigated the committee in her article for its presumed support for the obligatory provision in '*every school*' of 'Creole, Gujerati and Punjabi' and for the adoption by 'all local authorities' of 'reverse discrimination' [*sic*] in the recruitment of black teachers. For Kenny the apparent 'racial harmony' now existing between pupils in British schools would be put 'in jeopardy' should the government accept Swann's recommendations. Her advice was that: 'The whole report should be scrapped, lock, stock and barrel – in the interests of the ethnic minorities as much as anyone else.' Not that criticism of the report has been confined exclusively to right-wing ideologues. On the contrary, *Education for All* was also criticized by organizations such as the National Antiracist Movement in Education, which insisted that the report suffered from important omissions and commissions and that it inhibited rather than advanced the legitimation of antiracist education (NAME, 1985). A cursory glance at what is commonly termed the 'ethnic media' in the period immediately following publication of the report, and attention to the heated debates and critical rejoinders to *Education for All* at the various post-Swann conferences throughout England and Wales would reveal just how much black and white antiracists were dissatisfied with the report. Even members of the committee (past and present) have publicly attacked and/or dissented from some of the themes and conclusions of the report (for the range of responses to the report, see Brandt, 1987; Chivers, 1987; Verma, 1989).

Even more have dissociated themselves from Lord Swann's 'personal overview' of the full report; 'a guided tour' to the document which bears only tengential resemblance to its parent publication but which, because of its brevity, was always likely to be widely read.

In his article in the *New Statesman*, Barry Hugill (1985, p. 13) suggested that dissatisfaction about *Education for All* was well-based because 'The saddest aspect of the report is that the majority of recommendations have been made time and time again . . . At its weakest, the report perpetuates some of the myths that it is, in another context, intent on exploding'. Notwithstanding Hugill's criticism, it is difficult to dispute Brandt's (1987, pp. 61–2) view which, as we saw in the previous chapter is that: 'For good or ill, probably the most important document to emerge within the discourse of race and education is the Swann report'.

Yet, the pertinence and veracity of Hugill's comments are especially clear in relation to the committee's inquiry into black 'educational underachievement' and its development of the ostensibly new, unifying concept of 'Education for All'. The first of these constitutes a linking theme of governmental concern about the education of black students; we shall see that it inspired the setting up of the committee in the late 1970s and provided the platform on which 'Education for All' has been largely based. On the latter, neither the orthodoxy nor its constituent features are new in themselves. But with the growing demand for the maintenance and provision of community languages and separate schools, there was a correlative need for the state to construct an ideology to assuage the anxieties of black parents that the education system was failing to respond adequately or appropriately to the needs of their children. These issues should constitute the focus of a critical review of the report. At the same time we must not ignore the Secretary of State's official response to the report of the general implications of 'Education for All' in the mobilization of strategies geared towards the mitigation of racial inequalities in education. We shall soon see that the proliferation of support for initiatives associated with 'Education for All' constituted no more than a fleeting moment, effectively aborted by the rise of the New Right and its influence on the framing of the 1988 Education Reform Act.

To begin with, I want to spend some time in delineating the political history of the Swann (formerly Rampton) Committee since its inception in the late 1970s. *En route* I want to discuss why it was established, the role it was assigned in relation to the core of educational decision-making, and the political dramas with which it has been associated. As I shall argue, it was against this backcloth that hopes and expectations were formed.

The long voyage: from Rampton to Swann, 1977–85

Education for All was finally published in March 1985, at least two years late and more than eight years after the then Labour government had agreed to the request from the Select Committee on Race Relations and Immigration (1977, p. xx) that it should establish 'a high level and independent inquiry into the causes of the underachievement of children of West Indian origin'. It is important to reflect on the reasons why the Select Committee's concern with black 'educational underachievement' should have stimulated this positive response from central government.[1] After all, as we saw in previous chapters, this was not a new issue of concern. What was clear by 1977, however, was that, contrary to earlier diagnoses and prognoses, black 'educational underachievement' as measured by these researchers could no longer be considered an ephemeral problem, related casually to the disruptive effects of immigration on black students, their lack of familiarity with the UK, or because of discontinuities between British and Caribbean education systems. By the late 1970s the vast majority of school students of Afro-Caribbean origin had been born and brought up in Britain; despite this, they were still more likely than their white or 'Asian' counterparts to be represented in the lower streams of the secondary school, in ESN schools and among those leaving school with few or no formal qualifications. For black parents and community activists the reasons for 'underachievement' could be located within the state system of education which routinely and systematically miseducated their children. It is therefore no coincidence that, at precisely the same time as the government agreed to investigate this phenomenon, we were witnessing the mobilization of black community action in education and the accelerated growth of black supplementary or Saturday schools. In the words of Mel Chevannes, who helped to establish the Black Arrow Supplementary School in Wolverhampton in 1977: 'We believe black children aren't getting the best from local schools – they need the qualifications to get the jobs – and we aim to give it to them' (quoted in Tomlinson, 1984, p. 68). But while the pattern of black 'educational underachievement' and the consequent growth of supplementary schools clearly challenged the meritocratic credibility of the state's education system, it would be naive to assume that this alone precipitated the government's response. The typification of black youth in the educational term 'underachievement' resonated with broader and more politically based characterizations of these youths as 'alienated', 'criminalized', 'disaffected' and so on (see Solomos, 1988). Once the 'immigrant'/'stranger' hypothesis of 'underachievement' had been stripped, through the passage of time, of all explanatory power, the evidence of persistent inequalities of educational outcome and its implications for social and political cohesion became increasingly more obvious.

The Select Committee's request for an inquiry to focus on the causes of 'underachievement' among 'West Indian' students was modified by the government's insistence that this should be based within a more broadly conceived examination of 'the achievements and needs of all pupils for education for life in a multi-racial society' (1978, p. 7). At the same time, it was agreed that: 'priority should be given to identifying weaknesses in the education system affecting the achievement of pupils of West Indian origin' (1978, p. 7). Now this is interesting because when the formal terms of reference were announced by Mark Carlisle[2] in July 1979, this emphasis on the educational system had been eschewed in favour of an inquiry into 'the educational needs and attainments of pupils of West Indian origin' (DES, 1985, p. ii). Inevitably this had profound implications for the nature of the inquiry and for the reception accorded both the interim and final reports. After all, criticism has crystallized largely around the committee's failure to consider the manifest forms of racism in schools and the way these might impinge on the educational advancement of black students. If the original, albeit informal, terms of reference had not been changed by Carlisle, it is likely that the committee would have paid considerably more attention to precisely those in-school processes which black and white antiracists have argued have been ignored. What is more, as we shall see, it would have been more difficult for Carlisle and Sir Keith Joseph to reject claims that racism in education constitutes an important phenomenon for investigation and action.

On publication of the committee's interim report, *West Indian Children in Our Schools* in 1981, John Rex (1981) was prompted to write that: 'The most important thing about the Rampton committee, as it used to be called, is not its content, but the whole political drama which surrounded the publication of its first report'. I agree. To begin with, there was an inexplicable delay of four months between submission to the DES and publication. In the Parliamentary debate on the report (*HC Parl. Debs*, 4 July 1981, cols 261–262), Tom Ellis asked whether 'the report would have been published if there had been no Brixton . . . disturbances in the intervening period'. Ellis's criticism was based on the view that, first, the DES had provided inspired leaks to the press in this period which had served to discredit the report in advance, and second, the DES had failed to respond formally to the 20 recommendations aimed specifically at it. Controversy also surrounded the 'resignation' of the chairperson, Anthony Rampton, in May 1981; whether he jumped or was pushed is a question which continues to tantalize. Certainly there were suggestions that Carlisle was unhappy about the emphasis placed in the report on racism as an explanation of black 'educational underachievement'. Nevertheless, it is salutary to recall that 'racism' constituted only one of the possible contributors to 'underachievement' and that the others crystallized around a range of pathologies including poor family background, lack of parental support and understanding, inadequate socialization and so on. Rex's comment also draws our attention to the fact that the report suffered from a paucity of credible research evidence and an adequate interpretation of that which was at hand. The committee based its general argument about black 'educational underachievement' on data provided by the DES School Leavers Survey 1978/79. They purported to show – and the committee concurred with the impression – that in the six LEAs considered, students of Afro-Caribbean origin performed significantly less well in public examinations than either white indigenous students or those of South Asian origin. The failure of the committee to standardize these data along social class lines or to consider the results in relation to gender differences and individual schools' records of achievement has been highlighted and discussed elsewhere (Reeves and Chevannes, 1981; Troyna, 1984b). The point I want to make here is that the grossly insensitive use of the data, linked as it was to the provocative issue of teacher racism, undermined the credibility of the committee's argument, failed to pre-empt inevitable press criticism of the report, and incurred the anger of many teachers who perceived it as an (un-justified) attack on their professionalism.[3] We shall see later that, like the Bourbons, the committee chaired by Lord Swann since Rampton's 'resigna-tion' had 'learned nothing and forgotten nothing' in its handling of comparable data in the final report.

The response of the DES to the interim report – or, more precisely, its non-response – might also be seen as more significant than the content of the document. On its publication, Carlisle had insisted in response to a written question that he would 'consult widely on the report's implications' (*HC Parl. Debs*, vol. 6, 17 June 1981, col. 363) and this was reaffirmed by his Minister, Rhodes Boyson, in the Parliamentary debate less than three weeks later. But neither this nor a formal response from the DES to Rampton's recommen-dations took place. DES action was confined to circulating the report to LEAs without comment, and organizing a one-day conference! What we have, then, is a committee charged with making 'definite and positive recommendations' but which remained structurally peripheral to national policy-making and de-velopments in education (Dorn and Troyna, 1982). Again, this was confirmed by Sir Keith Joseph's perfunctory acknowledgement of the Swann Commit-tee's contribution.

These brief glimpses into the origins, activities and recommendations of the Rampton Committee and its official reception help to contextualize more appropriately the Swann Report, its emphases and ideological framework. It facilitates this for a number of reasons. First, we have seen that, at least after the Conservative Party secured power in 1979, the inquiry was never intended to focus on the school as an agent for the reproduction of racial inequalities. If anything, its official terms of reference geared it towards explicating cultural and social phenomena which might be associated with differential performance between students from different ethnic backgrounds. The legacy of Carlisle's reformulation of the committee's original terms of reference can be found not only in the final report but also in the nature of the research it attempted, but failed, to commission. Second, its relationship to formal decision-making struc-tures in education was, from its inception, minimal and subordinate. That is to say, as a consultative committee, first and foremost, it was expected to present recommendations for action – but the Secretary of State was not compelled to accept them. Third, and most significantly, its concern with black 'educational underachievement' was inextricably linked to the broader rather than specifi-cally educational implications of a discernible group of students doing badly at school. In this sense, Rampton/Swann shared many of the concerns and im-peratives associated with earlier government inquiries chaired by Hunt, New-som and Plowden, among others. The goal was to identify reformist policies which might secure an integrated society; to stabilize a society characterized by social, political and racial divisions.

The ideology of 'Education for All' and the recommendations it prompted need to be seen in this broader historical and sociopolitical context, one which is essentially reactive in its concern and pre-emptive in its goal: as the Swann Committee put it in their final report:

> We believe that unless major efforts are made to reconcile the concerns and aspirations of both the majority and minority communities along more genuinely pluralist lines, there is a real risk of the fragmentation of our society along ethnic lines which would seriously threaten the stability and cohesion of society as a whole.
>
> (DES, 1985, p. 7)

By the time Lord Swann and his colleagues submitted their final report to the DES, apprehensions of and reformist challenges to racial inequalities in education had shifted quite perceptively. No longer was the multicultural education debate framed exclusively around particularistic concerns. Instead, the last few years had witnessed the ascendancy of universalistic versions of this orthodoxy. At the same time, concern about the apparently immutable pattern of 'West Indian underachievement' persisted. In the period following publication of Rampton's interim report, both the Home Affairs Committee and Lord Scarman drew attention to this trend and to the disturbing political and social implications to which it apparently gave rise. In the words of the Home Affairs Committee (House of Commons, 1981), this was evidence that 'we have not got ethnic minority education right' (1981, p.1v). For Swann the imperative was clear: to delineate the extent of black 'educational underachievement', to specify its causes and to formulate an ideology which in practice would ameliorate this educational and social evil.

But this was a restricted and restrictive research paradigm. It is *restricted* because it demands attention to achievement along ethnic lines. Consequently, the committee's discussion and conclusions were based solely on a comparative investigation of the performance of 'Asian', 'West Indian' and 'all other leavers' (that is, mainly whites) in public examinations taken in five LEAs in 1981–2. Apart from the occasional nod in the direction of class and gender as explanatory, or at least moderating, variables, the focus was on explicating differences or otherwise between the achievement levels of students from these different ethnic backgrounds, nothing more or less. By replicating the Rampton Committee's mode of analysis, Swann and his colleagues showed a cynical disregard for the criticisms of this approach already voiced by Reeves and Chevannes (1981), Rex (1981a) and Troyna (1984b), among others. Also ignored was the important research of Roberts *et al.* (1983) which had shown that the national profile of black 'educational underachievement' could be 'attributable entirely to the fact that they reside in districts and attend schools where the attainment of all pupils is below average' (Roberts *et al.* 1983, p. 19). One final point needs to be made here. The committee's determination to look for differences between ethnic groups not only blinded it to the influences of gender, class and individual school performance records, but also led them to ignore the significance of age. As Tanna (1985) has shown, a critical reading of the data provided by the DES has revealed that 'Asians' tend to perform as well as 'all other leavers' only after investing more of their time in formal education. In other words, in order to achieve comparable results with 'all other leavers' they needed to stay on at school longer and give up the opportunities provided by apprenticeship courses and the Youth Training Scheme (YTS), both of which had an upper age limit which prevented entry.

The Swann Committee also operated within a *restrictive* paradigm. This is because, having concluded on the basis of the data that 'West Indians' perform less well and 'Asians' performed at least on a par with 'all other leavers', the committee was compelled to identify and attribute causal status to characteristics which were peculiar to particular ethnic groups. This has a number of unfortunate consequences, to say the least. First, it provided the space for critics to challenge the proposition that racism has an inhibiting effect on the educational progress of black students. As Simon Pearce (1985, p. 3) wrote in his policy papers for the Monday Club: 'Most Asians perform as well as whites, and considerably better than West Indians. What then of racism?' (for similar critiques, see Jeffcoate, 1984, p. 64; Palmer, 1986). Second, it steered the committee into commissioning an extensive review of literature and research on 'The IQ Question' simply to reaffirm that it is '*not* a significant factor in underachievement' (DES, 1985, p. 89; emphasis in original). One might have hoped that the committee would already have been sufficiently aware of the pseudo-scientific and racist predicates of intelligence testing through the writings of Flynn (1980), Kamin (1977) and Rose (1979). Finally, it led to the reproduction and quasi-legitimation of cultural stereotypes in a forlorn attempt to explain the different achievement levels of 'West Indians' and 'Asians'. The former, we are told, 'are given to "protest" and "a high profile" '; the latter are more concerned with ' "keeping their heads down" and adopting "a low profile" ' (DES, 1985, p. 86). Not only are these stereotypes offensive and racist, they are indisputably wrong.[4] But even if we suspend our judgement on this matter and tolerate Swann's conclusion that 'the reasons for the very different school performances of Asians and West Indians seem likely to lie deep within their respective cultures' (DES, 1985, p. 87), we are forced to ask how is it possible to account for the educational performance of Bangladeshi students – 'the one Asian sub-group whose school achievement was very low indeed', according to the committee (DES, 1985, p. 87).

The point I want to stress here is quite simple: the Swann Committee, unable to escape from the confines of its original problematic, generated and reproduced a number of untenable propositions and ended up in a cul-de-sac. Its failure to win the consent of the black communities for a piece of original research into the question of 'underachievement' can be explained largely in terms of its insistence that ethnic cultures as well as in-school processes needed to be examined. But did they? Surely the findings from the Thomas Coram Institute which showed that standards of literacy and numeracy among black children are as high as those of whites when they first go to school (*Times Educational Supplement*, 23 December 1983), coupled with Michael Rutter's conclusion that black students are prepared to invest extra years in their schooling after which they leave with a 'broadly comparable' set of qualifications to whites (Rutter *et al.*, 1982, p. 163), suggests that the problems which black students experience occur most vividly during the '15,000 hours' of their school career. From this perspective it is easier to appreciate why NAME (1985, p. 2) insisted that Swann should have commissioned research to consider 'some of the major factors which impinge on success or failure in schools': 'Institutional racism, gateways, barriers, "filter systems", streaming, setting, suspensions, expulsions, referral procedures, assessment centres, "Sin bins", remedial units, mixed-ability teaching, guidance and option choices, timetabling, levels of parental and community involvement, and consultation and pastoral care'. Only research could identify how far each of these derive from racist impulses or intent.

Swann's song of 'Education for All'

But Swann's conception of racism is based on an entirely different predicate, one which believes that it is derived from ignorance about different minority cultures; thus is it seen neither as a uniquely British phenomenon nor a problem peculiar to 'whites' (DES, 1985, p. 27). Instead, it is said to constitute little more than a lack of knowledge and misunderstanding about the lifestyles and cultural values of ethnic minority communities. The imperative for the education system, then, is 'to equip pupils with knowledge and understanding in place of ignorance and to develop [their] ability to formulate views and attitudes and to assess and judge situations on the basis of this knowledge' (DES, 1985, p. 14). Racism, in other words, is synonymous with prejudice in this ideological framework,[5] and the task becomes one of persuading different sections of the education system, and the state in general, of the educational efficacy of the orthodoxy, 'Education for All' (DES, 1985, pp. 87–8). But in order to ensure the success of this strategy the black communities, according to the committee, must play their part. Thus, despite considerable support for separate schools, especially from South Asian communities, the committee declined to support the initiatives, on the grounds that the ' "separate development" of all different groups would be unlikely to offer equality or justice to the members of all groups, least of all the numerically smaller minorities' (DES, 1985, p. 5). From this same vantage point of a commitment to 'a democratic pluralist society', the committee expressed reservations about 'mother tongue' teaching in schools. It supported neither 'the introduction of programmes of bilingual education in this country' nor the maintenance of 'mother tongue' in mainstream schools (DES, 1985, p. 406). Rather the committee maintained that:

> the key to equality of opportunity, to academic success and, more broadly, to participation on equal terms as a full member of society, is good command of *English* and the emphasis must therefore we feel be on the learning of English.
>
> (DES, 1985, p. 407; emphasis in original)

Without wishing to deny the importance of fluency in English it is important to point out – as earlier sections of the report indicated – that this ability has *not* helped students of Afro-Caribbean origin to secure 'equality of opportunity' in British society (see Brown, 1984). Nor can the denial of community language provision be sustained legitimately in the context of arguments for 'a democratic pluralist society'. As J. J. Smolicz has argued, language constitutes a core value for certain ethnic minority communities and, contrary to Swann's implicit assumption that the focus on learning English will facilitate the emergence of a stable and cohesive society, evidence drawn from the Canadian experience indicates that: 'Conflict and division arise not out of difference, but rather out of denial of the right and the opportunity to be different' (Smolicz, 1981, p. 137). Swann's rejection of community demands for the legitimation of 'mother tongue' provision and teaching in schools and for separate schooling for the purpose of maintaining the 'core values' of certain ethnic minority groups therefore seems likely to engender precisely those feelings of discontent, lack of identification with the state, frustration, and demands for structural separatism which 'Education for All' was intent on preventing.

And what does Swann offer in return for these community concessions? A conception of the state which is neutral, which will be responsive to the call for antiracism and which is waiting to be provided with the technical means by which it may operationalize this orthodoxy. As the committee asserted: 'countering racism within society must be a matter for the Law, for Government, Local Authorities, Employers, the Commission for Racial Equality and indeed many others, individually and collectively' (DES, 1985, pp. 87–8). This complacent, even cynical conception of the state's relationship with the black communities and its receptivity to calls for antiracism has been highlighted elsewhere in this volume. Suffice to say here that in presenting the report to Parliament, the Secretary of State carefully diminished the importance of racism in education, a point not lost on the then Labour spokesperson on education, Giles Radice. He asked Sir Keith Joseph why he had ignored racism, a factor 'which blights the prospects of many black and Asian children'. Joseph's reply came as little surprise, except perhaps to the Swann Committee:

> The hon. Gentleman has allowed himself to speak in far too absolute a fashion about what he calls 'racism'. He does an injustice to the teaching force, whose members are dedicated to the service of individual children and in whom I have seen precious little evidence of any racist prejudice.
> (*HC Parl. Debs*, vol. 75, 14 March 1985, col. 453)

The truth or falsity of Joseph's assertion has since remained a matter for empirical inquiry. The point I want to stress here, however, is that individual teacher prejudice is only part of the story of racism in the English educational system. Both Joseph and the Swann Committee failed, or refused, to consider the more insidious and covert forms of racism as they operate almost routinely in pedagogic, administrative and organizational features of school and college life.

In all, the arguments provided in *Education for All* circumvented the central problem of how to provide antiracist education in multiracial Britain. And it was avoided by two principal methods: first, through defining racism in terms of intentional and individual racial prejudice and recommending teaching strategies to combat those attitudes (among pupils) and racism awareness training

(RAT) courses to eradicate them (supposedly) from the teaching profession; and second, through the proposition that the state is willing to accept clearly formulated arguments for initiating and endorsing antiracism as an educational and political orthodoxy. Both are contentious, if not erroneous propositions. But in the course of this political chicanery the committee succeeded in denying the legitimacy of certain demands from Britain's black communities, obfuscated the thrust of the debate by failing to consider and identify how racism operates in the education system, and eschewed responsibility for reformulating the education system so that it might cater more effectively and appropriately for its ethnically diverse clientele. What we were left with, then, was a report which advocated certain superficial changes to the structure, orientation and content of the contemporary education system and further endorsement for those multiculturalists committed to the development of a pluralist society through the promotion and acknowledgement of ethnic lifestyles in the classroom. Put another way, Swann and his colleagues provided little support or encouragement for those interested and committed to the racialization of educational policy and practice. For educationists and bureaucrats, on the other hand, committed to 'cultural tourism' or the three Ss conception of educational change, 'Swann's song' constituted an important weapon in their ideological armoury.

The 'tradition of tolerance'

'We are not looking for the assimilation of minority communities into an unchanged dominant way of life', Swann and his colleagues insisted early on in their report; 'we are perhaps looking for the "assimilation" of *all* groups within a redefined concept of what it means to live in British society' (DES, 1985, p. 8).

A laudable aim, perhaps. But as responses to the report were to demonstrate, it demanded concessions from the state which were unlikely to be achieved. Of course, some ground was won by the cultural pluralists. In all democratic, culturally diverse societies the state has to tread a cautious path between two precipices. On the one side, too much allowance for cultural diversity can lead to fragmentation. On the other, too little leads to alienation and unrest. In his valedictory speech as Secretary of State for Education, Sir Keith Joseph confronted this dilemma head-on. He rejected the virulent assimilationist contention that 'our education system should in effect take no account of ethnic mix'. In his view: 'It cannot be right to require one set of British children to abandon their culture during their school years'. But he was also dismissive of the 'self-indulgent bias of those who . . . want to subvert out fundamental values and institutions'. He therefore rejected the position 'which asserts that our education system requires a total transformation before justice to ethnic minorities is possible'. The solution to this tantalizing problem was to be found in the 'tradition of tolerance which is one of British society's most precious values'. For Joseph, the imperative was to develop 'A British school for British citizens' which reflected and strengthened commonalities and transmitted 'to all its pupils a sense of shared values and traditions' (Joseph, 1986).

But how far was this an advance on monocultural education? Well, compared to the recommendations of the 1969 Select Committee on Race Relations and Immigration, Joseph's muted playing of the cultural pluralism refrain sounded little different. 'Deliberate efforts should be made', reckoned the Select Committee, 'to teach newly arrived immigrants about life in this country – our customs, social conventions and industrial activities, as well as our language' (1969, p. 42).

The departure from the 'immigrant'/host model of race relations in the 1960s was more apparent than real. Despite the (limited) injection of funds into multicultural education in the immediate post-Swann years (see Tomlinson, 1990), assimilationist concepts of the education system's role in a culturally diverse society continued to prevail, albeit in more subtle guises. The national state's circumspect support for 'evangelical' projects and courses to diffuse the orthodoxy of 'Education for All' contrasted dramatically with its enthusiastic championing of the antiracist campaigns mounted by Raymond Honeyford, Anthony Flew and the Hillgate Group which centred on events in Berkshire, Bradford, Brent and the ILEA. As Stephen Ball (1990, p. 40) has noted, 'cultural variation' became a 'social "problem"', a threat to the national identity'. Responsibility for the resolution of this problem rested fairly and squarely on the shoulders of the education system. And it was to the 1988 Education Reform Act that cultural restorationists looked for the realization of their demands.

The ERA: 'a window of opportunity'?

'The beginning of a new era' is how the Secretary of State for Education, Kenneth Baker, described the legislative package which comprised the Education Reform Act (*The Times*, 30 July 1988). And it is difficult to dissent from this view. In all, the legislation contained 238 clauses, 13 schedules and attracted more Parliamentary time than any other since 1945. And the result? It contrives to alter, to a greater or lesser extent, who teaches; what they teach; how; where; and to whom. Nor are these likely to be fleeting changes, episodic interventions in the educational milieu, contingent on the electoral pre-eminence of Thatcherism. On the contrary; as Richard Johnson has pointed out, the ideology of Thatcherism *will* pass, but the legacy of its conception of education is likely to endure. For Johnson, the transition into 'the new era' will 'be as fundamental as that of 1780–1840 (the birth of "mass schooling") or that of 1865–1880 (the creation of a civic education service)'. He continues: 'By the end of the century the "growth" of 1870–1970 may look like a specific historical phase, with its typical educational forms oddly relative to my children's children' (Johnson, 1989, p. 92). The ERA brings about a fundamental reconstitution of the institutional framework in which schools and colleges function and it is here that the challenges to antiracist (even multicultural) education and related egalitarian initiatives have been most effectively mounted.

'The whip hand': DES, LEAs and schools

The 1944 Education Act established an institutional arrangement in which the Minister of (now Secretary of State for) Education shared with representatives of local government and the teaching profession responsibility for decision- and policy-making. Within this tripartite partnership, central government retained enormous powers to influence the shape and nature of education in England and Wales. However, these tended to be 'reserve powers', to use Roger Dale's (1989, p. 97) phrase, rarely invoked in a period where a broad educational consensus prevailed. As we saw earlier, the recessive role of central government in educational decision-making during the post-war years permitted a considerable degree of autonomy at the local level. According to Lord Butler, who presided over the 1944 Act, the tendency for the centre to acquiesce to LEAs in determining policy priorities was fundamental to his conception of how a liberal democracy should operate. Almost a generation after the passing of the Act, he reaffirmed his conviction that

> it would be a great pity if we took away the interest and control of education from the Local Education Authorities. At the time of the passing of the Education Act, there was much discussion as to what the Minister was going to do. I was criticised for saying that the Minister was going to 'take a great interest'. I believe the Minister of Education will and should always have the whip hand as far as money goes, but I repeat, it would be a great pity to take away from the Local Education Authorities an interest in education, because it binds education to the Local Authority and thereby binds it to the district and makes it the responsibility of every resident.
>
> (Butler, 1968, p. 22)

It would be misleading to suggest that this centre–local relationship was sacrosanct or that the locus of control remained firmly with the LEAs. By the mid-1970s, for instance, as the economy was moving into recession, the DES made significant moves to reassert its control of the education system (see Ranson, 1985; Dunford, 1988). Even then, however, there were considerable opportunities for LEAs to exploit their position within this partnership. So how does the ERA alter this arrangement?

The legislation embraces two discrete though, as we shall see, complementary models of control. First, it sanctions the aggrandisement of the centre with the delegation of over 400 new powers to the Secretary of State. This centralist tendency is represented in its most spectacular (and novel) form by the introduction of the National Curriculum and the targets of attainment and assessment at ages 7, 11, 14 and 16. Centralism is also represented by the move from permissive to prescriptive modes of funding. I want to say more about this later. Suffice it to say here that by helping to ensure greater compatibility between central government policies and local practices, prescriptive funding plays a significant role in defining and confining educational priorities. The other side of the coin sees the ERA providing for a *laissez-faire* model of control. This permits a greater devolution of powers to parents and governors over the way educational institutions are organized, administered and funded. With the setting up of city technology colleges (CTCs); provision for schools to apply for grant-maintained status (GMS) and, if successful, receive funding directly from Whitehall; the introduction of open enrolment and, of course, delegated financial management to schools (LMS) we have a scenario for the 1990s and beyond in which 'consumer participation' figures prominently. Now, these represent different interpretations of the state's role as a regulatory instrument and stem from distinctive political traditions. However, both impulses reside in that loosely structured group of conservative politicians, journalists and academics popularly known as the New Right (Levitas 1986; Quicke 1988). The trend towards centralization draws its rationale from the neo-conservative group within the New Right and its commitment to strong government as a prerequisite for securing the unity of the nation, among other things. The neo-liberals, in contrast, are committed to 'rolling back the state'. They give priority to the freedom of the market and individualism and therefore champion consumer participation.

Despite their differences and respective priorities for action, exponents of these political principles cohere around a common purpose in the ERA: to erode the LEAs' political control over education. On this view, we can conceive of the ERA as a complement to and extension of the Conservatives' approach to central and local relations over a range of governmental functions. As Troyna and Carrington (1990, p. 85) have suggested:

> From the Local Government Finance Act, which replaces the rates with a community charge (or poll tax) and uniform business rate, through to the Housing Act which allows council tenants to 'opt out' of local authority management and control; from the Local Government Act which obliges local councils to put their catering, cleaning and other services out to competitive tendering and, in Section 27, bans them from publishing publicity material which might be deemed as 'political', through to the ERA and its redesignation of powers for LEAs, we are witnessing a scenario in which those who work in (or are elected to) County Halls have become agents rather than partners of central government.

What is more, the ERA is the culmination of a prolonged war of attrition against LEAs in which two main strategies may be discerned: circumvention and destabilization. On the first of these, we can recall how LEAs have been progressively marginalized from educational decision-making in the 1980s. The introduction of the Technical and Vocational Education Initiative (TVEI), Assisted Places Scheme (APS) and, in higher education, the setting up of the Polytechnics and Colleges Funding Council (PCFC) are classic reminders of this trend. With the TVEI, for example, LEAs were simply not consulted, despite the fact that the Initiative had profound implications for state secondary school curriculum practices and the allocation of resources. LEAs were also excluded from discussions about the setting up and operation of the APS which established a direct link between private schools, individual parents and central government (Fitz *et al.*, 1986). In higher education the replacement of the National Advisory Body (NAB) with the PCFC ensured that responsibility for the planning, management and resourcing of polytechnics and colleges was wrested from the hands of LEAs. Here, the Secretary of State aimed to ensure that 'polytechnics should be free from local constraints' (DES, 1987, p. 30).

Processes of circumvention such as these do little to stabilize LEAs as a power base in the education system. There have been other, more direct forms of destabilization, however. Among these, the change from permissive to prescriptive funding seriously undercuts the autonomy of LEAs. While it permits the LEA an opportunity to shape bids for funding in accordance with what it perceives as local needs, the criteria which central government specify as the basis for fund allocation remain non-negotiable. In short, it affirms the locus of control at the centre and allows little room for manoeuvre or initiative at the local level. As Brian Knight (1987, p. 212) points out, this style of funding constitutes 'a very powerful device . . . to effect change in education'. Above all, it rigidifies and reinforces the centre's conception of education.

The destabilization of LEAs has taken another form, represented in an enduring and insidious process of demonization. That is to say, in response to attempts in some socialist local authorities to develop alternative political and educational programmes linked, more or less, to egalitarianism, the Conservative government generated a 'moral panic' in which the sound of 'loony tunes' was heard loud and strong (Gordon and Rosenberg, 1989). 'It is the professional Left that now confronts us', warned Michael Hesletine at the 1982 Party Conference, and in a determined effort to counter their threat, Thatcherites went on the attack with a campaign which demonized LEAs – a vision diffused to a wider public through the tabloid press. In the caricatured imagery which this threw up, tales of how 'loony left' LEAs such as ILEA, Brent, Haringey, Manchester and Bradford had sacrificed the allegedly colour-, class- and gender-blind principles of universalism and individualism on the altar of minority rights and 'positive discrimination' became *de rigeur*. Little wonder, then, that the former Bradford headteacher, Raymond Honeyford, emerged as a *cause célèbre* and was invited to discuss educational policy at Downing Street. Above all else, his opposition to Bradford LEA's policy on multicultural education was predicated on a vigorous defence of universalism and individualism: the claim that we treat all children the same while responding to their individual needs. The racist, sexist and classist implications of those tenets were, of course, conveniently ignored.

The destabilization of LEAs in the formative years of the ERA has, then, proceeded along a clearly delineated path. First: attack the *credibility* of the policies (allegedly) pursued by these 'apostles of mediocrity and bigots of indoctrination', as Baker (1987) described them. Second: question their *legitimacy* as a policy-making body in the educational community. As Thatcher (1987) put it: 'There's no reason at all why local authorities should have a monopoly of free education. What principle suggests this is right? What recent experience or practice suggests it is even sensible?' Third: break this (apparent) monopoly with the creation of a more diverse – some might insist on the

epithet 'stratified' – schooling system and a reformed system of funding allocation which relocates decision-making about expenditure fairly and squarely in
the hands of governing bodies. And the consequences of these reforms? In the
words of Thatcher (1987), they strengthen the 'Conservative tradition of ex-
tending opportunity more widely'.

The 'conservative restoration'

As the 'conservative restoration' of educational principles begins to impact on
the daily lives of administrators, teacher-educators, teachers and pupils in England and Wales, it is tempting to romanticize about the past, yearn for a return
to the halcyon days before the ERA and, as a corollary, accept doom and
gloom as an inevitable consequence of the legislation. This would be myopic
and unfortunate politically. We saw in earlier chapters that even at the height
of LEAs' intervention in the area of racial equality it was easier to discern the
racialization of policy rhetoric than the racialization of everyday practices in
Authority administration.

We should also remember that in the period between the 1944 Education
Act and the Conservatives' legislation on school governance (the Education
Acts of 1980 and 1986) the relative autonomy of LEAs and teachers provided
the context for the development of what Ranson *et al.* (1987) describe as
'professional accountability'. Based on the exclusivist and elitist conviction that
only professional educationists should assume decision- and policy-making
roles, it was at best indifferent to, at worst entirely dismissive of, contributions
from parents and other laypersons. The events at William Tyndale School in
1974 showed, among other things, how an unswerving commitment to professional accountability might provoke an irreconcilable division between
teachers and parents. There is also some evidence to suggest that with professional accountability in the ascendancy, parent and lay governors committed to
antiracist education found their policy proposals falling on deaf ears in governors' meetings (Sharron, 1987).

Ranson and his colleagues suggest two alternative interpretations of accountability. 'Market accountability' is the model which underpins Conservative reforms of school governance in the 1980s. It is based on the conviction that
educational professionals (so-called 'producers' in the ideology of the New
Right) must be answerable to 'consumers' (parents and governors rather than
students). In contrast, 'public accountability' derives its legitimacy from a conception of the wider community as 'citizens' rather than 'consumers' with a
concern for 'others' and 'the health of society' in deliberations and formulation of
policy (Ranson, 1988). 'Public accountability' would, of course, provide a model
of decision-making which is compatible with the principles of community education – the institutional context which, I have argued elsewhere, is especially
conducive to the realization of antiracist education (Troyna and Farrow, 1991).

While it would be politically maladroit to accept, a priori, that the governance
of schools in the 1990s will be grounded in models of 'market accountability', we

cannot underestimate the various ideological, financial and legal pressures under which school governing bodies are convened and their decisions are reached. In short, there is enormous pressure to adhere to the Conservative agenda. As Hilda Kean (1991, p. 148) puts it, the function of school governors is more or less restricted to 'juggling meagre resources between competing demands or funds raising through poaching children . . . from other schools'.

The move towards prescriptive funding alongside reductions in the general grant has severely limited LEAs' resistance to the hegemonic domination of the Conservatives. As part of the 'new realism', the decision of a growing number of LEAs to retreat from the previous stance on antiracist education has been justified on the grounds of survival in 'the survivalist culture'. Consider the views, for instance, of the adviser for multicultural education in 'Cottontown', a local authority in the North West of England:

> to openly describe itself anti-racist the Authority might suffer the con-
> sequences of being branded 'left wing' and 'extremist' and experience the
> same negative treatment from central government and the media similar
> to that experienced by ILEA and Brent Education Authority.
> (quoted in Sikora, 1988, p. 52)

Manchester is another LEA which has adapted to the new realism by de-racializing its policy. In its effort to compete successfully for categorical funding offered through the Education Support Grants, it has accepted the need to accede to the terms imposed by the DES. Among other things, this has demanded a softening of its commitment to antiracist, rather than multicultural education in its submissions (Ball *et al.*, 1990). But as we saw in Chapter 2, it is in inner London that we find the most striking evidence of Conservative success in de-emphasizing the status accorded antiracist education in local policy proposals.

It might be contended that this concern with the status of antiracist education in LEA policy statements is misplaced and anachronistic. Misplaced because, as I noted earlier in this book, only rarely did policies operate as effective change agents. Against that, however, I am convinced that they have served an important function. Among other things, their existence in some LEAs has been used (or exploited) by local antiracist campaigners and activists. What is more, as we saw in Chapter 2, Richardson (1983, p. 3) has argued that policies became 'a petard by which an LEA consciously and deliberately seeks to be hoisted; a deliberate and calculated hostage to fortune; a stick for its own back to be beaten' (see also Troyna and Ball, 1985). Anachronistic? Well, I have already illustrated how the ERA loosens the relationship between LEAs and their individual schools and colleges. In this process local authorities are de-prived of the power, legitimacy and, to use Richardson's (1988) phrase, 'moral authority' to encourage their institutions to base policies and practices on those formulated at County Halls. Let us look briefly at three of the structural changes brought about by the ERA and consider their actual and potential effect on racial equality in education.

Schools which assume grant-maintained status are entirely independent of LEA control and are funded directly by central government. Whether or not they decide to invest part of their budget on the LEA's multicultural advisory, support and resource services – which had previously been provided free of charge – remains to be seen. At any rate, grant-maintained schools are bound by the 1976 Race Relations Act, and in Circular 10/88 the DES noted that governors should run these schools with 'due regard' to the need to eliminate unlawful racial and sexual discrimination. However, this does not obviate entirely the possibility that grant-maintained schools might enhance racial inequality in education. After acquiring GMS schools can apply to the Secretary of State for changes to their basic educational character: from comprehensive to grammar, co-educational to single-sex, non-denominational to denominational, for example. It is at this juncture, when criteria are established for admission into the school, that selection might (unwittingly?) take place along perceived racial lines. After all, selection is inherently discriminatory. School uniform, sex, religion, residence, performance in examinations, presence of siblings in the school, parental connection, catchment area boundaries might each be used as the basis of school admissions policy; and each has the potential to exacerbate racial inequality in access, treatment and outcome.

But the concern with LEA policy statements might also be mitigated by the introduction of a scheme for the local management of schools (LMS). Under this proposal, at least 85 per cent of the Potential Schools Budget is removed from the LEAs and placed in the hands of governing bodies. LEAs are required to develop a formula for the funding of schools. In this they are compelled by the DES to ensure that the overwhelming proportion of the budget allocated to individual schools is pupil-driven – that is, say, at least 75 per cent of each school's budget is determined by the number and ages of its pupil population. The remainder is allocated on the basis of other mandatory and optional factors – the latter including 'non-statutory special needs (e.g. social deprivation)' (DES, 1988).

The trend towards LMS compels our attention for a number of reasons. To begin with, the move towards a standardized formula for funding constrains the LEA's room for manoeuvre in responding to the particular needs and circumstances of individual schools. In short, it inhibits preferential treatment for allocating resources to schools in deprived areas. What is more, it is likely to result in a redistribution of resources from these schools to those in suburban and rural areas of the LEA. As Ian Langtry, education officer of the Association of County Councils, has noted (in Sutcliffe, 1989, p. 1): 'It is an arithmetical truth that if you go towards a formula it must hit some schools, and benefit others'. There is already evidence from Avon, in South West England, that in the absence of an understanding of social justice principles, LMS can precipitate a redistribution of resources from inner urban to suburban and rural schools (Guy and Menter, 1992). LMS, then, denies certain schools access to the resources needed to meet their special needs. By giving pre-eminence to liberal versions of equality, and equating equality of treatment with *sameness* in the allocation of budgets, the approach is bound to exacerbate *inequality*. As a corollary, of course, schools will become increasingly reliant on parental contributions to maintain and improve services – a process which must also widen the gulf between inner and outer ring schools.

The delegation of responsibility for school budgets to governing bodies provides the opportunity for schools to distance themselves from the LEA's multicultural and antiracist support services and deprioritize racial equality as a formal criterion for assessing school policy and practice. Emerging evidence suggests that LMS will reinstate particularistic conceptions of multicultural and antiracist education. Put another way, as the decision to use services such as the inspectorate, curriculum advisers and in-service training (INSET) trainers rests entirely with school governing bodies, it is likely that governors of schools with few, if any, ethnic minority pupils will be unwilling to give priority to expenditure on multicultural and antiracist education from their limited budgets (see Troyna, 1992).

Following on from this, we are likely to witness a decline, if not disappearance, of potentially underemployed LEA multicultural and antiracist support services. Indeed, this decline is already under way. In Manchester, for instance, there are rumours that the 'race' unit will be disbanded as part of the LEA's general deracialization policy. All in all, this suggests that advisers and specialist inspectors will be compelled to assume different roles in the post-ERA period. This is precisely what the Audit Commission (1989) recommended in its report on LEA inspectors and advisers. In the light of LMS it proposes that inspectors spend more time in schools and support more systematically the quality assurance provided by headteachers.

Finally, we come to open enrolment, a proposal which reflects the Conservative Party's conviction that parental choice should prevail within the institutional framework of education provided by the ERA. For the Conservatives, parental choice – or consumer participation, to be more precise – is unassailable even though it has the potential to encourage and legitimate racist mobilizations. Angela Rumbold, Minister of State for Education, made attempts to assuage fears that the government would allow parental preferences to operate along 'racial' lines (CRE, 1989, p. 2). But this concern sits uneasily with the views of other government spokespersons. Baroness Hooper, the government's spokesperson in the House of Lords (*The Times*, 4 December 1987), insisted, for instance, that 'we do not wish to circumscribe that choice in any way' despite the fact that it might precipitate 'white flight'. Her views found support in the High Court when, in October 1991, Mr Justice MacPherson made it clear that the 1976 Race Relations Act did not govern the 1980 (and, by implication, 1988) provisions for parental choice of school (Vincent, 1992). Coming at a time when exclusionist conceptions of British citizenship characterized media and 'common-sense' responses to some Muslim objections to *The Satanic Verses*, unequivocal support for open enrolment in the ERA seems likely to accelerate a trend towards racially segregated schools.

Conclusion

This critique of the ERA and its claims to provide a 'window of opportunity' for all students is based on a single proposition – that entitlement cannot be genuinely offered within an institutional and ideological framework which sanctions the maintenance, reproduction and extension of inequality. It is possible, but by no means certain, that the proposals for the National Curriculum are likely to discourage overt instances of discrimination and facilitate access of all pupils to the full range of core and foundation subjects. But these advances cannot be seen in isolation. Placed in their appropriate context, we see how opting out, LMS, open enrolment and other systematic changes will further disadvantage ethnic minority and other disfranchised pupils in a number of fundamental ways. The priority must now be to rethink our strategies, and campaign for the restoration of egalitarianism on the political, social and educational agenda. It would be foolhardy for antiracists to contemplate anything else.

Notes

1. My reservations about the conceptual precision and methodological basis of the term black 'educational underachievement' have been outlined elsewhere (Troyna, 1984a).
2. Although Shirley Williams, as Secretary of State in the Labour government, had agreed to the establishment of the committee and had appointed Anthony Rampton to the chair, it was her successor in the newly elected Conservative government who appointed the committee's members and specified its formal terms of reference.
3. The publication of the report coincided more or less with the School's Council decision to publish a heavily censored version of its commissioned study into multicultural education. It was censored precisely because it purported to show in the original version the prevalance of teacher racism, a finding which angered the teachers' unions.
4. Consider, for instance, whether a 'low profile' was adopted by Asians at the Imperial Typewriters dispute, Grunwick, Bradford, Newham and so on. See selected chapters in CCCS (1982) for discussion of the form of common-sense racism expressed in the Swann Report and other official and academic publications.
5. This overwhelming emphasis on competence in English as the key to equality of opportunity in the UK once again highlights the linkage between *Education for All* and previous government inquiries in this sphere (Troyna and Williams, 1986, Chapter 1).

4 Antiracism in Schools: Policy Evolution or Imposition?

So far I have looked at the racialization–deracialization couplet in the national and local state policy arena. In this final chapter of this part of the book I will shift the centre of attention to the 'chalkface'. In particular, I want to document and reflect on how one particular school in the post-Swann period responded to the recommendation that institutions should prepare policies which declare their commitment to and promotion of cultural pluralist ideals.

It is undoubtedly true that one of the most significant developments in contemporary educational thinking and planning has been the growing support for whole-school policies. The basic premise of this innovation is that schools should endeavour to ensure that there is coherence and consistency in the students' learning experiences within the institution. It is believed that this goal would be expedited by the setting up of a framework within which a consensus could be reached regarding the ethos, pedagogical and administrative orientation of the school. This is an attractive argument which in Britain has been in the ascendancy especially since the publication of the Bullock Report, *A Language for Life* (DES, 1975). There, a general policy was proposed for the promotion of language development in the school: 'language across the curriculum' constituted one of the important organizing principles of the report. Since then, recommendations for whole-school policies have figured prominently in a number of influential educational documents. Among these, the Cockcroft (1982) report into the teaching of mathematics, David Hargreaves's (1984) report for the ILEA, *Improving Secondary Schools*, and the DES White Paper, *Better Schools* (1985b), immediately spring to mind. In the first of these, for instance, Cockcroft and his colleagues were keen to ensure that consistency and some degree of uniformity underpinned the way in which mathematics was taught in schools. To facilitate this aim, they recommended the formulation of general strategies within the school which would comprise, among other things, 'liaison between teachers so that those who make use of mathematics in the teaching of their subjects do not use an approach or a language which conflicts with that which is used in mathematics lessons' (Cockcroft 1982, p. 148).

On the face of it, it is difficult to envisage many educationists dissenting from the principles on which whole-school policies are based. After all, few teachers would want to see their efforts in the classroom challenged or negated by their colleagues, however unwittingly this might occur. Nevertheless, in the absence of a broad consensus, facilitated by a greater dialogue between colleagues and enshrined in a whole-school policy, there remains the potential for contradictory messages to be conveyed by individual teachers to their pupils. The following incident, described by Kate Myers (1985, p. 30), demonstrates vividly the truth of this argument:

> A nursery teacher reported how she changed the 'Wendy House' to the 'home corner' and painstakingly encouraged the boys to use this area of the classroom. She was subsequently horrified to hear a classroom assistant tell two little boys who were playing with the dressing-up clothes that boys didn't do that sort of thing and wouldn't they prefer to play with the Lego.

For Myers, one way of preventing such a situation is through the formulation of an equal opportunities policy, with teaching and support staff all implicated in its formulation and implementation.

It is important to recognize the influence of this broad trend in contemporary educational policy on the development of initiatives and strategies for multicultural and antiracist education. In an area of debate characterized, as we have seen, by dissent and conflict, there is, as James Banks points out, at least one issue on which consensus has been reached, that is, 'that *total* school reform is needed' and that this embraces, minimally, a concern with 'the learning styles favoured by the school, the languages and dialects that are sanctioned, the teaching materials and the norms towards ethnic diversity that permeate the school environment' (Banks, 1986, p. 226). There is evidence that this holistic conception of school reform is currently being advanced in the United States, Canada and Australia as well as in Britain. In the latter, the 1980s, as we have seen, saw LEAs take an increasingly active role in their attempts to encourage local schools and colleges to reappraise their normal practices and procedures to bring them in line with multicultural and antiracist concerns.

It is clear, then, that the general trend towards the formulation of whole-school policies has impacted directly on current thinking in matters relating to 'race' and education. Further encouragement for this development was found in the Swann Report, which suggested that all LEAs should 'expect their schools to review the curriculum, both taught and "hidden", in the light of the principles we have put forward, to prepare appropriate policy statements and monitor their practical implementation' (DES, 1985, p. 352).

Dilemmas in the whole-school policy process

It seems to me that the development of whole-school policies as one element in the general move towards the institutionalization of multicultural, antiracist education in schools should be applauded. Such policies formalize and enshrine particular approaches and practices which provide the framework within which teachers might operate collaboratively in their attempts to mitigate racism in their schools. At the same time, it is also important to acknowledge that these policies are likely to make only a partial and limited impact on the general ethos and habitual practices of the school unless those involved in their implementation also participate in the formulation. This is an axiom of the literature on organizational change and picked up on in the specific literature on the effectiveness of policies in the process of educational change. As Brian Boyd has noted, many of the advocates of whole-school policies have not confronted the profound managerial and organizational implications of this process, which are particularly salient in the secondary sector. For Boyd (1985, p. 80), the problem centres on

> how one achieves the aim of persuading a school staff, made up of subject specialists with boundary maintenance a high priority, of 'restricted' and 'extended' professionals, of people with fundamentally different values, and indeed different ideas of the aim of education, to work together to produce effective whole-school policies.

For some involved in the antiracist struggle in education, Boyd's cautionary comments would seem at best irrelevant, and at worst a diversionary tactic designed to impede the progress of reforms along antiracist lines. Resistance to a whole-school policy on multicultural, antiracist education which rested on the managerial and organizational grounds which Boyd mentions would be seen as an exemplar of institutional racism. Such critics would contend that those who invoke 'explanations' such as these are providing reasons for not challenging directly and explicitly a system which reproduces racial inequality. Consequently, they are complying with and supporting that racist system, *ergo* institutional racism.

Institutional racism

Those few studies which have documented the formulation and impact of whole-school policies on multicultural and antiracist education have, with a couple of exceptions (Mitchell, 1982; Bagley, 1992) followed assiduously the analytical approach which I have just paraphrased. That is to say, in accounting for the success or otherwise of these policies in reorientating the concerns and priorities of school staff, the studies have focused exclusively on what Hochschild (1984) terms 'racially relevant variables'. Carrington and Short (1989, p. 237), for example, stress the issue of 'presentation' and recommend that antiracists assuage the anxieties of teachers (and parents) by considering 'the possible advantages of a change in nomenclature' in their efforts to expedite institutional support for their policies. Others go further. They centralize institutional racism as the determinant of the success or failure of multicultural or antiracist education policies to gain credence in schools (see, for instance, Lax, 1984; Straker-Welds, 1984; Willey, 1984).

Now I would not wish to underestimate or deflect attention away from the powerful role assumed by teacher racism in the process of institutional resistance to change towards multicultural and antiracist goals. Carl Bagley's (1992) evaluation of factors which contributed to limiting the development of multicultural policies in two schools is the latest testimony to the way in which racism might act as a barrier to change in this context. 'Racially relevant variables' must not be discarded or marginalized in accounts of the progress or otherwise of multicultural and antiracist education policies. On the other hand, I have grave reservations about the use of 'institutional racism' as the only explanatory framework within which such an analysis must be situated. I will return to this argument in Chapter 7. Here I want to make clear that it seems deterministic and reductionist to incorporate the array of themes and issues related to the complex matter of institutional change within this single formulation. The processes of change are far too complex and varied to be accommodated neatly within one interpretive model *unless* that model is expanded to such an extent that it loses precision and explanatory power. Indeed, as Jenny Williams and her colleagues have argued, this is the problem with the concept of institutional racism – It has been used in a taken-for-granted, cavalier manner to the extent that its conceptual precision has been lost (Williams, 1985; Troyna and Williams, 1986; Carter and Williams, 1987).

Williams (1985, p. 335) points out that institutional racism is 'a bridging concept, linking and blurring the distinction between the material and the ideological'. Thus while the existence of racial inequalities alerts us to the existence of institutional racism, the relationship between the various mechanisms said to exemplify this concept in operation and the *causation* of racial inequalities is rarely specified or demonstrated empirically. As Williams (1985, p. 335) indicates:

> differential catchment areas, stereotyping by teachers, monocultural curricula, narrow and particular standards of assessment, white monopoly of positions of authority, differential expectations by teachers of achievement, racist textbooks and the undervaluation of black experience and history, have all been used to illustrate normal institutional procedures which explain differential educational achievement . . . They are all examples of injustices and clearly should be removed from educational practices; but their exact relationship to racial inequality can only be theorised, not demonstrated at the moment.

The conflation of these various practices, and their ideological underpinnings within the unitary formulation of institutional racism, has meant that its existence has tended to be defined by its consequences. This impoverished approach to analysis therefore absolves the researcher from the responsibility of testing empirically the relationships between ideologies and practices, on the one hand, and the existence of inequalities in, say, educational outcomes, on the other.

In this chapter I want to demonstrate empirically some of the arguments I have proposed so far and contextualize the significance of 'racially relevant variables' in the routines of school processes. Here I will draw on some research which I carried out in a school where a group of staff was involved in the move towards a whole-school policy on antiracism. In the role of 'researcher-consultant' I was in a privileged position to observe and document the process of policy formulation. The analysis, then, is based on interviews and the recorded minutes of meetings. It points to the tensions which the process of policy-making generated and the compromises and settlements which were negotiated. The experience also confirmed my view, expressed some years earlier, that it is misconceived to presume that 'the non-institutionalisation of multicultural education derives entirely from the (unwitting) racist attitudes of teachers' (Troyna, 1985, p. 209).

The origins of the policy at 'Outskirts' Community College

'Outskirts' Community College is a coeducational comprehensive upper school in England. Formerly an old-established grammar school, it became fully comprehensive in 1968, four years after it moved into new buildings in a rapidly growing middle-class suburb about 5 miles south of the area's main urban centre. It is a community college, and at the time of the research catered for approximately 1,500 part-time students. Its 1,200 full-time pupils, aged between 14 and 19, were included in a catchment area which extends to villages about 8 miles away from the college. The principal estimated that around 90 pupils (7.5 per cent) were black – mainly pupils of Afro-Asian origin whose parents were expelled from Kenya and Uganda in the late 1960s and early 1970s.

The pastoral side of college life was based on mixed-ability tutor groups, while the academic structure of the college was organized on a faculty basis, of which there were six: Design; English; Mathematics; Humanities; Sciences; and Languages. It seems reasonable to label the college as a 'pressured academic environment', to use Lacey's (1974, p. 150) term. The size of the sixth form (around 400 pupils) and the relatively high number who proceeded to higher education are matters which were emphasized in the college publicity and information sheets. Similarly, the college handbook made it clear to prospective parents that: 'the college is *not mixed ability*. Students are put into sets by Heads of Faculty according to grades supplied to us by High School staff' (original emphasis). As the principal put it, one of the possible sources of staff resistance to change was that 'they're good at their jobs'. Thus in the Humanities faculty, the notion of a common-core curriculum had been rejected by staff in favour of retaining single-subject teaching. In the words of the principal, the reason for this was simple: these subjects 'show good performances'.

The college handbook provided an accurate indication of the importance attributed to credentialism within the institution. The same document provided clues regarding the commitment of the college to antiracist, antisexist values and modes of practice. After all, as Weeks (1982) has remarked, if an educational institution 'feels a strong duty to its ethnic minority pupils one would imagine that this would be expressed in a document going out to these parents'. The college handbook drew to the attention of its prospective and current pupils that the following was one of its rules:

> Behaviour of all members of the College Community is based on the fundamental principle of showing respect; that is respect for others, respect for the environment, respect for the law of the land, and last, but by no means least, respect for self. Respect for others involves rejection of all forms of prejudice whether it concerns a person's sex, class or race.

This rule was reaffirmed the following year, and although there was little evidence to suggest that it was enforced vigorously, or even adhered to as a procedural value of the college, nevertheless it suggested some degree of sensitivity and awareness. It is also important to point out that this rule was not formulated simply in response to the LEA's request for action in line with its own policy on multiculturalism (see Ball, 1986; Allcott, 1992). On the contrary, along with the formation of the college working party on antiracism, it was written well before the LEA had published its formal policy on this issue.

So why was a working party formed in the college? Undoubtedly, the initiative stemmed from the principal. To start with, her previous experience had been in a multicultural community college in a nearby LEA, and she considered that the college's well-publicized initiatives on multicultural matters had relevance to 'Outskirts'. But as I argued in the opening chapters of this book, 'policy entrepreneurship' operates effectively as a description, not an explanation, for change. In our discussions, the principal made it clear that the nascent policy was conceived in terms of a pre-emptory strike; like her counterparts at the level of the local state, she saw policies as a way of averting future disorders. 'I believe in it [multicultural education]', she told me. 'Our future as a society, as a UK citizen, depends on antiracism. The alternative is horrible; dissension and more of the Brixton riots.' Against this background, however, more immediate concerns impinged on the college. During the academic year 1983–4, the principal was approached by some fifth-year pupils of Afro-Asian origin who complained of discrimination at 'Outskirts' and wished therefore to transfer to another school to complete their studies. The principal was sceptical of the veracity of their accusations and suggested that the real reason for their request was that they 'wanted to be with their own folk'. Despite these reservations, the principal brought the matter to the attention of the Staff Association, which comprised all full-time teachers and which met once a month as a consultative and decision-making body. Having previously declared its opposition to 'any form of discrimination in terms of race, class or gender' the Association agreed to the setting up of working party on multicultural education to which members would volunteer.

The working party on antiracist education

The working party met formally in March 1984 for the first of what was to be a total of seven meetings. Its membership, coincidentally, comprised staff from each of the college faculties and divisions and included both junior and senior members of the teaching force. One of the defining characteristics of its membership, however, was that it contained recently appointed staff. In the absence of formal terms of reference, it was agreed at the first meeting that the group should be known as the antiracist working party, that is should extend its constituency to include representatives of the pupils, parents and governors as well as 'outside speakers who had experience of multicultural education and of dealing with racism in schools'. The group also agreed that its aim should be to: '(1) raise awareness within both the staff and the student body; (2) combat racism'. Subsequent meetings saw the working party extended to include representatives from the pupils and governors (who attended intermittently) and 'outside speakers', including the LEA adviser for multicultural education, some local specialist workers, and myself. During its meetings the working party studied relevant policy documents from other LEAs and educational institutions, discussed articles on antiracist and multicultural education, and watched videos used by the local Industrial Language Unit in its racism awareness training courses. By its seventh meeting in April 1984, the working party had agreed on a policy to be submitted for ratification by the Staff Association on 21 May and for subsequent inclusion in the 1984–5 college handbook.

The Proposed Policy Statement of 'Outskirts' Community College

The Principal and teachers of 'Outskirts' College have adopted the following statement:

We aim to develop education at 'Outskirts' College in assemblies, lessons and tutorials and to take all available opportunities to:

(1) impress upon all members of the college community that racism and the discrimination it leads to are offensive and unjust;
(2) explain the historical, political, economic and social backgrounds to racism in this and other societies;
(3) prevent wherever possible any abuse of a racist nature within the college community.

The community college should be a place that brings people together, increases understanding and promotes justice. We shall do all we can to protect this principle.

Staff reactions to the policy

The momentum and enthusiasm generated by the working party during its short but productive life was seriously undermined by the onset of industrial action in the final term of 1983–4. This prevented any further discussions among the working party about how the policy might be implemented and monitored. It also meant that the Staff Association did not meet until the beginning of the new academic year. In the light of these events, the working party reluctantly abandoned the hope that the policy would feature in the new college handbook.

By the beginning of the new academic year industrial action had receded and the policy was presented for ratification at the Staff Association meeting on 10 September 1984. It was introduced formally by a member of the working party who reminded the Association that it had provided a brief for the working party, that the group had representation from all faculties and departments and that 'the aim of today's meeting was to obtain ratification for the policy'. Clearly, however, members of the Staff Association did not share this view of their role. Overwhelmingly, the position taken was that the policy should be scrutinized by faculties, divisional and departmental members, its implications for pedagogy and curriculum content discussed and formulated and, with any revisions that may then be necessary, adopted formally by the staff and included in its next handbook. In contrast, most working party members had assumed that adoption of the policy constituted the basis for discussion. In other words, that the priority should be *ratification*, after which the minutiae of the policy, including its operationalization, should be discussed by members of individual faculties and departments. The debate, then, crystallized around the *style* of adoption, rather than the content of the policy. Indeed, only one member of the Association took issue with the substantive content of the policy, claiming that it was 'moving into the area of indoctrination and propaganda'.

The different positions were resolved when the Association accepted the proposal that: 'The policy should be discussed at departmental and faculty meetings and the results fed back to the next Staff Association meeting'. However, this proved to be an optimistic appraisal of future events. Although each faculty, department and pastoral division of the school discussed the policy and its implications for practice in their meetings, other matters intruded on the agenda of the Staff Association. So, by the end of the winter term of 1984–5 the issue had still not appeared before the Staff Association and the entire enterprise was in danger of collapse. Indeed, scrutiny of the minutes of departmental, faculty and division meetings where the policy was discussed suggested that there was little support for its adoption. The criticisms voiced by staff throughout 'Outskirts' covered a range of issues and themes. At the risk of oversimplification, they could be distilled into two main categories.

First, a reluctance to concentrate exclusively on racism as a matter for action. A number of staff insisted that there were other forms of discrimination in the college which also needed to be tackled, perhaps more urgently. The conclusion reached in one divisional meeting was that there should be a more broadly conceived equal opportunities policy: 'A more general statement that made reference to *any* discrimination (race, religion, sex, etc.) might be preferable.' This perspective was shared by the Science faculty: 'Racism as a particular discriminating attitude should not be singled out from other forms of prejudice such as fat people or others who did not conform to a norm.' Quite simply, staff in different areas of the college believed that the policy was too narrow in its concern and focus. Their conclusion does, of course, ignore the history of the policy initiative and the original brief provided by the Staff Association to the working party.

The other major bone of contention crystallized around the professionalism of the staff and their perceived role as mere operatives in the acceptance and implementation of the policy. This was the argument of some members of the English faculty. In their view, 'the policy implies ignorance and failure on the part of the staff in their current, existing attitudes and practices. It is therefore insulting.' These staff members also felt that 'the policy is prescriptive and intends to "force" staff into practices in the classroom as teacher and/or tutor which they may not want to be involved in'. Precisely the same issue was raised in the meetings of the various divisions of the college. In one of these it was claimed that the policy 'implied a lack of awareness on the part of the staff and as such could be interpreted as criticism of their professionalism'. In another the minutes of the meeting recorded: 'the purpose of the statement was questioned: is it merely to be approved?' A related issue concerned the protective attitude displayed by some staff towards their subject area. The minutes revealed how some staff were reluctant to engage in cross-faculty dialogue. For instance, Mathematics staff insisted that the policy had little relevance to their work and that they would resent the intrusion of other staff from different faculty areas into their deliberations and curriculum planning. Among other points raised in their meeting, Mathematics staff claimed that they had 'checked through syllabus and textbooks etc. for problems with course content but these are not really applicable to Maths' [*sic*].

The outcome of the 'Outskirts' policy initiative

For the latter part of the 1984–5 autumn term the debate about the policy was moribund and was destined to be consigned to the annals of the college's history. Events at the beginning of the new term altered that, however, and precipitated a more immediate commitment to the policy.

Early in that term, some pupils of Afro-Asian origin at 'Outskirts' called on their friends from the city to join them at the school in combating racist abuse from a group of white fifth-form pupils. What resulted can best be described as 'ritual violence' in the playground, and the groups soon dispersed. But the event alerted the vice-principal of the college to the need for 'Outskirts' to resurrect the policy on antiracism. He insisted that the policy be placed on the agenda of the next Staff Association meeting which was to be held in January 1985. In his words, the imperative was 'to demonstrate the college's rejection of racism' and he believed the policy could play a part in declaring publicly that stance.

The meeting on 21 January was poorly attended, with less than half of the full-time teaching staff present. In this context it was agreed that any decision of the policy could not be said to be democratically representative of the staff's view. The nature of this agreement helps to clarify the otherwise obscure phrasing of the recorded minutes of the meeting:

It was proposed that the policy statement developed by the Anti-Racist Working Party be adopted *by the meeting* with the exception of the *apparently* contentious second aim. The essential nature of democratic action was called into question. The *meeting* adopted the policy statement with 20 votes for, 0 against and 8 abstentions.

(emphasis added)

What emerged as the official policy of 'Outskirts' was an emaciated statement of principle which absolved staff from a commitment to 'explain the historical, political, economic and social backgrounds to racism in this and other societies'. Along with the LEA's recently published policy and guidelines on multicultural education, the college statement provided the framework in which the member of staff, subsequently designated with responsibility for this issue, operated.

Reflections on the career of an antiracist education school policy

This reconstruction of events leading to the adoption of a whole-school policy on antiracism reveals some of the complexities associated with policy innovation in schools. In this particular instance, these complexities were exacerbated by the politically contentious nature of the proposed innovation – a policy against racism. It is clear from the transcripts of meetings that some staff at 'Outskirts' were unwilling to engage explicitly with strategies designed to mitigate the effects of racism in the school. Whether this reticence derived directly from their attitudes on 'race' is impossible to say. After all, these same members of staff had already endorsed a Staff Association decision to oppose all forms of discrimination at the school. Against this, however, there were at least two occasions when pupils of Afro-Asian origin had felt that they were discriminated against in the school. Clearly, then, whatever the root cause of staff resistance, its manifestation cannot and should not be underplayed in the analysis. Nor should it be ignored in the development of future strategies to institutionalize antiracist principles in the school.

However, the narrative also pointed to the forms of resistance to change which, for reasons I have already suggested, should not be accounted for simply in terms of institutional racism. On the one hand, the narrative brings into sharp focus the part played by the established ethos of the school in facilitating or limiting the potential for change. On the other, it highlights the role of the professional culture of teachers in this scenario. In the extant literature on the formulation and implementation of whole-school policies on antiracism these matters have generally been accorded little significance. But they exert enormous power in determining the outcome of the innovation.

The professional culture of teachers

In one of the earlier attempts to link the debate about whole-school policies on antiracism to general theories of curriculum change and educational innovation,

Mitchell (1984, p. 32) observed that: 'The *sine qua non* of successful whole school policies is dialogue between staff across departments'. It is clear that some schools have neither the tradition nor the organizational structure to support the type of relationship to which Mitchell refers. This may be particularly true of secondary schools, which have become increasingly larger and more complex organizations. As David Hargreaves (1980, p. 142) indicates, 'Strong subject identities and weak pedagogical perspectives' prevail in these institutions, precisely the context which is anathema to the developmental approach on which the theory and practice of whole-school policy are based. Put another way, there are some schools which are not in the habit of organizing discussions about anything and have little experience of establishing or making public the procedural values which inform the way in which the institution and its constituent members operate. From this perspective, recommendations from the DES, LEAs, even the governing body, that schools provide evidence of an equal opportunities profile could go some way towards expediting greater collegiality, dialogue and collaboration. But to impose a stringent deadline on the completion of this process is foolhardy; it defeats the object and ignores the different stages of collaboration already reached in schools.

At a cursory glance, 'Outskirts' might have appeared the ideal institution for the successful introduction of a whole-school policy. The Staff Association, for example, had been established with the aim of facilitating dialogue among staff and increasing general participation in decision-making processes. But attendance at Staff Association meetings was voluntary and often poor. Nor did the college have any tradition for making its procedural values explicit – that is, with the exception of promoting its record as a 'high achieving' school. In fact, the 'pressured academic environment' of the institution was based in part on the maintenance of strict subject differentiation rather than cross-subject or inter-faculty exchange and collaboration. At closer inspection, then, 'Outskirts' cultivated an ethos which was hardly conducive to the infusion of practices which are cherished within whole-school policies. Against this background the innovation was almost bound to fail.

A closely related issue concerns the ways in which the professional culture of teachers can militate against embracing the tenets of whole-school policies. This is how Geoff Whitty (1985, p. 148) puts it:

> professional culture at the chalk face retains a certain capacity to be resistant to change initiated elsewhere, even if its role is essentially defensive. This poses a problem not only for governmental and industrial attempts to give schools a more utilitarian bias, it also poses problems for those who wish to see schools as a context within which critical insights into the nature of the wider society can be developed.

In his discussion of this issue, David Hargreaves (1980) conceives the occupational culture of teachers as being ordered around three themes: status, competence and relations. It is the relational theme which is of particular interest here. Hargreaves draws attention to the 'cult of individualism' in teaching where the 'live and let live' maxim is often axiomatic in schools. He claims that 'like sexual activity teaching is often seen as an intimate act which is most effectively and properly conducted when shrouded in privacy' (Hargreaves, 1980, p. 141). Naturally, the tenacity of a commitment to the cult of individualism within the professional culture of teaching is influenced strongly by the school's ethos and internal organization. In 'Outskirts' it was not challenged systematically or firmly. Rather, in the interests of the school's academic reputation, it was encouraged to persist. It is partly for this reason that a sizeable handful of 'Outskirts' teachers resented the perceived intrusion into their established practices and arrangements which the policy implied. It also helps to explain why they interpreted the policy as a critique of their current work. But this is not the whole story.

Equal opportunities and teaching

In recalling the experiences of the Girls into Science and Technology (GIST) project, Kelly (1985, p. 140) made the important point that: 'All innovation in schools includes, at least implicitly, a critique of teachers' previous practice, and is thus potentially threatening'. These fears are likely to be exacerbated in the present climate where there are perceptible moves towards centralization in decisions affecting curriculum content and pedagogy and, as a corollary, an erosion of teachers' relative freedoms in the classroom. Kelly goes on to suggest that these fears become more distinctive in discussions about equal opportunities and antiracist education. The reason: because 'However we [the GIST project team] tried to disguise it, the message to teachers was that they had been disadvantaging half their pupils all their professional lives' (Kelly, 1985, p. 139).

Again, there are close parallels with the experiences at 'Outskirts'. This helps to explain why some teachers refused to see racism in the school as a priority for ameliorative action and why, also, members of the Mathematics Department were reluctant to view the matter as relevant to their subject area. Both constituted strategies of resistance to the perceived challenge to the teachers' competencies in ensuring equality of treatment for all pupils. What I observed at 'Outskirts' resonates with one of my earlier arguments about multicultural and antiracist education initiatives:

> one of the covert messages conveyed to practitioners by the multicultural education movement is: you have failed demonstrably to ensure that black students enjoy equality of opportunity in education; therefore you need 'expert' assistance (from specialist advisers and inspectors, support staff and consultants) and pre-packaged materials to facilitate the realisation of this goal.
>
> (Troyna, 1985, p. 221)

In their efforts to minimize this threat the GIST team focused primarily on the professional concerns of teachers (the concept of equality of opportunity) and avoided 'the personal ramifications of sex stereotyping' (Kelly, 1985, p. 139). Similarly, the working party at 'Outskirts' drew attention in the policy to the integral role of antiracism in the principle of community education to which the school as a community college was geared. In both cases, this strategy met with limited success.

Conclusion

Mukherjee (1984, p. 6) directed the following criticism to white people: 'Your racism has been your silence . . . Inaction or silence, to me, means action. To me inaction means collusion'. His observations seem to resonate with the policy-making process at 'Outskirts'. Why? First, because staff prevaricated over the adoption of an antiracist school policy for over a year. Second, they rejected what was, arguably, the most important of the proposals for action in the policy. Third, they accepted only a diluted version of the original, and then only reluctantly, and for purely expedient reasons: to pre-empt the possible recurrence of racial tension within the institution. Despite the fact that these minor, even hesitant initiatives in 'Outskirts' went some way beyond what has happened in the majority of British schools, it is difficult to dispute the claim that the staff colluded with a system in which many of the rules, regulations and procedures encourage the reproduction of racial, gender and class inequalities. Nevertheless, to conflate the actions and attitudes of the staff with practices and actions which are racist in intent (such as 'colour bars') and designate them as 'institutional racism' seems to be an unproductive basis on which to develop change. 'The relationship between racist intent, racialist practices and racist effects (in the form of inequality)', I have argued elsewhere, 'is not as clear-cut as many would have us believe. The imperative must be to clarify empirically these relationships if realistic and productive antiracist policies are to be formulated' (Troyna and Williams, 1986, p. 56).

It is unfortunate that the debate about the evolution of antiracist policies in schools is often disarticulated from the routine concerns of those concerned with mainstream educational innovation and change. Variables such as the internal organization and ethos of schools, alongside the 'cult of individualism', constitute some of the most powerful obstacles in the process of change. In highlighting these variables my intention has not been to deny the existence of racism among the staff at 'Outskirts'. It has been to suggest that the struggle to achieve racial equality in education is more complex and treacherous than some antiracists might assume.

PART 2

Reflections on Research

5 Children, 'Race' and Racism: The Limitations of Research and Policy

The 'picturesquely anecdotal'

In this chapter my concern shifts from a close interrogation of policies on multicultural and antiracist education to an appraisal of some of the research studies which have helped to mould their form. I will also look at the methodological orthodoxy on which some of these more influential studies have been based.

On the face of it, it is not difficult to discern the influence of empirical research on race relations in schools in the nature and orientation of multicultural and antiracist education policies. The principal co-ordinates of policies aimed at enhancing the status of cultural diversity in schools and combating racism derive, in various degrees, from research into the following areas: children's racialized attitudes towards their own and other ethnic groups; the salience of ethnicity in the structure of school-based friendship groups; and the form and incidence of racist harassment by pupils and teachers.

This ostensibly impressive array of substantive issues was not enough to convince some observers in the 1980s that sufficient insights have been gained about the relations between children of different ethnic groups. For instance, following its small-scale study of race relations in five LEAs in 1984, Her Majesty's Inspectorate (HMI, 1984, p. 1) came to the provocative conclusion that 'little is actually known about race relations in schools'. Although this chimed discordantly with conventional wisdom, Michael Marland reckoned much the same three years later. In drawing up a provisional research agenda following the publication of *Education for All*, he characterized existing studies 'on the detailed texture of school life from the point of view of ethnicity' as comprising little more than the 'picturesquely anecdotal' (Marland, 1987, p. 119).

These propositions compel us to look rather more critically at the existing studies, and it seems to me that *The School Effect* (Smith and Tomlinson, 1989) provides a useful starting point for this exercise. The study presented a complex statistical analysis of the internal processes of 20 urban, multiracial comprehensive schools in Britain. The aim of the study was to try and identify those factors which contribute to an 'effective school'. Among its findings the authors emphasized that 'what school a child goes to makes far more difference (in terms of exam results) than what ethnic group he or she belongs to' (Smith and Tomlinson, 1989, p. 305). This seems to fly in the face of the customary rationale for the provision of both multicultural and antiracist education. For this reason alone, *The School Effect* demands careful scrutiny. But there are other reasons. It has, for instance, been enthusiastically received by both the Labour and Conservative Party spokespersons on education and been accorded exemplary status in discussions about the way in which research might be used in the framing of national policy agendas. It also provides one of the few, ostensibly systematic, analyses of the incidence of racist harassment in schools. Finally, I will argue that the study is emblematic of the failure of research, based on a positivistic paradigm, to capture sensitively the general nature of race relations in education, and particularly its dynamic in the social, cultural and institutional worlds of young people. This leads to commensurate weaknesses in policies designed to tackle structural inequalities in education. The way in which Smith and Tomlinson handle data relating to racism demonstrates vividly this argument.

Racist harassment

Empirical research into racist harassment in education has tended to be framed around two distinct methodologies. Over the last decade or so, local monitoring groups, the Commission for Racial Equality (CRE), journalists and campaigners, LEAs and specialist enquiry teams have collated an impressive range of evidence which demonstrates the tenacity and pervasiveness of racist and interracial conflict in schools. Quite often, this has taken the form of case studies such as those assembled by the CRE (1987) in *Learning in Terror*. The alternative approach is represented by those researchers who have developed more formal, quantitative methods of analysing racist harassment by pupils. These researchers have built up a statistical profile of these incidents through pupil responses to questionnaires, structured classroom observation and interviews with pupils, parents and teachers. Interestingly, the research built upon these more formal methodologies has been more circumspect about the prevalence of such incidents in schools.

Elinor Kelly's analysis of 'racial' name-calling among secondary school pupils in Manchester is a good example of this hesitancy. She distributed formal, self-completion questionnaires to 902 pupils and on analysis of the data concluded that: 'In thinking about the individuals who may become either "victims" or "aggressors' we are, it seems, talking about a small minority' (Kelly, 1988, p. 17). Smith and Tomlinson (1989) are even less impressed by claims that 'racial' incidents are a pervasive feature of life in British schools. In their study, parents of children in the 20 sample schools were asked in what ways they were satisfied or dissatisfied with their children's school. 'Just 1 per cent of parents mentioned racial attacks, or that black and white children don't get on', according to the authors (Smith and Tomlinson, 1989, p. 62). They contrast these findings with those derived from case studies and insist that, although their study 'did not include systematic classroom observation, there was little indication of overt racism in relations among pupils or between pupils and staff'. They go on to say:

> Thus, although some well-publicised reports have created the impression that overt racism is a serious problem in multi-ethnic schools, or in some of them, on closer examination there is little evidence on this matter, and no evidence at all of the size or extent of any problem.
>
> (Smith and Tomlinson, 1989, p. 62)

Their conclusions have not gone unnoticed, especially by those who have argued that the issue of racism in schools has been inflated by those with 'vested interests'. Anthony Flew, one of the more vociferous critics of LEA and school antiracist policies, applauded the authors' conclusions in his review of the book. 'The School Effect', wrote Flew (1989, p. 22), 'should remind us all of Hastie's Law: "The incidence of alleged racism in a given society will vary in direct proportion to the number of people generously paid and prominently positioned to find it." Never ask the barber whether you need a haircut'. But can the veracity of Smith and Tomlinson's widely cited critique be sustained?

There is no doubting that Smith and Tomlinson's scepticism about the methodological weaknesses of many of the extant studies on 'racial' incidents in schools is well founded. Both the anecdotal and supposedly more systematic empirical bodies of evidence on this issue are both partial and imprecise. What is more, the evidence fails to provide any indication of how common such incidents might be in schools. Against this, however, I am not convinced that *The School Effect* provides a more accurate, rigorous or sensitive insight. My reservations crystallize around three main considerations.

Smith and Tomlinson state that their interest in the study is with 'overt racism', by which I take them to mean observable, clear-cut instances of racist abuse, harassment and bullying, either by teachers or pupils. But this is a limited, almost superficial understanding. In recent years broader definitions of racist harassment have been formulated by the Home Office in association with other central government agencies, LEAs and individual schools in a variety of different situations. These definitions include not only physical and verbal instances of racist incidents but also what might best be described as 'hidden' or 'indirect' forms: mimicry, tone of voice, exclusion, teacher expectations, body language and so on (see Troyna and Hatcher, 1992).

The apparent absence of 'overt racism' should not, then, be used to counter claims about the seriousness or prevalence of racist incidents. The two phenomena are not synonymous. Rather the former is only one and not necessarily the most common expression of the latter.

Smith and Tomlinson's procedure for establishing the incidence of 'overt racism' is also problematic. In this part of the study, data were collected from parents, not pupils. But can parental views be legitimately accepted as a valid and reliable portrayal of racism in schools? It seems not.

As Smith and Tomlinson note elsewhere in their book, there is a tenuous relationship between what pupils experience at school and parental perceptions of those experiences. The researchers found a weak correlation between the 'child's enthusiasm (for school) . . . and the parents' assessment of how happy the child is at school' (Smith and Tomlinson, 1989, p. 106). This suggests that even if children discuss their schooling experiences with their parents they present them with a limited picture of their everyday reality of school. It is reasonable to assume that either pupils bracket out their experiences of racism from their conversations with parents or, alternatively, their parents reinterpret those experiences. Confirmatory evidence for this can be found in other studies, including the Macdonald inquiry into the murder of Ahmed Iqbal Ullah at Burnage High School in 1986. I will have more to say about this inquiry in Chapter 7. Here I want to point out that, in the course of collecting evidence for their report, the team of inquirers spoke with Ahmed's sister, Selina Ullah. She 'remembered that he would be very reticent about incidents which happened at school and that the family would have to press him *very strongly* in order for him to give any details about incidents which had occurred' (Macdonald *et al.*, 1989, p. 12; emphasis added). Elaine Sihera recalls a similar scenario. Her daughter had been the victim of racist name-calling in her school for some time before she shared the experience with the family. According to Sihera (1988, p. 29) 'she had not told us because we wouldn't have done much about it'. Sihera does not elaborate on the reasons why the family would have been reluctant to intervene, but Akhtar and Stronach (1986, p. 23) reckon that some parents might trivialize the significance of 'racial' incidents, especially racist name-calling, preferring to see it as no more significant than other routine forms of teasing and sarcasm between children at school.

It could also be that parents trivialize racist name-calling because they feel powerless to intervene in the light of the school's *laissez-faire* position on this matter. Whatever the reason, it seems that parents can only provide a limited guide to the extent and intensity of racism in their children's everyday experiences at school. While children may not discuss these experiences with their parents, this is insufficient reason to reject other, arguably more persuasive sources of data on this matter.

My final criticism of Smith and Tomlinson's position centres less on their strategy for establishing the incidence of 'overt racism' in schools than on their analytical framework. Here is the nub of my argument. I am sceptical about the application of quantitative research in this area because I believe it is too crude to capture the subtle and complex nature of racism in education. This critique is not meant to imply, as some writers might assume (Hammersley, 1992) an uncritical deference to qualitative research or a willingness to sacrifice the rigours of research methodology on the altar of 'political correctness'. It is to argue that quantitative research is a less appropriate research tool to tease out the salience and impact of racism in the cultural milieux of children.

Nor is this critique confined to the methodology used by Smith and Tomlinson. It extends to the research of Elinor Kelly which I mentioned earlier, Cohn's (1988) study of name calling, and various local and national projects on racist harassment. Each has concentrated on assembling statistical data on the observable, detectable and therefore easily measurable and quantifiable forms of racism.

This determination to use statistical tools of analysis might be useful in helping to mobilize action against racist attacks. At the same time, it might help to perpetuate and legitimate reductionist interpretations of these incidents. Perhaps I can express this argument more clearly by looking at parallel tendencies in the cognate field of sexist harassment.

In her critical appraisal of studies of woman battering, Pagelow (1979) claims that a reliance on statistical methods of investigation has led to superficial and impoverished understandings of this protracted and diffuse phenomenon. The emphasis on statistical profiles means that variables are only conceptualized according to what is easily questionable rather than what is theoretically significant. Thus 'woman battering' is typically defined in research only in terms of physical violence against women. But as Pagelow points out, this excludes verbal and psychological forms of 'woman battering', forms which are less amenable to quantitative analysis. She continues:

> Numerical tabulation of slaps or kicks produces raw material for the computer to feed upon, but we miss out on more than we get . . . what have we really learned about the interactional dynamics before and after those acts, the damage sustained (or lack of it) and the cognitions attached to the acts by both the actor and the receiver?
>
> (Pagelow, 1979, p. 346)

She contends that this research orthodoxy provides 'skewed results' because it offers limited answers to important questions. For Pagelow, a range of methodologies should be applied to this field of enquiry which would help to provide depth as well as breadth to our understanding.

The study of sexual harassment on the campus by Dzeich and Weiner (1984) reached similar conclusions. They argued that the self-imposed silence of female students subjected to 'sexual harassment' by male professors derived in part from uncertainty about how to label such experiences. Again, this highlights the need for a common definition and range of methodologies to facilitate empirical exploration of this complex phenomenon.

Whom do you like?

Quantitative approaches have also provided the main methodological tool for teasing out children's attitudes towards their own and other ethnic groups. These research studies resolve around two discrete though related concerns: the explication of black children's self- and group images; and insight into white children's attitudes towards ethnic minority groups.

Both research initiatives have a long history stretching back to experimental studies completed in the USA in the late 1920s and early 1930s. Moreover, both have generated data which have helped to shape the terrain on which multicultural education in Britain and the USA has flourished and derived legitimacy. In Chapter 1 I referred briefly to the impact of David Milner's identity studies on the nascent multicultural movement in Britain in the 1970s. His research was originally reported in *Children and Race* (Milner, 1975), was seemingly confirmed by later research embedded in the same methodological genre (for example, Davey, 1983), and assumed almost reverential status in policy and academic discourse. Milner's argument was based on children's responses to dolls of different colour. His recommendations for multicultural forms of education seem now to have a familiar refrain: black children are hostile towards their ethnic identity; therefore, policy should be directed towards ensuring that curricular and teaching materials help to promote a positive black identity by being more culturally sensitive. This would, in consequence, help to improve their commitment to school and improve their academic performance.

Putting to one side momentarily concern about the way in which researchers have interpreted the apparent predilection of black children to reject 'same-race' dolls and photographs in favour of representatives of the dominant ethnic group, it is my conviction that these studies suffer from delusions of grandeur. Implicitly or otherwise, researchers working in this methodological frame have encouraged a belief in the predictive powers of the studies. They presume that the nature of race relations in schools and elsewhere can be 'read off' from the findings. This sits uneasily with the well-established fact that there is only a tenuous relationship between attitudes (especially those expressed under experimental conditions) and actual behaviour. As Allport (1954) put it almost 40 years ago, children might articulate and reproduce a racist discourse but this need not necessarily operate as an informing principle of their day-to-day interaction. Now, if there is no necessary or automatic link between attitudes and actions we need to be cautious about reading too much into the policy recommendations of this research genre.

'Quantitative methods' according to Liz Gordon (1984, p. 106), 'can only report what is happening; qualitative look at the why and the how'. In both the identity studies and the more general investigation of children's 'racial' attitudes, researchers have given priority to the 'what'. Their main concern has been with eliciting and documenting the nature of children's perceptions and conceptions of race-related issues rather than exploring the processes which underpin those attitudes. Consequently, the stimuli presented to the children in these research inquiries – dolls, photographs, word-association tests, sentence completion tasks and so on – and the way the questions are framed ('Give me the doll/photograph that looks like a white child'; 'The English are . . .') give privileged status to physical features. Physical traits are decontextualized and disembodied but are presented to children as legitimate criteria for differentiating humankind; and the children, for reasons to do with the power relations between 'researchers' and 'researched', are constrained to respond in similar terms. Quite apart from the dubious ethical premises of this strategy, some of which I will discuss in Chapter 6, it seems inevitable that 'racial' and 'ethnic' characteristics will be used by children in their responses. After all, it is the only resource available to them! On this view, the research might be indicted for its manipulative techniques. It tends to ensure that children's perceptions are 'colour-bound'.

These caveats do not lead me to conclude that theories about children's 'racial' attitudes are simply an artefact of this methodology. As I will show in Chapter 7, there is a rich seam of evidence, adduced mainly from qualitative research, which demonstrates clearly children's racialized perceptions of social reality and the array of sources from which they derive. But I am concerned that researchers working within this positivistic paradigm, often under experimental conditions, subordinate an understanding of the racialization process in favour of description. Stephen Reicher makes a similar point in his critique of the identity studies. He maintains that the use of dolls and still photographs in these studies naturalizes 'race' and sex which are:

> the archetypes for justifying the physical categorisation of humanity. Such a method ignores that many alternative forms of categorisation, for instance class, depend on what people do rather than, principally, how they look. The only way to guard against such implicit bias is to start off by examining the ordinary language explanations of 'naturally' occurring events . . . Instead of simply applying quantitative techniques to limited response categories, it is necessary to use qualitative analyses in order to establish the categorical structure prior to statistical analysis.
>
> (Reicher, 1986, p. 165)

This seems imperative. The positivistic approach which informs and distorts the picture of children's racialized attitudes has helped to generate and legitimate impoverished understandings of this complex issue. It has also encouraged the development of policies which, at best, only scratch the surface of the salience and role of 'race' in the social worlds of children.

You need friends

In contrast to the extensive literature on the attitudes of children and young people concerning 'race' (see Aboud, 1988), there is little evidence about their behaviour and the significance of 'race' and ethnicity in their social interactions within and outside school. As we have seen, one strand of knowledge derives from recent studies of racist harassment. The other, more extensive, emerges from studies of the role of ethnicity in the structure of school-based friendship groups. Again, quantitative methods, with a few notable exceptions, have dominated this literature.

The favoured approach is sociometry. Children are asked to nominate their three best friends in school, whom they would like to sit or play with, or some such variant. The results are then presented in tabular form or in a diagram. These show the cluster of friendships both in numerical terms (the size and range of groups) and how they are constituted in relation to ethnicity (and other structural or organizational variables). Summing up the research findings on ethnicity and friendship groups in British schools, Tomlinson (1983, p. 129) writes that pupils 'do not appear to form inter-ethnic friendships to any great extent, being "racially aware" and preferring their own groups from an early age'. If this is true then it is especially worrying for those who subscribe to the 'contact hypothesis': that interpersonal contact across ethnic lines in, and of, itself brings about better race relations by attenuating individual racial prejudice. If segregated groups continue to prevail in multiethnic schools, as Tomlinson's distillation of sociometric research findings suggests, then there seems little hope of improved race relations in the future – at least according to this theory of intergroup behaviour. My concern with sociometry and the contact hypothesis with which it articulates in both research and policy is that it is an oversimplified and distorted interpretation of intergroup behaviour.

To start with, in interpreting the rationale underpinning the structure of friendship groups in multiethnic settings, sociometrists constantly place 'race' or ethnicity in the driving seat. Their results are presented and analysed primarily in relation to these variables. In so doing, interpersonal behaviour is explained in terms of group characteristics. Put another way, children's motivation for selecting friends is seen in relation to group categories, not personal attributes. Is this a valid and reliable interpretation?

It seems not. We cannot presume that pupils' immersion in interethnic friendships is indicative of positive racial attitudes among their members. Why? Because this conflates interpersonal relationships with an individual's perception and valuation of groups. As Turner (1987) emphasizes in his critique of the contact hypothesis, it is important to differentiate between interpersonal attraction, by which he means favourable attitudes towards people as unique individuals, and group cohesion, the mutual attraction between in-group members *qua* group members. In applying their results to wider discussions about the state of race relations, sociometrists have failed to acknowledge that the relative importance of interpersonal attraction and intergroup relations may vary from one situation to another according to the salience of group membership to individuals in different contexts. Quite simply, ethnic homogeneity in school-based friendship groups cannot be assumed automatically to signify negative racial attitudes or intergroup hostility. Ethnicity may or may not be a significant variable to individuals in that particular setting.

As a corollary, sociometrists encourage us to believe that interethnic friendships are not only accompanied by but also signifiers of the absence of racial prejudice. An appealing proposition, perhaps, but one which must be treated with caution. This is because it is based on correlational not causal links. There might be an observable, statistical connection between interethnic friendships and the positive racial attitudes of participants, but it is another thing to presume that one exists in a causal relationship to the other. Even if we could infer causality, precluded, of course, by the quantitative perspective, in what direction would it operate? To paraphrase Reicher (1986), does pupils' involvement in ethnically mixed friendships attenuate their racial prejudice or is it only those (white) pupils who are not racially prejudiced who immerse themselves in interethnic friendship groups? Sociometry, and the positivistic paradigm in which it is embedded, is ill equipped to answer this complex and critical question.

Conclusion

I have argued three things in this chapter. First, we have only a limited insight into the nature of interethnic relationships in schools. Second, the knowledge that we do have available derives from research which is underpinned by a positivist paradigm. Third, the quantitative studies which dominate the literature on this theme are ill equipped to deal with such a complex matter: they provide descriptions rather than understanding of the racialization process and children. Despite these limitations it is the quantitative research of Smith and Tomlinson, Milner, and the sociometric school of analysis which has played the most significant role in determining the shape of national and local policies in what is generically known as 'multicultural education'. Policies on dispersal (or 'bussing'), culturally diverse curricular and teaching materials, disciplinary procedures on 'racial' harassment and 'effective' schools initiatives have assumed credibility largely in terms of what I have argued is a crude and therefore inadequate research basis. As Bhavnani (1991, p. 10) insists in her study of the ways in which young working-class people discuss issues in 'the domain of the political', if studies 'are operationalised from an inadequate theoretical discussion, there is a danger that the quantitative analyses which follow will mask the paucity of the theoretical basis' for the research.

The way in which 'race' shapes and constrains the social world of children can only be successfully explored by identifying its place in the totality of children's lives, teasing out the ideological lens through which children make sense of that world and act within it. I will have more to say on this in Chapter 7. Here I want to emphasize that this imperative demands a mode of analysis which is equipped both theoretically and empirically to locate the ideologies and behaviour of children in the context of the home, school and community. Such studies are beginning to emerge. However, in the continuing reluctance of policy-makers to acknowledge these studies or utilize their insights in the framing of policies, efforts to understand and combat the insidious and corrosive effects of racism in education are likely to remain, at best, limited and partial, at worst, obfuscatory.

6 'Whose Side Are We On?' Ethical Dilemmas in Research on 'Race' and Education

BARRY TROYNA WITH BRUCE CARRINGTON

'There is another problem, too, I think,' she went on, opaquely. He waited. 'I think they don't think it's interesting. The project, I mean. No, that's not quite right. People like talking about themselves, as you know,' she glanced at him in order to acknowledge his professional superiority, 'but they don't see the point of it. Why do we want these accounts of everyday routines? What are we going to use them for?'

'Have you been telling the truth, then?' he asked.

'The truth about the project? Of course. Isn't that what you wanted me to do?

'Not really,' he admitted, faintly.

'But isn't it unethical to do anything else?'

'Delia,' he said, getting up and strutting around the room, patronisingly, 'life is full of ethical problems. So is work. Sometimes, in order to achieve the ends we want to, we have to be unethical.'

(Oakley, 1991, p. 106)

In this chapter the ethical dilemmas facing researchers in antiracist education will be examined and the tensions and contradictions which currently exist between antiracist theory and practice highlighted. To bridge this gulf, we draw particularly upon the sociological insights of Gouldner (1975) and the contributions of critical theorists such as Lather (1986). We argue that their respective conceptions of research provide not only the basis for a critical appraisal of available substantive work on 'race' and education in the UK, but also a framework within which the following, essentially ethical, questions might be addressed. First, how can antiracist researchers reconcile their partisanship with objectivity? Second, what role (if any) should white researchers play in antiracist research? Third, what role should research play in promoting racial equality in educational access, treatment and outcomes? Fourth, to what extent ought the research act itself *actively* challenge common-sense (for example, stereotypical, racist, populist) beliefs and perceptions? Fifth, can antiracist principles be reconciled with the need for external sponsorship and funding? Finally, what steps can be taken to facilitate the development of greater reciprocity and collaboration between the antiracist researcher and those whom she or he researches?

Partisanship and objectivity

It is our contention that an antiracist educational ideology is congruent with research informed by critical theory. For example, as the work of Lather (1986), among others, has indicated, research within this paradigm is essentially 'transformative' in nature: researchers not only seek to highlight forms of inequality and injustice, but also view the research act itself as constituting a deliberate challenge to the status quo. From this standpoint, the ultimate purpose of research is to contribute to a body of empirically grounded 'emancipatory knowledge'. This knowledge, by interrogating common-sense conceptions of the world (as well as more systematic forms of 'distorted communication'), may serve to 'empower the oppressed' by enabling them 'to come to understand and change their own oppressive realities' (Lather, 1986, pp. 261–2). Lather stresses that such research, as a 'response to the experiences, desires and needs of oppressed people' should aim to achieve maximal reciprocity between researcher and researched. She advocates a democratization of the research process. In her view, research should be seen as a 'dialogic enterprise' in which the traditional division of labour between research and researched (and its attendant status differential) is abandoned. Lather claims that if subjects (as active, purposive agents) are to be encouraged to be reflexive and question their own taken-for-granted beliefs and assumptions, then researchers must ensure that the 'researched' play a full part in the 'construction' and 'validation' of 'emancipatory knowledge': that is to say, both parties contribute to the analysis of data and formation of theory. It can be seen, then, that this research paradigm bears a strong resemblance to conceptions of an antiracist pedagogy.

While we accept Lather's views about the 'educative' purpose of such collaborative research and respect her unequivocal partisanship, we believe that there are some problems with this position. Above all, it declares a commitment to 'underdogs' which is idealist and could be construed as relativist. Criticisms along these lines formed the thrust of Gouldner's (1975) reflections on the work of Howard Becker. It seems to us that Gouldner's strictures are also important in facilitating an exploration of and resolution to the ethical questions associated with research on 'race' and education.

Briefly, when addressing the question 'Whose side are we on?', Becker had contended that the researcher was compelled to affiliate to the perspectives of either 'subordinates'/'underdogs' or 'superiors'/'overdogs'. The inference drawn from his studies of deviance is a sentimental commitment to the 'underdog': marijuana users, jazz musicians, prostitutes and so on. In recognizing

Becker's genuine concern to expose injustices through his research, and the potential conflict that such an enterprise entails, Gouldner nevertheless argues that it is possible to reconcile such explicit forms of partisanship with objectivity. Gouldner contends that if (partisan) sociologists are to act in the role of arbiter between interest groups ('underdogs' and 'overdogs') there must be some appeal to a body of ethical principles if justice is to be realized. Ultimately, Gouldner (1975, p. 68) insists that: 'It is to values, not to factions, that sociologists must give their most basic commitment'.

We take Gouldner's imperative as the starting point for our appraisal of research on 'race' and education. Specifically, this demands that the researcher's pre-eminent commitment should not be to black or white youth, teachers or administrators, but to the fundamental principles of social justice, equality and participatory democracy. In short, we are arguing for the establishment of principles which are common both to antiracist pedagogy and research. From this perspective, we can now explore the remaining opening questions which highlight, in our experience, the main ethical dilemmas facing researchers in this area. An appropriate starting point for two white researchers contributing to this area is a consideration of the extent to which the 'race' or ethnicity of researchers has a bearing on the realization of these principles.

The role of white researchers

Quite clearly, important strategic, moral and political decisions need to be taken about how research might best expedite the attainment of these principles, and it is around this issue that trenchant criticisms about the involvement and concerns of white researchers in 'race relations' and antiracist research have crystallized. In Britain, the USA and Australia (see Bell and Nelson, 1989) a common criticism of such research has been that white researchers have tended to direct their energies towards the study of black people rather than white racism. In Britain, such criticisms were voiced during the 'palace revolution' of the early 1970s when black community activists and others criticized the political orientation and research agenda of the Institute of Race Relations (IRR). At the time, the IRR was, in the words of Mullard (1985, p. 1), 'a white prestigious body'. It was engaged in various activities which, its opponents argued, rested on a pernicious and misleading identification of 'the problem'. For those involved in the struggle for control of the IRR the fundamental issues to be considered differed from those which the Institute's researchers had addressed. Bourne (1980, p. 339) has noted:

> It was not black people who should be examined, but white society; it was not a question of educating blacks and whites for integration, but of fighting institutional racism; it was not race relations that was the field of study, but racism.

Clearly these were not simply differences in interpretation which might be resolved by rational, disinterested discourse. They reflected diametrically opposed political positions regarding the cause and nature of racial inequality in Britain and the political actions which were needed to combat this reality. The critique rested mainly on the presumption that (white) social science scholarship had authenticated a scenario in which black citizens played an active role in the generation and maintenance of racial inequality. It was not an unfamiliar debate; the research of Daniel Moynihan and James Coleman in the USA had prompted similar critiques in the 1960s (see Billingsley, 1970). In Britain, the dispute continued into the 1980s and formed the leitmotiv of *The Empire Strikes Back* (CCCS, 1982). Here, black members of Birmingham University's Centre for Contemporary Cultural Studies (CCCS) attacked the research problematics of various white sociologists. Although one of the authors suggested in an accompanying article that he did not insist that 'white sociologists cannot study black people' (Lawrence, 1981, p. 9), his colleagues were less concessionary in their contributions to the main text.

Essentially, the critique comprises three parts. First, that white researchers cannot elicit meaningful data from black respondents because of status and power differences between them. Thus, the absence of shared socialization and critical life experiences inevitably impairs the nature and value of the data. The problem of symmetry, of course, is not merely confined to this particular research relationship. It also features in discussions about the interview relationship between feminist researchers and female interviewees. Some feminists, such as Finch (1984) and Oakley (1981), tend to concur with the view that symmetry provides the *sine qua non* of valuable and reliable data. Others, such as Davies (1985), are more doubtful. Davies, for instance, indicates the possible advantages of the 'cultural stranger' role. The argument here is that those issues and concerns of girls and women which female researchers might take for granted are more likely to be probed and made problematic by a male researcher. Davies also shares with Cashmore and Troyna (1981) a sceptical view of how one might assess the extent to which a male/white researcher might alter the shape and nature of an interview with girls/blacks. As Davies (1985, p. 87) says: 'It would be impossible to state with certainty . . . the specific effect of gender on any research relationship; all one can ask for again is that it might be borne in mind in planning and execution'.

A second and more significant criticism is based on the way in which the data elicited from black respondents are generally interpreted by white researchers. Here, Parekh (1986, p. 24) has argued a forceful point: 'Most researchers in the field are white. They have no experience of what it means to be black, and lack an intuitive understanding of the complex mental processes and social structures of the black communities'. Consequently, we find accounts of black communities – written, in the main, by white researchers – which are not only ethnocentric but caricature these communities by centralizing empirically questionable concepts such as 'identity crisis', 'negative self-image', 'intergenerational conflict', 'unrealistic and high aspirations' and 'culture conflict' (see Stone, 1981; Lawrence, 1982). Analyses embedded within such frameworks have the potential to generate policy and political responses which do little, if anything, to combat racial inequalities or the structures and ideologies from which they stem. On the contrary, they contribute to the maintenance of 'pathological' conceptions of black communities.

The third and final element of this critique questions the white researcher's self-appointed role as 'ombudsman', to use Gouldner's (1975, p. 40) term. It is a criticism which has been directed mainly at John Rex and his colleagues at the former SSRC Research Unit on Ethnic Relations. Rex has consistently maintained that his work on 'race' is underpinned by an explicit commitment to racial equality and justice. In Rex's (1981b, p. 51) words, he wants 'to use empirical research on racialism and racism in contemporary British society to help all of those engaged in fighting against that racialism'. However, Bourne (1980), Lawrence (1982) and the CCCS collective are impatient with this view. They have suggested that by bringing into the public eye the life situations and life chances of black people, Rex and his colleagues provide the state with essential data which may be used to maintain racial inequalities. Indeed, they go on to assert that this is almost inevitable in so far as Rex and his colleagues were dependent on funding from the state to pursue *policy-*orientated research. Irrespective of the declared commitment of Rex and his colleagues to social justice, the likelihood of their research being appropriated by the state to sustain and legitimate the status quo is enhanced by their relatively powerless position *vis-à-vis* the state.

These are important criticisms of the role of white researchers in 'race relations'. What they identify is the profound difficulty in reconciling a genuine commitment to antiracist values and principles with research which focuses on the black communities. The convergence between the taken-for-granted assumptions and values of white researchers about black communities, on the one hand, and the delicate situation they occupy as policy-orientated researchers, on the other, suggests almost immovable obstacles to the realization of these goals. This is how Lawrence (1982, p. 134) sees it:

> In a situation where *state racism* has intensified, it is disingenuous for policy-oriented researchers to expect that their racist and patriarchal conceptualizations of black people will not be of interest to the state institutions which oppress black people.

This is not to deny the role of white researchers in the antiracist struggle; it is to suggest that the principles they avow are in danger of violation should they focus their research activities on the black communities. This constitutes an important ethical issue in the future formulation of research projects and programmes. Nevertheless, a tantalizing question remains: to what extent do we need to have systematic evidence of racial inequality before strategies can be developed to tackle it?

Ethics and black educational experiences

As we saw in Chapter 3 and elsewhere in this book, concern about the apparently poor performance of black students (especially those of Afro-

Caribbean origin) at all levels of their school career has figured prominently in the literature on 'race' and education. The last twenty-five years have seen the publication of numerous empirical studies of this issue which range from localized case material of performance within and between schools, to comparisons which are both regional and national in nature. As Troyna (1984b, p. 153) has noted: 'even the most cursory perusal of the literature in this field would show the notion of black educational underachievement is widely accepted as an irrefutable fact'. Nor as we saw in Chapter 3 was this observation disturbed by the publication of *Education for All* (DES, 1985). On the contrary, the data collected by the committee on ethnic differences in examination performance at 16+ and 18+ endorsed Taylor's (1981, p. 216) insistence that 'research evidence shows a strong trend to underachievement of pupils of West Indian origin on the main indicators of academic performance'.

Unfortunately, what this particular statement fails to acknowledge are the conceptual and methodological weaknesses often characteristic of research into this issue. For instance, although it is widely accepted that parental social class and educational level have an important bearing on the school performance of students (Halsey *et al.*, 1980), the bulk of research into this specific feature of school achievement has failed to take these factors into account. Thus, despite claims to the contrary, there continues to be some confusion as to whether Afro-Caribbean students *qua* Afro-Caribbean students are relatively low academic attainers. As we saw in Chapter 3, it could be that factors other than what Hochschild (1984) terms 'racially relevant variables' have greater salience.

Clearly, if researchers are concerned to challenge racial inequality in education, it is important that they demonstrate unequivocally the salience of 'racially relevant variables' in the determination of the educational experiences of black students. The ethical issue which this highlights is that, if a 'problem' is to be researched and, more importantly, obviated, then it is imperative that the work undertaken is rigorous and clear. It is simply insufficient to infer cause from effect; this merely absolves researchers from responsibility for testing empirically the relationship between, say, ideologies and practices, on the one hand, and the existence of inequalities, on the other (Troyna and Williams, 1986).

However, if we remain unsure about those factors which are casually related to the educational *outcome* of black students, we are more confident about the existence of differential *treatment* accorded black and white students in school. The research of Carrington (1983), Green (1982) and Wright (1987) has suggested how teacher expectations about black students' presumed academic deficiencies and concomitant sporting prowess may be reflected in teacher strategies, assessment procedures, and in decisions about setting and option allocation. Green's research is especially important, but by no means exceptional (see also Biggs and Edwards, 1992; Ogilvy *et al.*, 1992), in this context for it provides crucial evidence of how racial attitudes and beliefs not only influence the behaviour of teachers towards black pupils but also how they may affect the pupils' self-concepts and, possibly, academic achievements (for a critique of these studies see Foster 1990; 1991). Green's fieldwork was conducted in six schools (junior and middle). His sample comprised 70 teachers (all of whom were white) and their 1,814 pupils (of whom 940 were white, 449 of Asian descent and 425 of Afro-Caribbean descent). Using a Flanders Schedule, Green began by analysing the characteristics of interaction between teachers and boys and girls from each ethnic group. He then invited his teacher respondents to complete a revised version of the British Ethnocentrism Scale. On the basis of these results, he was able to identify two distinctive groups – 'ethnically highly tolerant teachers' and 'ethnically highly intolerant teachers'. A comparative analysis of the classroom behaviour of these groups revealed that highly intolerant teachers gave their Afro-Caribbean pupils less individual attention, only minimal praise, more authoritative directions and fewer opportunities to initiate contributions to class discussions. Green also found that the mean self-concept scores of Afro-Caribbean pupils taught by 'highly intolerant teachers' were significantly lower than those of their black peers who were taught by 'highly tolerant teachers'. If, as Green's research suggests, teachers' racial attitudes are translated into classroom action, then this is likely to circumscribe the level of educational attainment of black children. Following on from this, and its relationship to our stated ethical position, the imperative must be for educational researchers to develop interventionist strategies which mitigate these clear-cut forms of unequal treatment and contribute towards equity in the treatment of all students within educational settings. This takes us on to our fourth area of concern: the extent to which the 'research act' itself ought *actively* to challenge common-sense beliefs and perceptions.

Reinforcing or challenging stereotypes?

As we have already indicated, the aim of 'emancipatory knowledge' should be to encourage researchers to be reflexive and question their own taken-for-granted beliefs and assumptions. In effect, the 'research act' is conceived as educative. A perusal of studies into teachers' racial attitudes in the UK shows clearly that this conception has not been in the forefront of researchers' minds. As we will now show, researchers have limited their interventions to encouraging, reinforcing or even forcing subjects to employ prevailing racial stereotypes. We are not aware of any study which has attempted to challenge or undermine directly teachers' racial beliefs and perceptions.

A clear example of how researchers have encouraged teachers to construe the world in racial terms is Brittan's (1976) Schools Council/NFER survey undertaken in the early 1970s. A questionnaire, comprising mainly items amenable to Likert scaling, was administered to a national sample of teachers drawn from both primary and secondary schools. It sought to gauge their opinions about ethnic differences in pupils' and parents' responses to education. The survey showed that Afro-Caribbean pupils were generally seen in a less favourable light than their white or Asian peers. What is more, they were often stereotyped as having lower academic ability and as creating disciplinary problems. By inviting teachers to indicate the extent to which they agreed or disagreed with statements such as 'Asian pupils are usually better behaved than

English pupils', 'West Indian pupils resent being reprimanded more than English pupils do', and 'West Indian pupils tend to raise the academic standard of this school', Brittan not only encouraged her respondents to employ racist and ethnicist frames of reference but also may have given spurious legitimacy to the process of differentiation along ethnic lines.

Similar criticisms may be levelled against smaller-scale studies, such as that of Edwards (1978). She presented 20 student teachers with tape-recordings of speakers from different social and ethnic backgrounds: a bidialectal British-born girl of Barbadian descent (who spoke both in Creole and with a working-class Reading accent); an English boy with a working-class Reading accent; a professor's son who spoke received pronunciation (RP); and a recently arrived female Creole speaker from Jamaica. The respondents were asked to consider 'the relative academic potential of the speakers' and 'their desirability as members of a class'. Not surprisingly, when invited to employ stereotypes of 'race' and class, they behaved 'in accordance with widely-held social stereotypes'. The middle-class male speaker, for example, was perceived as having the highest academic potential and the Barbadian girl was judged less favourably when speaking Creole than in the local working-class accent.

Headteachers were also encouraged to articulate (but not to question) their taken-for-granted assumptions about 'race' and ethnicity in Tomlinson's research on 'special education' in Birmingham. The 30 heads in the sample were asked to describe 'their perceptions of the problems West Indian and Asian children *in general* presented in school . . . The questions were designed to elicit the cultural beliefs of heads about the children' (Rex and Tomlinson, 1979, pp. 198–9, emphasis added). When asked to generalize, the headteachers obliged by stereotyping Afro-Caribbeans as 'less keen on education than Asians', 'slower than Asian children, not as bright', and 'volatile, disruptive and easily stirred'.

Carrington and Wood's case study of ethnic differences in extracurricular sports participation at 'Hillsview School' exhibits similar flaws (Carrington, 1983; Carrington and Wood, 1983). They attempted to probe teachers' racial frames of reference by inviting them to indicate whether they varied their approach to suit pupils of different ethnic backgrounds. Their responses indicated that 'there were some teachers at the school who operated with pejorative stereotypes of West Indian pupils and viewed their behaviour, academic activities and parent culture in a negative manner' (Carrington, 1983, p. 50). Although some members of the school's staff were unwilling to condone these stereotypical rationalizations, the research, along with those others we have cited, did little to facilitate dissent from such images and perceptions of black and white pupils. By implication, at least, it provided a context for the expression and reproduction of racist and ethnicist views of pupils and their families.

A more explicit example of how research might reinforce such views can be found in Hartley's (1985) study of a Scottish urban primary school. Referring to his respondents' (teachers) use of the term 'immigrant' to describe British Asians, Hartley (1985, p. 19) noted:

In addition to this matter of nomenclature, there is an argument which says that by the very act of treating ethnic-minority groups as units of analysis in a research undertaking, the researcher may be culpable of unconscious racism. That is, he [*sic*] may actually create a difference associated with ethnicity that might not have occurred to those whom he is researching. He may make an issue out of something that hitherto had not been perceived as such by the participants in the situation he observes. This is a dilemma which is difficult to overcome. My stance here is to state that it was the teachers themselves who offered the 'immigrant'/ white dichotomy . . . Our purpose is not to condone the teachers' inaccurate nomenclature, nor their use of the ethnicity of the pupil as a basis for differentiation, rather it is to see what consequences these had for the school experience of children labelled in this way.

We appreciate that Hartley felt restrained, as an ethnographer, by the self-imposed methodological imperative of adopting 'a position akin to an observer who was both detached and involved'. Leaving aside what we see as the limitations of this paradigm, our main cause for concern is Hartley's lack of consistency. He defends his refusal to combat teachers' racial differentiation by insisting that he wanted to contribute 'nothing to the day to day proceedings of the school' (Hartley, 1985, p. 51). At the same time, however, he appropriates the racist terminology of some teachers, transmits it to the pupils and therefore may have contributed directly to the way those pupils construed relationships at the school. The following extract (Hartley, 1985, p. 170) shows that although he is aware of the ideological significance of the term 'immigrant' he nevertheless introduces it to a discussion with pupils. It is our contention that this reinforces and extends its legitimacy within the context of that school:

White boy: The teachers take more time with learning the blacks English than with us. My mum and dad says they spend more time with the blacks than they do with us.
DH: Do you think the teachers treat the 'immigrants' any differently?
Girls (3): Yes.
Girl: They are not as strict.
Girl: I think they're petted.
Girl: Mrs . . . favours 'immigrants' more than whites.

The studies of teachers' racial attitudes and typifications discussed above show how researchers have both encouraged and reinforced prevailing stereotypes of 'race' (and class). Figueroa's (1986; 1991) investigation of student teachers' images of ethnic minorities raises further ethical questions. Figueroa administered three questionnaires to a cohort of PGCE secondary students who had attended a short course on multicultural education. The questionnaires were designed to elicit views on the student teachers' perceptions of and attitudes towards 'West Indians' and 'Asians' together with other race-related issues. In common with other studies in the area, Figueroa encouraged respondents to articulate stereotypes by completing open-ended statements such as 'when I think of Asians I think . . .'. Semantic differential techniques were also used. Figueroa's previous research had shown that when respondents were asked to rate 'white British pupils', 'West Indian pupils' and 'Asian pupils', many refused and elected to use the 'can't generalize' option. As a result, the sample described in the paper under discussion was *not* provided with this option: respondents were *forced* into a situation where they could do nothing but stereotype. Despite this constraint, Figueroa (1986, p. 15) reports that 'several respondents made comments about this question indicating that they didn't want to be forced into producing stereotypes'. Although Figueroa is frank in his presentation of the research, he nevertheless conveys the impression that his primary concern is to ensure that his sample generates racial stereotypes. Surely such an approach with an incoming generation of teachers is hardly conducive to changing the status quo in education?

In this section we have focused on research on teachers' and student-teachers' racial attitudes and beliefs. It is our contention that the criticisms of these studies also apply to research on children's racial attitudes (see Troyna and Hatcher, 1992, pp. 18–49, for a critical overview) and professional responses to the role of the school in a multicultural society (Giles, 1977; Troyna and Ball, 1985; Carrington *et al.*, 1986). At best, the research has merely highlighted ways in which teachers, policy-makers and pupils tend to evaluate black people in Britain in a negative or dismissive manner. Another problem with this research is its elitist and undemocratic nature, which is especially exemplified by the denial of subjects' capacity to scrutinize and change the mode of the research act and their role within it. Ultimately, we are sceptical of the value of this research because it separates conception from execution, theory from practice. Lather's (1986) epithet, 'the rape model', seems to be appropriate to research such as this which takes rather than gives, describes rather than changes, transmits rather than transforms. Whether or not the ethical principles we have espoused here can be reconciled with the demands of external funding agencies and sponsors is, of course, an open question.

Sponsors: whose side are they on?

It may seem a truism to note that at a time of severe contraction, expenditure on educational research is highly susceptible to major cuts, and competition for an increasingly limited supply of external funds has intensified. What is more, as Hargreaves (1986, p. 15) rightly points out, this same period has seen a concomitant decline in 'government interest in investing in independent questioning and self-criticism'.

The implications for researchers genuinely committed to implementing educational research based on the antiracist principles we have outlined here should be clear. First, the potential for external funding for radical antiracist research is limited. This is especially the case when one considers the DES (now Department for Education) as an important source of research funds.

After all, it is significant that a commitment to antiracist educational research (or practice) did not appear in the Secretary of State's oral statement on the Swann Report of 14 March 1985 (DES, 1985) which sets out the government's approach and priorities in this area (see Chapter 3 of this book). Second, it is increasingly likely that successful applications for external funds would have been compelled to assume explicitly policy-orientated goals. For those researchers working on social administration or policy analysis projects (Dale, 1986), this would not constitute a problem. However, as we noted earlier, it does pose a particular dilemma for those researchers who may not wish to assume the so-called role of 'ombudsman'. For many antiracists, committed to the principles of research specified by Lather and others (for example, Ball, 1991), the imperative is to 'empower' oppressed groups, enabling *them* to take action rather than present the research findings to the 'powerful' (for example, policy-makers and professionals) in the (forlorn) hope that they might shoulder some responsibility. Third, the contraction in external funding enhances the researcher's reliance on patronage from sponsoring agencies. Put another way, it has progressively constrained the autonomy of the researcher, not only to initiate research, but also to retain control over its orientation and dissemination. The consequences of restructuring of the Social Science Research Council (now Economic and Social Research Council) in 1982 demonstrate this point clearly. The reappraisal of the way the Council allocates its limited funds led to a greater proportion of its money being distributed through its Research Developments fund (where the Council identifies research areas to which proposals are invited) and to a lesser amount allocated to its Research Grant Scheme (where applications on any topic within the Council's remit are considered). The current economic and, more importantly, political context strengthens Platt's (1976, pp. 64–5) conviction that the course of research is affected strongly by external factors, especially those which centre on the relationship between sponsoring bodies and the researcher.

Three examples of how sponsoring agencies can constrain, even control, the nature and dissemination of research on 'race' and education should be sufficient to illustrate the argument. Although two involved the relationship between researchers and one sponsoring body (the now defunct Schools Council) they are instructive in that one of these examples involved Robert Jeffcoate, a self-declared liberal whose antipathy towards radical antiracist principles has been well publicized (see, for example, Jeffcoate, 1984). The research revealed extensive racism among staff in sample schools. Because of this, the Schools Council chose to delay publication of its commissioned report, *Education for a Multicultural Society*, for three years. Moreover, the published version (Schools Council, 1981) was a heavily censored document. A similar fate was experienced by Dawn Gill, then a geography teacher at Quinton Kynaston School in London, who was commissioned by the Schools Council to 'investigate how (geography) syllabuses and examinations at 16+ can meet the needs of all pupils in a multiracial society'. Her eventual report, however, eschewed this defining and confining perspective. Instead, it gave primacy to an antiracist perspective in preference to multicultural considerations and specified the limitations of examination reform in the promotion of racial justice and equality in education. The Schools Council refused point-blank to publish this report.

Seen from this perspective, it is hardly surprising that the Swann Committee was not given access to John Eggleston's report on the educational and vocational experiences of black 16–18-year-olds which the DES had commissioned and had available some months before the Committee provided its final report (Eggleston, *et al.*, 1985). In view of the difficulties encountered by these researchers, we can only wonder whether future research based on an overt commitment to antiracism would be likely to attract 'official' sponsorship.

A new direction for research on 'race' and education

Let us conclude by briefly summarizing our argument and suggesting a possible future direction for research on 'race' and education. As well as criticizing much existing research in the area for its failure to provide evidence on the specific effect of 'racially relevant variables' on educational outcomes, we have also shown that it has tended to reinforce populist images of Afro-Caribbean and South Asian people and culture and done little to surmount the traditional (asymmetrical) division of labour between the researcher and researched. Because of its essentially elitist and conservative form, the research may be regarded as being at variance with antiracist practice. We have argued that both theory *and* practice in this sphere should be informed by the same principles: that is, a commitment to social justice, equality and participatory democracy.

Our analysis suggests that a collaborative, action-research model such as that employed in the GIST project (for example, Whyte, 1986), or by Chisholm and Holland (1986) in their work on antisexist curricula, might also provide the basis for future research on 'race'. This approach, as Chisholm and Holland (1986, pp. 358–9) have noted, 'can be seen as fostering change during the course of the research process, which includes monitoring or evaluating the change process or outcomes'. In the case of antiracist education, it could offer various advantages. First, in planning, evaluating and appraising an initiative *with* teachers, researchers would find themselves in a position where they could intervene *directly* to influence attitudes and behaviour. As well as providing a forum for reflecting critically on 'race'-related issues, this approach could help to obviate the misgivings that many teachers appear to have concerning antiracist education and, to a lesser degree, multicultural education. Advocates of antiracist education, teachers and researchers alike, may then be better placed to persuade those 'lukewarm' or outwardly hostile towards the initiative of its compatibility with a 'good' education – that is, an education predicated upon humanitarian, democratic principles and a commitment to equipping young people to play a full part in community life as decent, fair-minded, responsible and rational citizens. Furthermore, antiracists might also argue that pedagogical strategies compatible with their ideology, such as collaborative group work, not only serve to enhance young people's social awareness, interpersonal and ethical skills, but do so without any apparent adverse effect on their level of attainment (Yeomans, 1983). In recent years, antiracist policies have been criticized because of the often ambiguous and generalized nature of their prescriptions. The form of research that we envisage would seek to overcome these problems by helping schools to devise, implement and evaluate their own antiracist policies. As well as providing invaluable data on, for example, the influence of *situational* constraints (school ethos, phase, type, ethnic composition) on such innovations, it would also serve to remind researchers of the varied *institutional* constraints under which teachers currently work. Collaborative action-research would help to ensure that antiracist education is better understood (and thus accepted) by teaching staff and its *effects* more systematically monitored. Antiracist theory and practice cannot be founded upon mere articles of faith: both must be reflexive and subject to rigorous empirical scrutiny if their transformative potential is to be realized. This will only be achieved when the present division between theory and practice is eliminated.

7 In Defence of Antiracist Education: The 'Language of Possibility'?

Holding back the years

By the start of the 1990s the liberal hour was in terminal decline. The ERA had presaged a sustained and virulent attack on all forms of progressive education. Child-centred education, mixed ability teaching, approaches to the teaching of reading, assessment by coursework and comprehensive education were each subjected to critical scrutiny in the early years of the new decade. Nor was teacher education immune to these attacks. In October 1991 one of the Conservative Party's informal advisers on education, Anthony O'Hear, spoke to the Education Conference of the teachers' union, the National Association of Schoolmasters/ Union of Women Teachers (NAS/UWT), of his concern that teachers education courses had a 'harmful preoccupation with "irrelevant" issues such as race, gender and homophobia'. A year later, Prime Minister John Major was even more emphatic in his celebration of equiphobia. 'Primary teachers', he told delegates at the 1992 Conservative party conference, 'should learn how to teach children to read, not waste their time on the politics of gender, race and class.'

This confrontation with the so-called pernicious and pervasive influence of progressive ideas in education derived from revisionist interpretations about the 'golden days' of schooling. That is, the period before the introduction of 'destabilizing' educational innovations in the 1960s.

Equiphobia figured prominently in this scenario. However, if the 1988 ERA and associated legislative attacks on local government left antiracism as a faint light on the burner, the publication, a year later, of the findings of the inquiry into the murder of Ahmed Iqbal Ullah at a school in Manchester in 1986 all but extinguished the flame.

On 17 September 1986 Ahmed was stabbed to death in the playground of Burnage High School in Manchester. His assailant was Darren Coulbourn, a 13-year-old white pupil at the school. Coulbourn celebrated his 'triumph' by exclaiming to fourth- and fifth-year pupils: 'I've killed a Paki'. Manchester City Council immediately set up an independent inquiry to report on the antecedents and consequences of the murder. Chaired by Ian Macdonald QC, the inquiry team completed its deliberations and submitted its 500-page report to the Council within 18 months of the murder. On receipt of the report, *Murder in the Playground*, the Council decided that it contained libellous material and decided not to proceed with its publication. As a result, Macdonald and his inquiry team – Rheena Bhavnani, Lily Khan and Gus John – formed their own company (Longsight Press) and arranged for the publication, advertising and distribution of the report. By the time the report (Macdonald *et al.*, 1989) finally appeared, much of it had been leaked to the press. Here its main findings were reconstituted and popularized in ways which were compatible with the contemporary hegemonic denunciation of antiracism as anathema to 'good education', divisive, doctrinaire and, above all, deprecating of 'our' culture. The veracity of these condemnatory statements hinged on the allegedly causal link between the school's antiracist policies and the racist murder of Ahmed Iqbal Ullah. This paradox emerged as the central problematic of press coverage and, at the same time, the answer. The following headlines give some flavour of how the press displaced *racism*, the central concern of Macdonald *et al.*, with *antiracism*, as the root cause of the tension at Burnage: '*Anti-racist policy "led to killing"* ' (*Daily Telegraph*, 26 April 1988); '*Anti-racism teaching "a disaster"* ' (*The Independent*, 27 April 1988); '*How anti-racist rules failed our kids*' (*The Sun*, 28 April 1988); '*This Dangerous Obsession*' (*Daily Mail*, 26 April 1988).

This discrediting of antiracist education not only accelerated the rise of equiphobia but seemed to complement and strengthen the central state's impatience with the perceived 'loony tunes' of the Left. After all, did it not provide substantive, on-the-ground evidence of the misplaced and ultimately tragic activities of antiracist zealots?

Needless to say, press coverage of the report bore only a passing resemblance to the arguments presented in the report. This is not to deny that the inquiry team was critical of the way antiracist education had been conceived and put into operation at Burnage High School. It was. At the same time, it pointed out that this was one, possibly idiosyncratic, version of antiracism – which privileged black cultures and denied and devalued those of white, working-class pupils. The team also pointed out how the link between this approach and the normative status of physicality and masculinity in the school heightened the potential for tension, particularly between members of different ethnic groups.

What is especially important, however, is that, contrary to the full report, the press conveyed to its readers a totalized conception of antiracist education. In this way, it dissolved every distinction within this broad conception of educational reform into an uncontested, monolithic entity which prescribed only one course of action: and that was to be found at Burnage High School. This consolidated populist interpretations of antiracist education which rendered it as a synonym for essentialist and reductionist arguments such as: 'all whites are racist' and 'black cultures should have privileged status in the curriculum' (see Connolly, 1992). At the same time it 'legitimated' images of antiracists as confrontational, excessive and illiberal.

Press converge of *Murder in the Playground*, if not the report itself, simply represented one in a series of the media's valedictory statements on antiracist education. But the Macdonald inquiry's critique of Burnage's version of antiracist education was also significant in that it came from the Left. In this sense, it helped to pave the way for Leftists to take a more critical stance on antiracist education. Recent writings on 'race' have consolidated the inquiry's view that the theory of antiracism and the strategies to which it has given rise need to be scrutinized carefully. Some writers have gone further, insisting that antiracist education is in need of fundamental revision, if not abandonment. For instance, in his provocatively titled essay, 'The End of Anti-Racism', Paul Gilroy (1990, p. 191) criticized the 'moralistic excesses' and 'dictatorial character' of antiracism. Cohen (1992) and Rattansi (1992) argue along similar lines in their contributions to the Open University course reader, *'Race', Culture and Difference*. Cohen (1992, p. 92) talks of the need for 'critical revision', while Rattansi (1992, p. 11), recognizing that we are in 'a period of transition', exhorts antiracists to 'take stock and to reflect on the theoretical, pedagogic and political foundations of multiculturalism and antiracism'. As part of their new project, Cohen and Rattansi want to lay bare what they see as the theoretical and pedagogical weaknesses of both multicultural and antiracist education.

Although writing from a markedly different theoretical perspective, Short's (1991) arguments correspond with some of those of the 'critical revisionists'. They all dispute the claim that there is a significant divide between multicultural and antiracist education. Short attacks antiracists for distinguishing themselves from multiculturalists when, in his view, they share remarkably similar understandings of racism and views on the pedagogical tools which might be used to tackle effectively this ideology and its attendant range of discriminatory practices.

Interestingly, many of the arguments and strategies associated with antiracists in these articles remain unattributed. The following passage from Short's paper is a clear example. He begins by addressing the alleged shortcomings of my own work but then eschews this specificity in favour of an attack on the apparently distinctive and characteristic antiracist theoretical stance proposed by a number of (anonymous) writers:

> Troyna, in common with *the majority of anti-racists*, recognises prejudice as a major problem. But in contrast to multi-culturalists, *they* resort to an economic reductionist argument and locate the roots of prejudice within the mode of production: prejudice is held to be functional to capitalist class relations and oppression.
>
> (Short, 1991, p. 13; emphasis added)

This assertion begs a number of questions. To begin with, is my own work located within this economic reductionist paradigm? If so, where is the empirical evidence for this proposition? Certainly, it is not to be found in my book with Ellis Cashmore, *Introduction to Race Relations* (2nd edition), in which we argue that 'racism has, over the years, been a great servant of capitalism in splitting working class loyalties and introducing antagonisms between workers. *Yet we do not view this as in any way a pure product of some conspiracy of capitalism*' (Cashmore and Troyna, 1990, p. 210; emphasis added). Nor can it be discerned from my work which deals specifically with education. I do argue that antiracist education should be geared towards an understanding of the social and racial formation of the state and how it might be possible to challenge and, ultimately, transform it (Troyna, 1989, for instance). But to give primacy to certain sociopolitical structures in explaining the development and reproduction of racial inequalities is not the same as reductionism. To suggest otherwise is to oversimplify, distort and ignore the variants within Marxist thought.

Nor does Short give us any help in trying to identify which writers comprise 'the majority of anti-racists'. In the absence of this information, we are bound to ask who they are (and who is excluded from this grouping) and where they articulate the claim that the roots of prejudice are located 'within the mode of production'. The lack of precision in this part of Short's paper is a serious weakness. Among other things, it disempowers those who might wish to trace the specific location of this theoretical stance in the literature.

From what I have said earlier about the prevailing political culture of the late 1980s and early 1990s, it is not surprising to find certain writers on the Left now characterizing antiracist education as bankrupt. The alleged failure of Leftist politics to dislodge the hegemonic status of Thatcherism has led to the evolution of arguments and strategies which might accommodate the new political culture. This provides at least part of the context in which the critiques are best understood. Nevertheless, I would be taking a Luddite position if I were either to ignore these criticisms or reject them all out of hand. At the same time, they contain a number of misrepresentations of antiracists' work and reproduce many of the essentialist and reductionist arguments which they perceive in my own and others' writings on this theme.

I will suggest in this chapter that some of the approaches adopted by these critics of antiracist education often reproduce two intellectually dubious devices. The first is 'obloquy'. According to Geras (1991, p. 1), obloquy is 'something very pronounced: speaking ill of a person or – as it may also be . . . – tradition of thought'. Geras encountered seven broad types of obloquy in contemporary, Leftist critiques of Marxist thought. These take the form of 'off-the-cuff, belittling – and, upon examination, feeble' analysis (Geras, 1991, p. 5). Among them are what Geras (1991, p. 8) terms the 'Amazing Reductions' critique in which Marxism is construed as 'irredeemably reductionist'. I have already noted, and will go on to elaborate later, that this same criticism is applied, quite unfairly in my view, to theories of antiracist education.

Emergent criticisms of antiracist education also share the properties of what Glaser and Strauss (1967) refer to as 'exampling': the practice of 'fitting out' an already formulated theoretical position with supporting evidence. The process of 'exampling' takes the following form:

> A researcher can easily find examples for dreamed up, speculative or logically deduced theory after the idea has occurred. But since the idea has not derived from the example, seldom can the example correct or change it (even if the author is willing) since the example was selectively chosen for its confirming power. Therefore one receives the image of a proof

when there is none, and the theory obtains a richness of detail which it
did not earn.

(Glaser and Strauss, 1967, p. 5)

In responding to the observations of these 'critical revisionists' I will draw
particularly on two empirical research projects with which I have been involved. The first is *Racism in Children's Lives* (Troyna and Hatcher 1992). I
mentioned this book in Chapter 5, where I embarked on a critique of research
into race relations in schools. Briefly, the book explores the salience of 'race' in
the way in which young children perceive and interpret their social worlds.
Our main concern was to tease out why, and under what circumstances, 'race'
emerges as a plausible and appealing mode of reasoning for young people. The
analysis derives from a series of discussions with young children, aged 9–11, in
predominantly white primary schools. The research is especially relevant in this
context because it provides one of the clearest statements of my own (and
Richard Hatcher's) theoretical positioning on racism and endorses McCarthy's
(1990, p. 121) inferences about the influence of Gramsci on my work. It also
provides clearer insight into the question which has remained at the heart of
much of the research on 'race' and education: what are the factors which
contribute to the differential status of racism in the way people make sense of
their lives?

The second project is *Implementing Multicultural and Antiracist Education in
Mainly White Colleges* (Troyna and Selman, 1991; but see also Troyna, 1989;
and Troyna and Selman, 1989). The research explicates a pedagogical strategy
for antiracist education in a geographical region and post-16 college where, in
the words of one of the lecturers, 'You'll hardly see a dark face in the place'
(Troyna and Selman, 1991, p. 11). The origins of the project are to be found in
my dissatisfaction with antiracists' (and multiculturalists') engagement with
issues of racism in predominantly white educational contexts. It seemed to me
that an antiracist intervention should not blame white youngsters (*qua* white
youngsters) for racial inequalities. Ironically, in view of the criticisms now
levelled at my work, I saw this perspective as essentialist and reductionist.
Instead, I argued that it should try to provide the context which might enable
white students to recognize not only the specific nature of racial discourse and
practice but also the forms of inequality they themselves experience and share
with black people – as women, students, young people, residents in an economically depressed region of Britain and as members of the working class. In
other words, the aim was to distil experiential commonalities within a framework where differences are recognized. In one of his more disparaging comments, Short (1991, p. 12) asserts that I assume in this initiative that 'as soon as
the white working class realise . . . that its problems are not caused by black
people, but rather by the "capitalist system", an alliance will form across racial
(and other) lines to confront the real enemy'. A more sympathetic reading of
the research reveals a rather more realistic aim in the short term: one that
encourages moves from the 'language of critique' to the 'language of possibility' (Giroux, 1989).

I will structure the discussion around three distinctive themes: conceptions of racism; understanding racism in children's lives; and pedagogical strategies to tackle racial inequality in education.

Conceptions of racism

Central to the critiques of Short, Cohen and Rattansi is the conviction that antiracists operate with an impoverished understanding of their main theoretical and analytical concept: racism. According to Short, antiracists differentiate themselves from multiculturalists through their attachment to institutional racism as a central explanatory tool. Short (1991, p. 10) maintains that the concept 'is useful to the extent that it enables us to identify the causes of racial inequality. Conversely, it is useless, indeed positively harmful [*sic*], to the extent that it misleads us in our search for such causes'. As we have already seen, Short also attacks the allegedly economic reductionism of antiracism.

Cohen's critique centres on similar themes. He draws on the responses of his students to racist material collected during his research into the culture of racism among young white males and from an 'unofficial lampoon' circulating in a police training college soon after the publication of the Scarman (1981) report on the Brixton disturbances. From them he constructs a typology of models used to explain racist discourse. He asserts that his students' formulations of racism bear a close resemblance to those found in the extant literature. These formulations are reductionist, according to Cohen (1992, p. 77), because they 'claim that complex and multi-faceted phenomena can be explained by a single, simple cause. These explanations are therefore limited. They tell only part of the story and leave out any elements which do not fit into their line of argument'. He goes on to suggest that typical explanations of racism are constrained within one of the following restrictive (and restricted) interpretative straitjackets: radical holism and methodological individualism. These categorizations are drawn from the work of Levine *et al.* (1987) and approximate to the macro–micro dichotomy in the social sciences. Radical holism accords 'explanatory relevance to social "totalities", in apparent opposition to the strictures of individualist forms of analysis'. Methodological individualism, on the other hand, insists that 'only relations among individuals can be irreducibly explanatory' (Levine *et al.*, 1987, pp. 67–84).

Cohen maintains that the emphasis on institutional racism in the antiracist paradigm exemplifies the radical holist position, while those who focus on deficit models of working-class culture accord primacy to methodological individualism. The two are not mutually exclusive, however, according to Cohen. For those who want 'to get their argument out of a tight corner, and make for a less fatalistic scenario' (Cohen, 1992, p. 78), the two positions can be reconciled within a single discourse. A clear example of this expedient conjunction of the two stances is found in the formula: Racism = Power + Prejudice. A pithy and seductive formula, in Cohen's view, but reductionist (and essentialist) nevertheless.

Ironically, few antiracists would dissent from the critique mounted against holistic and individualist conceptions of racism. For this reason it could be argued that Cohen (and Short) are themselves both reductionist and essentialist in characterizing antiracist education in these terms. Let me elaborate.

It is undoubtedly the case that in the nascent antiracist position of the early 1980s, institutional racism functioned as a compelling and plausible concept. For some it operated as a heuristic device; for others, as a framework within which one could explain both how the routine operations, procedures and practices of institutions such as schools might, unwittingly and indirectly, perpetuate and reproduce racial inequality, and how the interrelationships between institutions might reinforce racial inequality (see Troyna and Williams, 1986, pp. 48–52). The criteria governing the delineation of catchment areas, admissions policies, allocation of pupils to ability groups and the designation of pupils with 'special needs' often had the effect, if not the explicit intention, of discriminating along perceived racial lines. These processes were often designated as exemplars of institutional racism. As Short points out, the concept received its most enthusiastic and uncritical support from the ILEA. In its 1983 policy document, the ILEA gave prominence to institutional racism in its determination to alert employees to the ways in which their taken-for-granted assumptions and ground rules could disadvantage black pupils and staff. By the time the policy was published, however, 'institutional racism' had already attracted the critical eye of a growing number of antiracists. They were increasingly dissatisfied with the cavalier and imprecise manner in which the ILEA and others had adopted the concept (see Troyna and Williams, 1986, pp. 54–9). In my analysis of the development of an antiracist education school policy in Chapter 4 of this book, I drew attention to the weaknesses of institutional racism as an explanatory framework. There I noted that Jenny Williams and her co-authors (Williams, 1985; Troyna and Williams, 1986; Williams and Carter, 1987) had written extensively about the wide range of policies and approaches habitually conjoined within the term and concluded that the concept had no discriminatory power. It is, therefore, empirically wrong for Short and Cohen to assert that this holistic interpretation of racism remains pre-eminent in the antiracist paradigm. Following their disenchantment with the way institutional racism has been inflated, to the extent that it has lost its precision and explanatory edge, antiracists have developed more sophisticated models of how racial inequality is reproduced, within and beyond education (see also Miles, 1989, pp. 50–61; Cashmore and Troyna, 1990, pp. 18–19; Essed, 1991, pp. 36–7).

In this respect, the work of McCarthy (1990) in the United States deserves to be mentioned. He has been concerned with identifying more specifically the ways in which 'race' operates within the institutional setting of schools. McCarthy therefore rejects the bifurcation between macro- and micro-perspectives on racial inequality and generates a theoretical model located at what Hall (1986) refers to as the 'middle range'. McCarthy recognizes the intersecting and relational impact of class, gender and 'race' in the production and reproduction of educational inequality. He goes on to argue that the articulation of these structural characteristics is fraught with 'tension, contradiction and discontinuity in the institutional life of the school setting' and should not be conceived in a 'static and simplistically additive way' (McCarthy, 1990, p. 82). Drawing on the work of the feminist writer, Hicks (1981), McCarthy cautions against the notions of double and triple oppression and centralizes the concept of nonsynchrony to explain the discontinuous, contradictory and reconstitutive power of the interaction between class, gender and 'race'. He argues that their intersection 'at the local level of schooling can lead to interruptions, discontinuities, augmentations or diminutions of the original effects of any one of these dynamics' (McCarthy, 1990, p. 85).

By introducing the 'noise' of multidimensionality into our understanding of the dynamics of educational inequality, McCarthy provides a firmer theoretical purchase on the differential impact of racism on, say, the academic performance levels of black pupils. From this perspective, racism is seen as a contingent variable. As McCarthy's account shows, its potential to enhance or subdue performance levels derives from its particular intersection with the relations of competition, exploitation, domination and cultural selection which operate in 'the everyday practices of minority and majority school actors' (McCarthy, 1990, p. 84). In Britain, Mac an Ghaill's (1989) conceptualization of black youths' experiences of schooling provides an empirical demonstration of McCarthy's thesis. The education system, along with 'race', class, gender and age, constitute an interlocking series of constraints on the life chances of black youth. However, 'there are no pre-determined outcomes', according to Mac an Ghaill (1989, pp. 284–5).

In another context, Philomena Essed's exploration of 'everyday racism' in the lives of black women in the United States and the Netherlands advances our understanding of the complex relations between the macro and micro dimensions of racism. Along with those who emphasize the influence of macro structures on 'race relations', she argues that because 'race' constitutes an organizing principle of social relations these relations are often likely to be racialized. However, she introduces an important caveat:

> it is only when these racial or ethnic dimensions of social relations are called upon or activated through practice that racial and ethnic relations are created, reinforced or reproduced. In other words, even when specific relations are racialized and when these relations underlie and structure social situations, racism *does not necessarily* have to occur in a specific time or place.
>
> (Essed, 1991, p. 52; emphasis added)

The failure to acknowledge these important theoretical contributions to understandings of the complex processes of racism within and beyond educational contexts seriously undermines the credibility of the arguments adduced by Cohen and Short. An equally serious defect in their critiques is the assumption that antiracists invoke the Racism = Power + Prejudice formula in their analyses. Even the most cursory glance at the literature would show that while this interpretation might have had some heuristic value a few years ago its status as a theoretical proposition has been discredited by a large number of anti-racists. The formula emerged as the credo of the racism awareness training (RAT) movement which originated in the United States in the 1970s (Katz, 1978) and underpinned the RAT courses introduced in Britain in the early to mid-1980s. While it continues to have credibility with some multiculturalists (Grugeon and Woods, 1990), antiracists such as Carter and Williams (1987), Gurnah (1984) and Sivanandan (1985) have mounted significant attacks on RAT and the oversimplified, essentialist formulation on which it is based. This is how Gurnah (1984, p. 12) exposed the deficiencies of the formula:

> Though at first sight this formula appears useful, various difficulties arise as soon as one starts to probe it. For example, when blacks have prejudice and power, does that make them racist? Does it mean that everytime a powerful white dislikes a black person, that this is racist? What if a powerful white man dislikes a black man because of the perfume the black wears, does this make the white a racist? What if the same white man despises a black woman because of her gender?

In short, the formula, like institutional racism, is too crude and lacks analytical precision. Although both seem to provide immediate explanations for the oppression of black citizens and their children, there is a fundamental essentialism implied in both. The work of McCarthy and Essed, among others, alerts us to the fact that the processes of racism are far too complex to be reduced to this single formula. Unfortunately, however, the antiracist critique of these concepts is silenced in the work of Short and Cohen (and Rattansi).

The unwillingness of antiracists to embrace these shorthand conceptions of racism parallels some of the recent feminist correctives to interpretations of women's oppression. There, writers such as Connell (1987) and Wolpe (1988) have voiced their dissatisfaction with the tendency for some feminists to attribute the source of male power exclusively to patriarchy. As Wolpe (1988, p. 11) argues, the introduction and use of 'the concept of patriarchy appeared to make it unnecessary to explore gender differences more fully. It is as though the act of acknowledging unequal power relations between men and women is sufficient'. In blunt terms, patriarchy, along with institutional racism and the Racism = Power + Prejudice formula have the effect of deproblematizing the issue. The inference drawn from the distorted review presented by Short, Cohen and, to a lesser extent, Rattansi, is that antiracist theorists subscribe to the essentialist view that whites *qua* whites are racist.

There is a third strand to the critique of antiracist education which figures in the articles of Cohen and Rattansi and is mentioned in passing by Short. This focuses on the alleged tendency for antiracists to explain working-class, or popular, racism as a manifestation of 'false consciousness'. Rattansi (1992, p. 30) suggests that there are several variants on this theme, although they coalesce around a class reductionist argument:

> In the crudest analyses, working class racism is interpreted as composed of a set of falsehoods perpetrated by one, or a combination, of

the following agencies: capital, the ruling class, the mass media and the state.

Notice here Rattansi's exclusive concern with 'crudest analyses' – the reductionist forms of explanation to which some antiracists, though who we are not told which, have succumbed. This 'Amazing Reduction' version of obloquy provides Rattansi with a (spurious) base on which to implicate all antiracist positions in his critique. But then he goes on:

> These are conceptualised as unified, non-contradictory, omniscient 'actors', unified by the common objective of dividing the working class along racial lines so as to facilitate the economic exploitation of both sections of the class. The state is viewed as an instrument of capital and state policies such as immigration and race relations legislation are seen as the outcome of deliberate, thus 'rational', manipulation by agents of capital and the capitalist state.
>
> (Rattansi, 1992, p. 30)

It is difficult to find what Rattansi finds objectionable here. Is he disputing the claim that immigration and race relations policies were the outcome of 'deliberate manipulation' by the state? If so, his dissent runs contrary to a significant body of research in the sociology and politics of race relations in Britain. For example, the recent publications of Bob Carter, Clive Harris and Shirley Joshi on state race-related policies in the 1940s and 1950s have revealed that the state was neither absent nor 'played a minimal role in the emerging discourse about "coloured colonial immigration" ' to Britain (Carter *et al.*, 1987, p. 1). On the contrary, it took an active part in the development of 'a racialised construction of "Britishness" which excluded and included people on the grounds of "race", defined by colour' (Carter *et al.*, 1987, p. 16). And this was translated into specific immigration control measures and an opposition to legislation designed to combat racial discrimination and protect the rights of Britain's black citizens.

Finally in this passage, Rattansi (1992, p. 30) concludes that such 'crude' analyses reduce the 'working-class racist' . . . 'to a cultural dope'. Cohen argues that this idea of the working class as a 'cultural dope' can be found both in the radical holistic and methodological individualist versions of antiracist education theory, although he does not tell us where. Both versions project deficit views of the working class. Once again, this constituted part of the *raison d'être* of RAT. As Cohen rightly points out, neither of these holistic or individualist theories can respond adequately to the question: what makes some (working-class) individuals receptive or resistant to racist ideas. The radical holist, according to Cohen, presents an overdetermined view of structure and fails to explain why there 'are plenty of white working class boys . . . who do not hold pronounced racist views' (Cohen, 1992, p. 80). The methodological individualist, on the other hand, tries to come to grips with this dilemma but often degenerates into a pathological conception of the individual's immediate environment. On this view, the nature of the individual's socialization, level of education or cultural milieu is said to be 'inferior' or 'deprived', according to particular and contrived versions of normality. Of course, it is possible to find vestiges in the literature of these explanations of working-class racism. Harrop and Zimmerman's (1977, p. 13) description of the 'ideal-typical National Front supporter' as 'young, ungifted and white' typifies the stance which Cohen attacks. An even more vivid example is provided by Marsland (1978, p. 96) in his 'explanation' of why racist politics attract white working-class male youth:

> White youth is neither educated nor guided firmly or effectively towards racial equality, by parents or teachers. (Nor even, alas, by teachers with deep commitments to a more abstract notion of equality). Instead, they are merely threatened with high mindedness and law, and (ultimately as a response to this failure) recruited into racialist parties.

The important point to make here, however, is that these analyses have been superseded by more sophisticated theoretical and empirical accounts of the complex ways in which 'race' enters into the social life of working-class communities. In this respect, Cohen's own work with working-class youth in London has been highly significant and acknowledged as such in the literature on antiracist education (Troyna and Carrington, 1990; Troyna and Hatcher, 1992). The critique of his work by Short, a staunch supporter of multicultural education, is further testimony to this. However, Cohen has not been on his own in ploughing this furrow and it is disingenuous of the 'critical revisionists' to suggest that analyses along these lines have not impacted on theories of antiracist education. I now want to provide some examples of recent conceptualizations of the way 'race' operates differentially in the judgements and day-to-day actions of young people.

Racism in children's lives

The empirical research of Cashmore (1987) in Birmingham focused explicitly on the differentiated response of white working-class youth to racism. He came up with tentative support for the contact hypothesis in concluding that while the 'idea of ethnic proximity as a recipe for ethnic harmony' should not be overemphasized, there was some evidence to suggest that direct contact between white and black people might play some role in modifying the racist precepts and images circulating in parental, media and youth culture.

Other researchers, such as Back (1991), Hewitt (1986) and Troyna and Hatcher (1992), have gone much further than Cashmore. Their studies have raised even more serious questions about the significance of the contact hypothesis in explaining the status of 'race' in the way young people make sense of their world and act within it. Their ethnographic analyses have attempted to tease out the complex processes associated with the way young people, especially in working-class milieux, differentially engage with and select from the 'race' repertoire. Along with Back and Hewitt, Hatcher and I eschewed both the radical holism and methodological individualism paradigms in drawing up a theoretical framework for our research. In different ways, we drew critically on the theoretical perspectives developed by Billig (1988) and van Dijk (1987) to help us understand and disentangle the complex processes involved in the transmission and acceptance of racist discourse.

In our analysis of the events leading up to the tragedy at Burnage High School, for instance, Hatcher and I took issue with those theorists who accord explanatory power exclusively to either macro- or micro-perspectives in accounting for the pattern of racist harassment in Britain. Indeed, Cohen's criticism of the failure of radical holists to explain the differential presence of racist ideas within working-class male cultures simply echoes our observations on the weakness of structural theory to explain the 'outbreak of (racist) violence under certain conditions' while ignoring 'its absence in other periods characterized by similar complexion' (Troyna and Hatcher, 1992, p. 37). In *Racism in Children's Lives* (and an earlier article which focuses specifically on Burnage High School (Troyna and Hatcher, 1991a)) we make some effort to synthesise macro- and micro-analyses by adapting the 'flashpoints' model developed by Waddington *et al.* (1989). This proved to be eminently serviceable in helping us to identify the various levels of social processes which come together in specific combinations in each racist incident, whether these incidents are exceptionally spectacular, such as the murder of Ahmed Iqbal Ullah, or more routine, such as the incidence of racist name-calling in schools throughout Britain.

We then proceeded to build on this model by drawing on the theory of hegemony: the process by which people's everyday common-sense understandings are shaped by, and brought into conformity with, the existing social and economic system. Questions of ideology are central to the concept of hegemony. Gramsci (1977), in his development of this theory, made a distinction between 'elaborated ideologies', the coherent bodies of thought produced and disseminated by intellectuals, and 'common-sense ideologies'. As Gramsci pointed out, common-sense understandings are neither rigid nor immobile; they are continually transforming themselves. Nor are they uniform. Common-sense ideologies are contradictory, ambiguous and multiform, according to Gramsci. They also lack 'reflective underpinning' (Essed, 1991, p. 147). Further, common sense contains both elements of dominant ideologies and elements of critical or potentially critical ideologies. So, for example, in the context of racism, elements of liberal discourse – such as 'rights' – may be interpreted in ways that either confirm racist discourses (such as the objection to children of South Asian origin speaking in their 'mother tongue') or provide a basis for challenging them. Common sense, then, does not work exclusively at the level of ideas; it is tested on the ground. Thus racist, and antiracist, ideologies gain their foothold and legitimacy because they are enacted in and seem to work in everyday social behaviour. In this way, 'race' may become an important lens through which young people perceive and interpret their social worlds. But, as a corollary, racism can only occupy a conditional status in people's lives.

In our attempt to establish the conditions under which 'race' might figure as an organizing principle and explanatory framework in the complex worlds of young children, we spent a term in each of three 'sample' primary schools and held discussions with 160 9–11-year-old children. Although the main concern was with children's view on 'race' and its salience in the organization and structure of their lives, we explored this issue through a range of diffuse discussions. 'Race' was an enduring but not always central or explicit theme in our conversations with the children.

The schools where we carried out our research were similar to many hundreds of primary schools in British towns and cities. They were similar, too, in containing a minority of black children, perhaps up to half a dozen in each class. A visitor in the classroom and playground, observing children working and playing together, black and white, might have concluded that 'race' was an insignificant feature of their lives. They would be wrong. 'Race' and racism figured prominently in the cultural and social lives of the children. The experience for white children of being in everyday contact with black children generated contradictory dynamics: towards racial equality and the deracialization of relationships, but also towards the racialization of existing social processes within children's cultures. In particular, racist name-calling was an important strategy within many white children's interactional repertoire and consequently one in relation to which all children had to take up a position. The meaning of this and other forms of racist behaviour can only be understood in the context of children's cultures, relationships and processes of interaction.

Racist name-calling takes place in a range of different types of social situation. These can be defined by a number of criteria: high or low level of friendship; the extent to which the user regards racist name-calling as a legitimate part of their interactional repertoire; and motivation in terms of harassment or self-defence. At one end of a continuum of name-calling situations is the deliberate, 'cold', repeated harassment of black children in order to assert dominance over them. Such incidents tended to be in the minority, however. More common forms of racist name-calling were to be found at the other end of the continuum. There, incidents of racist name-calling took place during heated arguments, usually in the context of other forms of verbal abuse on both sides. It could occur between children who were otherwise friendly to each other. Some white children who used racist name-calling in this 'hot' context did not regard it as a legitimate interactional strategy, because it was too hurtful and contrary to their own racially egalitarian beliefs. They were regretful afterwards. Others viewed it as legitimate in 'self-defence', and not necessarily different from other forms of hurtful verbal abuse.

Between these two points of the continuum were incidents of racist name-calling that occurred on a casual basis, often with the aim of asserting dominance in order to get the recipient to do something: move out of the way, return a ball, go away and so on.

What emerged from these discussions was that many children display inconsistent and contradictory repertoires of racial attitudes, containing both elements of racially egalitarian ideologies and elements of racist ideologies. In order to theorize these complex processes, we adapted Billig's (1988)

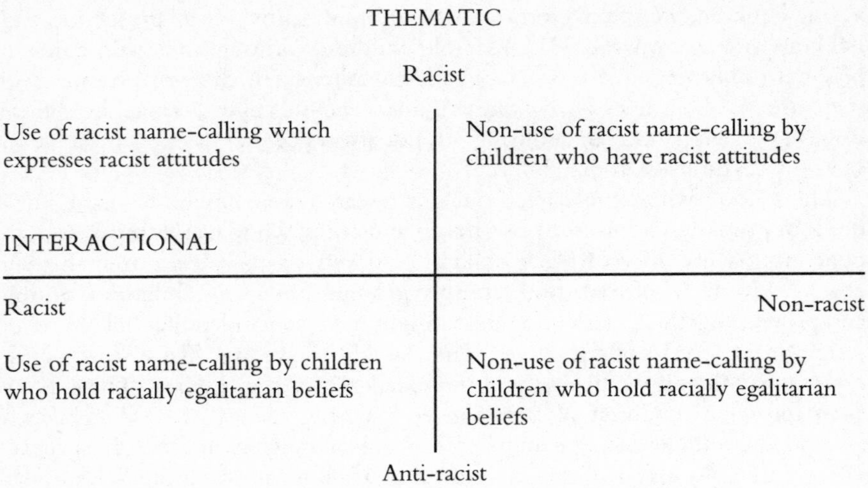

THEMATIC

Racist

Use of racist name-calling which expresses racist attitudes	Non-use of racist name-calling by children who have racist attitudes

INTERACTIONAL

Racist	Non-racist
Use of racist name-calling by children who hold racially egalitarian beliefs	Non-use of racist name-calling by children who hold racially egalitarian beliefs

Anti-racist

Figure 1   A model for locating racist name-calling

distinction between 'thematic' and 'interactional' ideologies in our analysis of children's cultures. The former refers to children's knowledge, values, beliefs and attitudes towards certain social issues; the latter to the repertoire of social knowledge and strategies for evaluating social situations which govern children's interpersonal exchanges. However, we departed slightly from Billig's position because he does not address the contradictions within ideologies of 'race' themselves.

As Figure 1 shows, the relationship between 'thematic' and 'interactional' ideologies of 'race' is not one of simple and direct correspondence. On the contrary, interactional ideologies have their own logic, which may be more or less congruent with the children's thematic beliefs and attitudes. A combination of attitudes and behaviour is possible, ranging from children who hold racist beliefs but do not express them in behaviour, to children who hold racially egalitarian beliefs but use racist name-calling in certain situations. Within children's culture, it is primarily interactional ideologies – those that govern their interpersonal exchanges with other children (and adults) – that animate racist ideologies and translate them into social practices. This is clearly the case with interactional ideologies of dominance, which can harness elements of racist ideologies in order to exert power over black children. But racist ideologies can also colonize interactional ideologies of equality. Examples of this in the research occurred when children spoke of using racist name-calling in self-defence; in their opposition to the use of 'Asian' languages on the grounds that it gives an unfair advantage; and their criticism of school policies that seem to privilege the interests of black children.

All in all, the research highlighted the need to view racism as a highly contingent aspect of children's cultures. Elements of elaborated and common-sense ideologies, both racist and anti-racist, deriving from direct and vicarious experiences – the family, television and local community – enter into and circulate within children's cultures. Here they interact with common-sense understandings which have emerged from everyday social interactions among children. It is in this context that children *differentially* affirm, diffuse and legitimate 'race' as a way of seeing and making sense of their day-to-day lives. To reiterate: this eschews the deterministic models which Cohen and others ascribe to the antiracist theorists. Children are neither the passive recipients of the dominant culture as the radical holist position suggests, nor does methodological individualism, and its deficit conception of working-class culture, play the leading role in our understanding of the significance of 'race' in the lives of children.

Pedagogical issues in antiracist education

Short, Cohen and Rattansi are united in their conviction that antiracists have failed to develop either a distinctive or appropriate pedagogy. This criticism should not be taken lightly. Writers such as Brandt (1987) and Mullard (1984), in their pioneering attempts to differentiate antiracist from multicultural approaches, paid scant attention to pedagogy. They provided little guidance for teachers on how to translate antiracist education into practical classroom-based strategies. Nor did LEAs or individual schools and colleges give sufficient space to these considerations in their policies. Indeed, pedagogy assumed such marginal significance in nascent antiracist policies that even those researchers who scrutinize their content failed to recognize the absence of clear-cut recommendations for classroom practice (see, for example, Dorn, 1983; Mullard *et al.*, 1983).

At least two factors helped to compound this sorry state of affairs. First, LEA policies and directives in the 1980s. Their weaknesses were twofold: as we saw in earlier chapters, they typically blurred the theoretical and conceptual distinctions between multicultural and antiracist education; in addition, they failed to provide specific guidance on classroom practices. Theorists working in this field also helped to complicate an already complex matter. They detected subtle, though important inflections within the two categories of multicultural and antiracist education. For instance, Hatcher (1987) drew a distinction between the 'old' and 'new' multiculturalism; while Bonnett (1990) identified differences between 'non-radical anti-racism' and 'radical anti-racism'. Confusion prevailed. Theoretical advances in this area often tended to conceal rather than clarify differences, especially for teachers. It came as no surprise, therefore, when empirical studies revealed that teachers, allegedly working within one or other of the multicultural or antiracist discourses, were unable to spell out the distinctively different classroom practices implied by these approaches (Bonnett, 1990). Those who were attracted to antiracist education theories were more likely to assert that they were compatible with their existing educational philosophies and practices (Troyna and Ball, 1985).

The late 1980s and early 1990s have seen antiracist theorists pay greater attention to pedagogy. And, in contrast to earlier antiracist initiatives, they

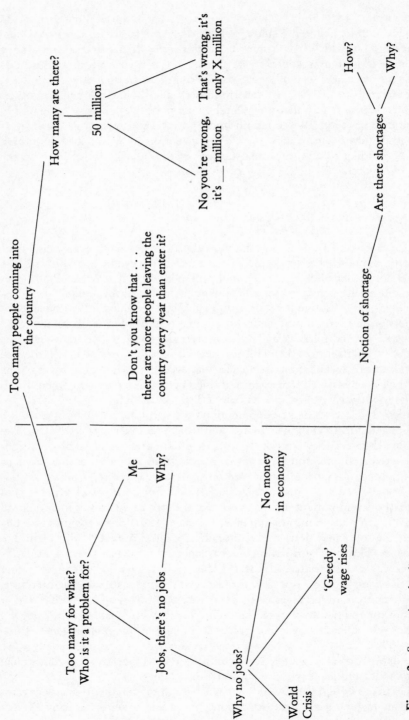

Figure 2 Structuring the discussion: what to avoid (Robson (1987) p. 130)

have not confined their scope to multiethnic classrooms. The Association for Curriculum Development (ACD, 1989) and Development Education Centre in Birmingham (Epstein and Sealey, 1990) have published material representing genuine attempts to harness classroom strategies to antiracism. Antiracists have also given more guidance about the specific orientation and direction of classroom-based work. To use Mullard's terms, antiracism assumes a *periscopic* stance in that it seeks to make 'a connection between institutional discriminations and inequalities of race, class and gender'. Multiculturalism, in contrast, is *microscopic*, focusing narrowly and intently on issues relating to culture, especially within ethnic minority communities (Mullard, 1984, p. 37). Robson (1987) makes this distinction crystal-clear in specifying how antiracists and multiculturalists typically respond to the often cited assertion in the classroom that 'there's too many of *them* coming into the country' (see Figure 2). In contrast to the multicultural approach, which centralizes race-relations matters, antiracists develop an approach which lays 'bare the *various* forms of oppression' (John, 1987, p. 21) without losing sight of the salience and specificity of racial inequality. My own work with Selman in Monkwearmouth College of Further Education was informed, in part, by these perspectives. We collaborated with the Liberal Studies Department in developing initiatives which centralized the concepts of 'bias', 'rights' and 'discrimination'. Our concern was with content and process. We aimed to encourage co-operation in pursuit of a common group product which, it was hoped, might expedite the learning of concepts and ideas, and the development of general procedural and social skills. Figure 3 gives a summary of the theoretical framework on which we based our initiative.

These recent advances, however, have failed to assuage the anxieties of the multiculturalists or 'critical revisionists' regarding the efficacy and distinctiveness of an antiracist pedagogy.

The essence of Short's scepticism about antiracist pedagogy is that, despite protestations to the contrary, it operates on the same terrain as that occupied by multiculturalists. That is to say, it is dependent on rationalism to dislodge the racist understandings of pupils. This is how Short (1991, p. 7) puts it:

> Prominent anti-racists such as Hatcher ([1987], p. 190) insist that 'the core of anti-racist education is learning about the racism of British culture' and Troyna & Williams (1986, p. 47) similarly note that 'a politicised curriculum would discuss the origins and manifestations of racism and would be directed as much to white as (to) black students.' But if children's prejudices are not amenable to rational discourse, why should it be thought that learning about racism will achieve anything worthwhile? What is learning about racism if not a form of rational discourse?

Short does not dispute the efficacy of rationalism. His aim is to encourage antiracists to admit that they predicate their intervention on this ground. Rattansi and Cohen, on the other hand, reckon that both multiculturalists and antiracists have been seduced by the potential of a rationalist pedagogy, despite what they perceive as its limitations in tackling racism in the classroom. These

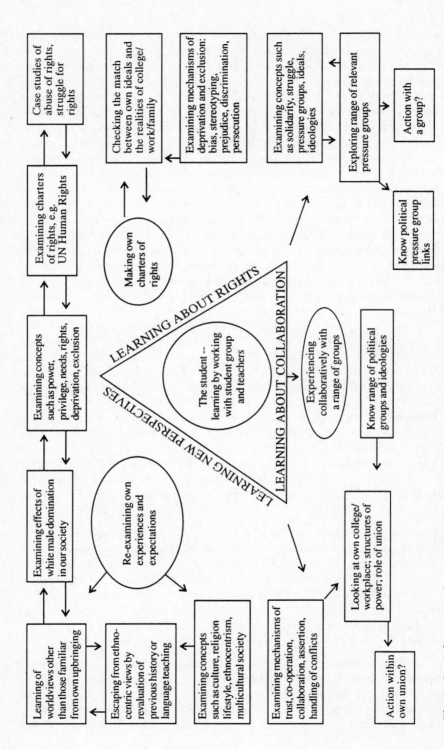

Figure 3 A framework for multicultural and antiracist education (Troyna and Selman, 1991, p. 7)

limitations derive from three sources: first, an erroneous conception of the irrationalism of the racist pupil; second, the failure to recognize that 'working class students' resistance to antiracist curricula and classroom discussions' may be 'bound up with a more generalised resistance to the degrees of surveillance, discipline, authoritarianism and class domination involved in conventional forms of schooling'; third, the 'patchy evidence' of success associated with rationalist pedagogy in tackling racism (Rattansi, 1992, p. 33).

Limitations, of course, do not equate to failure, and in the cautious tenor of Rattansi's critique it is possible to detect some appreciation of the pedagogical initiatives taken by antiracists. He is correct in suggesting that pupils' resistance to antiracist strategies might be tied in with their more generalized unwillingness to comply with the oppressive routines of formal schooling. But where does this leave teachers committed to tackling the racism of some of their pupils? In the absence of a fundamental reconstitution of formal schooling, are we to disenfranchise teachers entirely from antiracist and associated progressive education ventures? Clearly, this puts teachers in an invidious position. It also leaves Rattansi's observations marooned in the 'language of critique'. In concluding his article, he asserts the need 'to move beyond both multiculturalism and antiracism'. But he then falls short in providing an alternative:

> I have not provided a manifesto for that next phase in this article. I have merely tried to unravel what I take to be *some* of the main underlying oversimplifications which have informed educational practices in the field of 'race' and education.
>
> (Rattansi, 1992, p. 41)

There are more constructive alternatives; namely, trying to ensure that antiracist education constitutes more than an episodic intervention in the lives of the pupils. This is precisely what Troyna and Selman (1989, p. 35) argued in the context of their study:

> however sophisticated these [curricular and pedagogical] initiatives might be their effectiveness is dependent to a significant degree on the institutional context in which they reside. It is important that antiracism is accepted as a procedural value where policies for combatting racist incidents, tackling racist name-calling, and more generally, for handling controversial issues are developed by and for the constituent members of the institution.

In the absence of any supporting data, I am not sure of the grounds on which Rattansi claims that the 'antiracist project' has 'so far amassed only patchy evidence of success'. Nor am I sure of what would constitute 'success' in this context. Selman and I deliberately eschewed evaluation techniques which would focus on any causal links between the intervention and individual attitude changes. This approach would have legitimacy only if we had supported conceptions of racism which locate it purely and simply at the level of the individual. Our preferred strategy was to accelerate institutional developments and changes along antiracist lines. Without wishing to claim too much for the project, we did find that it had a catalytic effect in shifting the stance of the institution in relation to equal opportunities matters. By the end of the project the Students' Union had decided to formulate an equal opportunities policy and appoint an officer with responsibility for encouraging its diffusion. Senior management recognized the need for a similar policy to cover the appointment of staff, curricular development and student placements. And the library staff agreed that a reappraisal of existing library stock and principles governing future purchases were long overdue. Now these are not earth shattering developments. But in a college and region where even liberal conceptions of equal opportunities were disparaged prior to our modest intervention, they do constitute something more than 'patchy success'.

As we saw earlier, Rattansi's assertion that antiracists conceive of the racism expressed by certain young (working-class) people as irrational simply does not hold water. For many people, irrespective of their class background (Cashmore, 1987), racism functions as a common-sense ideology. It informs many of their routine judgements and actions. For them, racism is both logical and rational. Antiracist education projects are not designed to engage with the irrationalism of (young working-class) people – they are concerned with providing them with alternative explanatory frameworks. This leads us to the nub of the 'critical revisionists' ' critique of extant pedagogy: the contention that antiracists follow multiculturalists in privileging a rationalist pedagogy. A forceful assumption underlying a number of antiracist initiatives (including my own) is that providing pupils with the opportunity of perceiving things through an alternative and more plausible lens is likely to provoke changes in their racist construction of the way things are. Robson's view of the differing trajectories of multicultural and antiracist education (see Figure 3) implicitly hitches its wagon to the star of rationalism as a pedagogical tool.

But 'rationalist pedagogy' is a diffuse term which comprises a number of properties. It does not necessarily imply commitment to didacticism or teacher exposition. On the contrary, it can, and often does, assume a more student-centred edge with the development of more democratic and collaborative pedagogies (ACD, 1989; Troyna and Carrington, 1990). As I have indicated, this needs to be located in an institutional setting which supports and extends this initiative, with regard to its other constituent members. The project thus becomes grounded in a view of democracy based on relations which support the exploration and understanding of inequality and oppression. In Giroux's words, the institution becomes a site in which 'students learn the skills and knowledge needed to live in and fight for a viable democratic society'. He goes on to suggest that the priority for schools is 'to cultivate a spirit of critique and a respect for human dignity that is capable of linking personal and social issues around the pedagogical project of helping students to become critical and active students' (Giroux, 1989, p. 146). The crucial word here is 'cultivate'. Rattansi caricatures and belittles antiracists by suggesting that their project is anathema to this process. Why? Because like multiculturalists they attempt to 'combat racial prejudice by the provision of "positive images" ' and the presentation of 'black histories primarily as narratives of resistance and struggle against racism' (Rattansi, 1992, pp. 33–34).

Conclusion

The critique of antiracist education by Short and 'critical revisionists' such as Cohen and Rattansi demands our full attention. It follows the Burnage Report in providing a sustained critique of this orthodoxy from the Left. It differs from the report, however, in so far as it has failed to recognize the various inflections, and recent advances made, within this conception of education reform. In these terms, then, it has failed to provide a more persuasive basis on which to mount counterhegemonic struggles within schools.

References

Aboud, F. (1988) *Children and Prejudice*. Oxford, Blackwell.

Akhtar, S. and Stronach, I. (1986) 'They call me blacky'. *Times Educational Supplement*, 19 September, p. 23.

Allcott, T. (1992) Anti-racism in education: the search for policy in practice. In D. Gill, B. Mayor and M. Blair (eds), *Racism and Education Structures and Strategies*, pp. 169–82. London, Sage.

Allport, G. (1954) *The Nature of Prejudice*. Cambridge, MA, Addison-Wesley.

Amir, Y. (1969) Contact hypothesis in ethnic relations. *Psychological Bulletin*, 71, 319–42.

Assistant Masters and Mistresses Association (1987) *Multi-Cultural and Anti-Racist Education Today*. London, AMMA.

Association for Curriculum Development (1989) *Antiracist Strategies in Education*. London, ACD.

Audit Commission (1989) *Assuring Quality in Education – The Role of Local Education Inspectors and Advisers*. London, HMSO.

Back, L. (1991) Social context and racist name-calling: an ethnographic perspective on racist talk within a South London adolescent community. *European Journal of Intercultural Studies*, 1, 19–38.

Bagley, C.A. (1992) In-service provision and teacher resistance to whole-school change. In D. Gill, B. Mayor and M. Blair (eds), *Racism and Education: Structures and Strategies*, pp. 226–50. London, Sage.

Baker, K. (1987) Speech to annual Conservative Party Conference. Blackpool, 7 October.

Ball, S. (1990) *Politics and Policy-making in Education*. London, Routledge.

Ball, W. (1986) *Policy Innovation on Multicultural Education in 'Eastshire' Local Education Authority*. Policy Papers in Ethnic Relations (No. 4). Centre for Research in Ethnic Relations, University of Warwick.

Ball, W. (1991) The ethics and politics of doing antiracist research in education: key debates and dilemmas. *European Journal of Intercultural Studies*, 2, 35–49.

Ball, W. and Solomos, J. (eds) (1990) *Race and Local Politics*. London, Macmillan.

Ball, W., Gulam, W. and Troyna, B. (1990) Pragmatism or retreat? Funding policy, local government and the marginalisation of anti-racist education. In W. Ball and J. Solomos (eds), *Race and Local Politics*, pp. 78–94. London, Macmillan.

Banks, J. (1981) *Multi-ethnic Education*. New York, Allyn and Bacon.

Banks, J. (1986) Multicultural education and its critics: Britain and the United States. In S. Modgil, G.K. Verma, K. Mallick and C. Modgil (eds), *Multicultural Education: The Interminable Debate*, pp. 221–31. Lewes, Falmer Press.

Banton, M. (1988) Assimilation. In E. Cashmore (ed.), *Dictionary of Race and Ethnic Relations* (2nd edn), pp. 25–7. London, Routledge.

Barker, M. (1981) *The New Racism*. London, Junction Books.

Bell, C. and Roberts, H. (eds) (1984) *Social Researching: Politics, Problems, Practice*. London, Routledge and Kegan Paul.

Bell, D. and Nelson, T.N. (1989) Speaking about rape is everyone's business. *Women's Studies International Forum*, 12(4), 403–16.

Ben-Tovim, G., Gabriel, J., Law, I. and Stredder, K. (1986) *The Local Politics of Race*. London, Macmillan.

Berkshire Education Authority (1983) *Education for Racial Equality: General Policy Paper*. Reading, Berkshire Education Authority.

Bhavnani, K.–K. (1991) *Talking Politics: A Psychological Framing for Views from Youth in Britain*. Cambridge, Cambridge University Press.

Biggs, N. and Edwards, V. (1992) I treat them all the same: teacher-pupil talk in multi-ethnic classrooms. *Language and Education*, 5, 161–76.

Billig, M. (1988) The notion of 'prejudice': some rhetorical and ideological aspects. *Text*, 8, 91–110.

Billig, M., Condor, S., Edwards, D. *et al.* (eds) (1988) *Ideological Dilemmas*. London, Sage.

Billingsley, A. (1970) Black families and white social science. *Journal of Social Issues*, 26, 127–42.

Bonnett, A. (1990) Anti-racism as a radical educational ideology in London and Tyneside. *Oxford Review of Education*, 16, 255–67.

Boston, T. (1987) *Race, Class and Conservatism*. London, Unwin Hyman.

Bourne, J. (1980) Cheerleaders and ombudsmen: the sociology of race relations in Britain. *Race and Class*, 21, 331–52.

Boyd, B. (1985) Whole school policies. *Forum*, 27, 79–81.

Bradshaw, J. (1990) *Child Poverty and Deprivation in the UK*. London, National Children's Bureau.

Brandt, G. (1987) *The Realization of Anti-racist Teaching*. Lewes, Falmer Press.

Briault, E. (1973) *An Education Service for the Whole Community*. London, ILEA.

Brittan, E. (1976) Multiracial education – 2. Teachers' opinions on aspects of school life. *Educational Research*, 18, 182–91.

Brown, C. (1984) *Black and White Britain: The Third PSI Survey*. London, Heinemann.

Bryman, A. (1988) *Quality and Quantity in Social Research*. London, Allen and Unwin.

Bullivant, B. (1981) *The Pluralist Dilemma in Education*. Sydney, Allen and Unwin.

Burgess, R. (ed.) (1985) *Field Methods in the Study of Education*. Lewes, Falmer Press.

Butcher, H., Law, I.G., Leach, R. and Mullard, M. (1990) *Local Government and Thatcherism*. London, Macmillan.

Butler, Lord (1968) The 1944 Education Act in the next decade. In P. Bander (ed.), *Looking Forward to the Seventies: A Blueprint For Education*, pp. 13–22. Gerards Cross, Colin Smythe.

Carrington, B. (1983) Sport as a side-track: an analysis of West Indian involvement in extra-curricular sport. In L. Barton and S. Walker (eds), *Race, Class and Education*, pp. 40–65. Beckenham, Croom Helm.

Carrington, B. and Short, G. (1987) Breakthrough to political literacy: political education, antiracist education and the primary school. *Journal of Education Policy*, 2, 1–13.

Carrington, B. and Short, G. (1989) Policy or presentation? The psychology of anti-racist education. *New Community*, 15, 227–40.

Carrington, B. and Wood, E. (1983) Body talk – images of sport in a multiracial school. *Multiracial Education*, 11, 29–38.

Carrington, B., Millward, A. and Short, G. (1986) Schooling in a multiracial society: contrasting perspectives of primary and secondary teachers in training. *Educational Studies*, 12, 17–35.

Carter, B., Harris, C. and Joshi, S. (1987) *The 1951–1955 Conservative Government and the Racialisation of Black Immigration*. Policy Paper 11, Centre for Research in Ethnic Relations, Coventry, University of Warwick.

Carter, B. and Williams, J. (1987) Attacking racism in education. In B. Troyna (ed.), *Racial Inequality in Education*, pp. 170–83. London, Tavistock/Routledge.

Carter, T. (1986) *Shattering Illusions*. London, Lawrence and Wishart.

Cashmore, E. (1987) *The Logic of Racism*. London, Allen and Unwin.

Cashmore, E. and McLaughlin, E. (eds) (1991) *Out of Order?* London, Routledge.

Cashmore, E. and Troyna, B. (1981) Just for white boys? Elitism, racism and research. *Multiracial Education*, 10, 43–8.

Cashmore, E. and Troyna, B. (1990) *Introduction to Race Relations* (2nd edn). Lewes, Falmer Press.

Centre for Contemporary Cultural Studies (1982) *The Empire Strikes Back*. London, Hutchinson.

Chevannes, M. and Reeves, F. (1987) The black voluntary school movement: definition, context and prospects. In B. Troyna (ed.), *Racial Inequality in Education*, pp. 147–69. London, Tavistock/Routledge.

Chisholm, L. and Holland, J. (1986) Girls and occupational choice: antisexism in action in a curriculum development project. *British Journal of Sociology of Education*, 7, 353–65.

Chivers, T. (ed.) (1987) *Race and Culture in Education: Issues Arising from the Swann Committee Report*. Windsor, NFER/Nelson.

Clark, N. (1982) Dachwyng Saturday School. In A. Ohri, B. Manning and P. Curno (eds), *Community Work and Racism*, pp. 121–7. London, Routledge and Kegan Paul.

Coard, B. (1971) *How the West Indian Child Is Made Educationally Subnormal in the British School System*. London, New Beacon Books.

Cockcroft, W.H. (1982) *Mathematics Counts*. London, HMSO.

Cohen, P. (1988) *Tackling Common Sense Racism*. Centre for Multi-Cultural Education, University of London.

Cohen, P. (1992) 'It's racism what dunnit': hidden narratives in theories of racism. In J. Donald and A. Rattansi (eds), *'Race', Culture and Difference*, pp. 62–103. London, Sage.

Cohn, T. (1988) Sambo – a study in name-calling. In E. Kelly and T. Cohn, *Racism in Schools – New Research Evidence*, pp. 29–63. Stoke, Trentham Books.

Cole, M. (1989) Class, gender and 'race': from theory to practice. In M. Cole (ed.), *Education for Equality*, pp. 1–24. London, Routledge.

Commission for Racial Equality (1987) *Learning in Terror*. London, CRE.

Commission for Racial Equality (1989) *Racial Segregation in Education: Report of a Formal Investigation into Cleveland Educational Authority*. London, CRE.

Community Relations Commission (1974) *Unemployment and Homelessness*. London, CRC.

Connell, R. (1987) *Gender and Power*. Oxford, Polity Press.

Connolly, P. (1992) Press coverage of 'Murder in the Playground'. Unpublished MA dissertation in race and ethnic relations, Coventry, University of Warwick.

Craft, M. and Craft, A. (1983) The participation of ethnic minority pupils in further and higher education. *Educational Research*, 25, 10–19.

Dale, R. (1986) *Introducing Education Policy: Principles and Perspectives*. Milton Keynes, Open University Press.

Dale, R. (1989) *The State and Education Policy*. Milton Keynes, Open University Press.

Davey, A. (1983) *Learning To Be Prejudiced*. London, Edward Arnold.

Davies, L. (1985) Ethnography and status: focusing on gender in educational research. In R. Burgess (ed.), *Field Methods in the Study of Education*, pp. 79–96. Lewes, Falmer Press.

del Tufo, S., Randle, L. and Ryan, J. (1982) Inequality in a school system. In A. Ohri, B. Manning and P. Curno (eds), *Community Work and Racism*, pp. 75–87. London, Routledge and Kegan Paul.

Department of Education and Science (1971) *The Education of Immigrants* (Education Survey No. 13). London, DES.

Department of Education and Science (1975) *A Language For Life*. London, HMSO.

Department of Education and Science (1977) *Education in Schools: A Consultative Document*. London, HMSO.

Department of Education and Science (1981) *West Indian Children in Our Schools*. London, HMSO.

Department of Education and Science (1985a) *Education for All*. London, HMSO.

Department of Education and Science (1985b) *Better Schools*, Cmnd 9453. London, HMSO.

Department of Education and Science (1987) *Higher Education: Meeting the Challenge*. London, HMSO.

Department of Education and Science (1988a) *Education Reform Act: Local Management of Schools*, Circular 7/88. London, HMSO.

Department of Education and Science (1988b) *Education Reform Act: Grant Maintained Schools*, Circular 10/88. London, HMSO.

Department of Education and Science (1989) *National Curriculum: From Policy to Practice*. London, HMSO.

Dhondy, F. (1982) The black explosion in British schools. In F. Dhondy, B. Beese and L. Hassan (eds), *The Black Explosion in British Schools*, pp. 43–52. London, Race Today Publications.

Dorn, A. (1983) LEA policies on multi-racial education. *Multi-ethnic Education Review*, 2, 3–5.

Dorn, A. and Troyna, B. (1982) Multiracial education and the politics of decision-making. *Oxford Review of Education*, 8, 175–85.

Driver, G. (1980) *Beyond Underachievement*. London, Commission for Racial Equality.

Duncan, C. (1986) *Pastoral Care: An Antiracist/Multicultural Perspective*. Oxford, Blackwell.

Dunford, J.R. (1988) *Central/Local Government Relations 1977–1987 with Special Reference to Education: A Review of the Literature*. Stoke, Trentham Books.

Dzeich, B.W. and Weiner, L. (1984) *The Lecherous Professor: Sexual Harassment on Campus*. Boston, Beacon Press.

Edelman, M. (1964) *The Symbolic Uses of Politics*. Urbana, University of Illinois Press.

Edwards, V.K. (1978) Language attitudes and underperformance in West Indian children. *Educational Review*, 30, 51–8.

Eggleston, J., Dunn, D., Anjali, M. with Wright, C. (1985) *Education for Some*. Stoke-on-Trent, Trentham Books.

Elliott, J. (1990) 'Validating case studies', *Westminster Studies in Education*, 13, 47–60.

Epstein, D. and Sealey, A. (1990) *Where It Really Matters: Developing Anti-racist Education in Predominantly White Primary Schools*. Birmingham, Development Education Centre.

Essed, P. (1991) *Everyday Racism*. London, Sage.

Figueroa, P. (1986) Student teachers' images of ethnic minorities: a British case study. Paper presented to World Congress of Sociology, New Delhi, 18–22 August.

Figueroa, P. (1991) *Education and the Social Construction of Race*. London, Routledge.

Finch, J. (1984) 'It's great to have someone to talk to': the ethics and politics of interviewing women. In C. Bell and H. Roberts (eds), *Social Researching: Politics, Problems and Practice*, pp. 70–87. London, Routledge and Kegan Paul.

Fitz, J., Edwards, A.D. and Whitty, G. (1986) Beneficiaries, benefits and costs: an investigation of the Assisted Places Scheme. *Research Papers in Education*, 1, 169–93.

Flew, A. (1989) The School Effect: review. *Ethnic Enterprise*, November/December, pp. 21–2.

Flynn, J.R. (1980) *Race, IQ and Jensen*. London, Routledge and Kegan Paul.

Foster, P. (1990) Cases not proven: an evaluation of two studies of teacher racism. *British Educational Research Journal*, 16, 335–48.

Foster, P. (1991) Cases still not proven: a reply to Cecile Wright. *British Educational Research Journal*, 17, 165–70.

Geras, N. (1991) Seven types of obloquy: travesties of Marxism. In R. Miliband and L. Panitch (eds), *The Retreat of the Intellectuals*, pp. 1–34. London, Merlin Press.

Gibson, D. (1987) Hearing and listening: a case study of the 'consultation' process undertaken by a local education department and black groups. In B. Troyna (ed.), *Racial Inequality in Education*, pp. 77–91. London, Tavistock/Routledge.

Gibson, M. (1976) Approaches to multicultural education in the United States: some concepts and assumptions. *Anthropology and Education Quarterly*, 7, 7–18.

Giles, R. (1977) *The West Indian Experience in British Schools*. London, Heinemann Educational Books.

Gilroy, P. (1990) The end of anti-racism. In W. Ball and J. Solomos (eds), *Race and Local Politics*, pp. 191–209. London, Macmillan.

Giroux, H. (1984) Ideology, agency and the process of schooling. In L. Barton and S. Walker (eds), *Social Crisis and Educational Research*, pp. 306–34. Beckenham, Croom Helm.

Giroux, H. (1989) *Schooling for Democracy: Critical Pedagogy in the Modern Age*. London, Routledge.

Giroux, H. (1991) Democracy and the discourse of cultural difference: towards a politics of border pedagogy. *British Journal of Sociology of Education*, 12, 501–20.

Glaser, B.G. and Strauss, A.L. (1967) *The Discovery of Grounded Theory*. Chicago, Aldine.

Gordon, L. (1984) Paul Willis – education, cultural production and social reproduction. *British Journal of Sociology of Education*, 5, 105–16.

Gordon, P. (1985) *Policing Immigration: Britain's Internal Controls*. London, Pluto Press.

Gordon, P. and Rosenberg, D. (1989) *Daily Racism: The Press and Black People in Britain*. London, Runnymede Trust.

Gouldner, A. (1975) *For Sociology: Renewal and Critique in Sociology Today*. Harmondsworth, Penguin.

Grace, G. (1984) Urban education: policy science or critical scholarship? In G. Grace (ed.), *Education and the City*, pp. 3–59. London, Routledge and Kegan Paul.

Grace, G. (1987) Teachers and the state in Britain: a changing relation. In M. Lawn and G. Grace (eds), *Teachers: the Culture and Politics of Work*, pp. 193–228. Lewes, Falmer Press.

Gramsci, A. (1977) *Selections from Political Writings 1910–1920*. London, Lawrence and Wishart.

Green, P.A. (1982) Teachers' influence on the self-concept of pupils of different ethnic groups. Unpublished PhD thesis, University of Durham.

Green, S.J.D. (1988) Is equality of opportunity a false ideal for society? *British Journal of Sociology*, 39, 1–27.

Grugeon, E. and Woods, P. (1990) *Educating All: Multicultural Perspectives in the Primary School*. London, Routledge.

Gurnah, A. (1984) The politics of racism awareness training. *Critical Social Policy*, 11, pp. 6–20.

Guy, W. and Menter, I. (1992) Local management of resources – who benefits? In D. Gill, B. Mayor and M. Blair (eds), *Racism and Education: Structures and Strategies*, pp. 151–68. London, Sage.

Hall, S. (1980) Teaching race. *Multiracial Education*, 9(1), 3–13.

Hall, S. (1983) Education in crisis. In A.M. Wolpe and J. Donald (eds), *Is There Anyone There from Education?*, pp. 2–10. London, Pluto Press.

Hall, S. (1986) Gramsci's relevance to the analysis of race. *Communication Inquiry*, 10(2), 5–27.

Hall, S., Critcher, C., Jefferson, T., Clarke, J. and Roberts, B. (1978) *Policing the Crisis*. London, Macmillan.

Halsey, A.H. (1972) Political ends and educational means. In A.H. Halsey (ed.), *Educational Priority*, Vol. 1, pp. 3–12. London, HMSO.

Halsey, A.H., Heath, A.F. and Ridge, J.M. (1980) *Origins and Destinations*. Oxford, Clarendon Press.

Hammersley, M. (1992) A response to Barry Troyna's 'children, "race" and racism: the limits of research and policy'. *British Journal of Educational Studies*, 40, 174–7.

Hargreaves, A. (1986) Research, policy and practice in education: some observations on SSRC-funded education projects. *Journal of Education Policy*, 1, 115–32.

Hargreaves, D.H. (1980) The occupational culture of teachers. In P. Woods (ed.), *Teacher Strategies*, pp. 125–48. London, Croom Helm.

Hargreaves, D.H. (1984) *Improving Secondary Schools*. London, ILEA.

Harland, J. (1985) The new inset: a transformation scene. *Journal of Education Policy*, 2, 235–44.

Harrop, M. and Zimmerman, G. (1977) Anatomy of the National Front. *Patterns of Prejudice*, 11, 12–15.

Hartley, D. (1985) *Understanding the Primary School*. Beckenham, Croom Helm.

Hartnett, A. (ed.) (1982) *The Social Sciences in Educational Studies*. London, Heinemann Educational Books.

Hassan, L., and Beese, B. (1982) Who's educating whom? In F. Dhondy, F. Beese and L. Hassan, *The Black Explosion in British Schools*, pp. 21–35. London, Race Today Publications.

Hatcher, R. (1987) 'Race' and education: two perspectives for change. In B. Troyna (ed.), *Racial Inequality in Education*, pp. 184–200. London, Tavistock/Routledge.

Henriques, J. (1984) Social psychology and the politics of racism. In J. Henriques, W. Holloway, C. Urwin, C. Venn and V. Walkerdine (eds), *Changing the Subject: Psychology, Social Regulation and Subjectivity*, pp. 60–89. London, Methuen.

Her Majesty's Inspectorate (1984) *Race Relations in Schools: A Summary of Discussions at Meetings in Five Local Authorities*. London, DES.

Hewitt, R. (1986) *White Talk, Black Talk*. Cambridge, Cambridge University Press.

Hewstone, M. and Brown, R. (eds) (1986) *Contact and Conflict in Intergroup Encounters*. Oxford, Blackwell.

Hicks, E. (1981) Cultural Marxism: nonsynchrony and feminist practice. In L. Sargeant (ed.), *Women and Revolution*, pp. 219–238. Boston, South End Press.

Hochschild, J.L. (1984) *The New American Dilemma: Liberal Democracy and School Desegregation*. New Haven, CN, Yale University Press.

Home Office (1978) *The West Indian Community: Observations on the Report of the Select Committee on Race Relations and Immigration*. London, HMSO.

House of Commons (1981) *Fifth Report from the Home Affairs Committee Session 1980–1981: Racial Disadvantage* (Vol. 1). London, HMSO.

Hugill, B. (1985) Five years' frustration. *New Statesman*, 18 January, pp. 12–13.

Inner London Education Authority (1977) *Multi-Ethnic Education*, 8 November. London, ILEA.

Inner London Education Authority (1983) *Race, Sex and Class*. London, ILEA.

Jeffcoate, R. (1984) *Ethnic Minorities and Education*. London, Harper and Row.

John, G. (1987) Antiracist education in white areas: a movement in search of a focus. *Sage Race Relations Abstracts*, 13, 17–24.

Johnson, R. (1989) Thatcherism and English education: breaking the mould or confirming the pattern? *History of Education*, 18, 91–121.

Jones, K. (1989) *Right Turn*. London, Hutchinson.

Joseph, Sir Keith (1986) Without prejudice: education for an ethnically mixed society. Unpublished speech.

Kamin, L.J. (1977) *The Science and Politics of IQ*. Harmondsworth, Penguin.

Katz, J. (1978) *White Awareness: A Handbook for Anti-Racism Training*. Oklahoma, University of Oklahoma Press.

Kean, H. (1991) Managing education – the Local Authority dimension. *Journal of Education Policy*, 6, 145–54.

Kelly, A. (1985) Changing schools and changing society: some reflections on the Girls Into Science and Technology Project. In M. Arnot (ed.), *Race and Gender: Equal Opportunities Policies in Education*, pp. 137–46. Oxford, Pergamon Press.

Kelly, E. (1988) Pupils, racial groups and behaviour in schools. In E. Kelly and T. Cohn, *Racism in Schools – New Research Evidence*, pp. 5–28. Stoke, Trentham Books.

Kirp, D. (1979) *Doing Good by Doing Little*. London, University of California Press.

Kirp, D. (1982) *Just Schools*. London, University of California Press.

Knight, B. (1987) Managing the honeypots. In H. Thomas and T. Simkins (eds), *Economics and the Management of Education: Emerging Themes*, pp. 205–13. Lewes, Falmer Press.

Kogan, M. (1975) *Educational Policy-making*. London, Allen and Unwin.

Lacey, C. (1974) Destreaming in a 'pressured' academic environment. In J. Eggleston (ed.), *Contemporary Research in the Sociology of Education*, pp. 148–66. London, Methuen.

Lather, P. (1986) Research as praxis. *Harvard Educational Review*, 56, 257–77.

Lawrence, E. (1981) White sociology, black struggle. *Multiracial Education*, 9, 3–17.

Lawrence, E. (1982) In the abundance of water the fool is thirsty: sociology and black 'pathology'. In CCCS, *The Empire Strikes Back*, pp. 95–142. London, Hutchinson.

Lax, L. (1984) Anti-racist policies. In All London Teachers Against Racism and Fascism (ALTARF), *Challenging Racism*, pp. 207–18. London, ALTARF.

Leicester, M. (1989) *Multicultural Education: From Theory to Practice*. Windsor, NFER/Nelson.

Levine, A., Sober, E. and Wright, E.O. (1987) Marxism and methodological individualism. *New Left Review,* 62, 67–84.

Levitas, R. (ed.) (1986) *The Ideology of the New Right.* Oxford, Polity Press.

Little, A. (1975) The educational achievement of ethnic minority children in London schools. In G.K. Verma and C. Bagley (eds), *Race and Education Across Cultures,* pp. 48–69. London, Heinemann Educational Books.

London Borough of Brent (1983) *Education for a Multicultural Democracy: Book 1. The Need for a Change from a White Ethnocentric Approach.* London, Borough of Brent.

London Borough of Haringey (1978) *Racialist Activities in Schools.* London Borough of Haringey.

London Voluntary Service Unit/Afro-Caribbean Community Development Unit (1989) *The 1988 Education Reform Act and its Impact on London's Black Communities.* London, LVS/ACDU.

Lynch, J. (1987) *Prejudice Reduction and the Schools.* London, Cassell.

Mabey, C. (1981) Black British literacy. *Educational Research,* 23, 83–95.

Mac an Ghaill, M. (1989) Coming-of-age in 1980s England: Reconceptualising black students' schooling experience'. *British Journal of Sociology of Education,* 10, 273–86.

Macdonald, I., Bhavnani, T., Khan, L. and John, G. (1989) *Murder in the Playground: The Report of the Macdonald Inquiry into Racism and Racial Violence in Manchester Schools.* London, Longsight Press.

Manchester Education Authority (1978) *Education for a Multicultural Society.* Manchester, Manchester Education Authority.

Marland, M. (1987) The education of and for a multi-racial and multi-lingual society: research needs post-Swann. *Educational Research,* 29, 116–29.

Marsland, D. (1978) Youth's problems and the problems of youth. In M. Day and D. Marsland (eds), *Black Kids, White Kids, What Hope?,* pp. 93–103. Leicester, National Youth Bureau.

McCarthy, C. (1990) *Race and Curriculum: Social Inequality and the Theories and Politics of Difference in Contemporary Research in Schooling.* Lewes, Falmer Press.

Miles, R. (1988) Racialization. In E. Cashmore (ed.), *Dictionary of Race and Ethnic Relations* (2nd edn), pp. 246–7. London, Routledge.

Miles, R. (1989) *Racism.* London, Routledge.

Milner, D. (1975) *Children and Race.* Harmondsworth, Penguin.

Milner, D. (1983) *Children and Race: Ten Years On.* London, Ward Lock.

Mishra, R. (1977) *Society and Social Policy.* London, Macmillan.

Mitchell, P. (1982) Developing an anti-racist policy: the secondary experience. *Multi-ethnic Education Review,* 1, 16–17.

Mitchell, P. (1984) The headteacher's role as curriculum manager. In J. Maw, M. Fielding, P. Mitchell *et al.* (eds), *Education Plc? Headteachers and the New Training Initiative,* pp. 25–34. London, Bedford Way Papers No. 20.

Mould, W. (1987) Multicultural education: an LEA response. In T. Chivers (ed.), *Race and Culture in Education,* pp. 44–60. Windsor, NFER/Nelson.

Mukherjee, T. (1984) I'm not blaming you – an antiracist analysis. *Multicultural Teaching,* 2, 5–8.

Mullard, C. (1982) Multiracial education in Britain: from assimilation to cultural pluralism. In J. Tierney (ed.), *Race, Migration and Schooling,* pp. 120–33. London, Holt, Rinehart and Winston.

Mullard, C. (1984) *Anti-racist Education: The Three O's.* Cardiff, National Antiracist Movement in Education.

Mullard, C. (1985) *Race, Power and Resistance.* London, Routledge and Kegan Paul.

Myers, K. (1985) Beware of the backlash. *School Organisation,* 5, 27–40.

Myers, K. (1990) Review of 'Equal Opportunities in the New Era'. *Education*, 5 October, p. 295.

National Antiracist Movement in Education (1985) *NAME on Swann*. Nottingham, NAME.

National Union of Teachers (1983) *Combating Racialism in Schools*. London, NUT.

National Union of Teachers (1989) *Anti-racism in Education: Guidelines*. London, NUT.

Oakley, A. (1981) Interviewing women: a contradiction in terms. In H. Roberts (ed.), *Doing Feminist Research*, pp. 30–61. London, Routledge and Kegan Paul.

Oakley, A. (1991) *The Men's Room*. London, Flamingo.

Ogilvy, C., Boath, E., Cheyne, W., Jahoda, G. and Schaffer, H.R. (1992) Staff-child interaction styles in multi-ethnic nursery schools. *British Journal of Developmental Psychology*, 10, 85–97.

Oldman, D. (1987) Plain-speaking and pseudo-science: the 'New Right' attack on antiracism. In B. Troyna (ed.), *Racial Inequality in Education*, pp. 29–43. London, Tavistock/Routledge.

Olneck, M. (1990) The recurring dream: symbolism and ideology in intercultural and multicultural education. *American Journal of Education*, February, pp. 147–74.

Pagelow, M. (1979) Research on woman battering. In J. Fleming (ed.) *Stopping Wife Abuse*, pp. 334–49. Garden City, NY, Anchor Press.

Palmer, F. (ed.) (1986) *Anti-racism: An Assault on Education and Value*. London, Sherwood Press.

Parekh, B. (1986) Britain's step-citizens. *New Society*, 1 August, pp. 24–5.

Parkinson, M. (1982) Politics and policy-making in education. In A. Hartnett (ed.), *The Social Sciences in Educational Studies*, pp. 114–26. London, Heinemann Educational Books.

Pearce, S. (1985) *Education and the Multi-racial Society*. London, The Monday Club.

Platt, J. (1976) *Realities of Social Research*. Brighton, University of Sussex Press.

Pollard, A. (ed.) (1987) *Children and their Primary Schools*. Lewes, Falmer Press.

Quicke, J. (1988) The New Right and education. *British Journal of Educational Studies*, 36, 5–20.

Ranson, S. (1985) Changing relations between centre and locality in education. In I. McNay and J. Ozga (eds), *Policy-making in education: The Breakdown of Consensus*, pp. 103–23. Oxford, Pergamon Press.

Ranson, S. (1988) From 1944 to 1988: education, citizenship and democracy. *Local Government Studies*, 14, 1–19.

Ranson, S., Hannon, V. and Gray, J. (1987) Citizens or consumers? Policies for school accountability. In S. Walker and L. Barton (eds), *Changing Policies, Changing Teachers*, pp. 3–21. Milton Keynes, Open University Press.

Rattansi, A. (1992) Changing the subject? Racism, culture and education. In J. Donald and A. Rattansi (eds), *'Race', Culture and Difference*, pp. 11–48. London, Sage.

Reeves, F. (1983) *British Racial Discourse*. Cambridge, Cambridge University Press.

Reeves, F. and Chevannes, M. (1981) The underachievement of Rampton. *Multiracial Education*, 12, 35–42.

Reicher, S. (1986) Contact, action and racialization: some British evidence. In M. Hewstone and R. Brown (eds), *Contact and Conflict in Intergroup Encounters*, pp. 152–67. Oxford, Blackwell.

Rex, J. (1981a) Culture clashes. *Times Educational Supplement*, 7 August, p. 4.

Rex, J. (1981b) Errol Lawrence and the sociology of race relations: an open letter. *Multiracial Education*, 10, 49–51.

Rex, J. (1987) *Race and Ethnicity*. Milton Keynes, Open University Press.

Rex, J. and Tomlinson, S. (1979) *Colonial Immigrants in a British City*. London, Routledge, and Kegan Paul.

Reynolds, K. (1991) Restructuring the Welfare State – the case of the abolition of the Inner London Education Authority. *Critical Social Policy*, 32, 72–81.

Richards, C. (1986) Antiracist initiatives. *Screen*, 27, 74–9.

Richardson, R. (1983) Worth the paper it's written on? *Issues in Race and Education*, 40, 1–5.

Richardson, R. (1988) 'Opposition to reform and the need for transformation: some polemical notes. *Multicultural Teaching*, 6, 4–10.

Roberts, K., Noble, M. and Duggan, J. (1983) Young, black and out of work. In B. Troyna and D. Smith (eds), *Racism, School and the Labour Market*, pp. 17–28. Leicester, National Youth Bureau.

Robson, M. (1987) *Language, Learning and Race*. London, Longman/Further Education Unit.

Rose, S. (1979) Race, intelligence and education. *New Community*, 7, 280–3.

Rutherford, J. (ed.) (1990) *Identity: Community, Culture and Difference*. London, Lawrence and Wishart.

Rutter, M., Gray, G., Maughan, B. and Smith, A. (1982) School experiences and achievements and the first year of employment. Unpublished report to the DES.

Saggar, S. (1991) *Race and Public Policy*. Aldershot, Avebury.

Scarman, Lord (1981) *The Brixton Disorders: 10–12 April 1981*. London, HMSO.

Schools Council (1981) *Education for a Multicultural Society*. London, CRE.

Select Committee on Race Relations and Immigration (1969) *The Problems of Coloured School Leavers*. London, HMSO.

Select Committee on Race Relations and Immigration (1978) *The West Indian Community*, Vol. 1. London, HMSO.

Sharron, H. (1987) Governing prejudices. *School Governors*, November, pp. 30–1.

Sheffield Multi-Cultural Support Group (1982) *Education in Schools in Multicultural Sheffield*. Sheffield.

Short, G. (1991) Power, prejudice and racism: some reflections on the anti-racist critique of multicultural education. *Journal of Philosophy of Education*, 25, 5–15.

Short, G. and Carrington, B. (1987) Towards an antiracist initiative in the all-white primary school: a case study. In A. Pollard (ed.). *Children and their Primary Schools*, pp. 220–35. Lewes, Falmer Press.

Sihera, E. (1988) The trouble with you people. *Times Educational Supplement*, 16 September, p. 29.

Sikora, J. (1988) An assessment of one LEA's attempts to promote multicultural education in its secondary schools. Unpublished MEd dissertation, University of Manchester.

Simons, H. (1989) Ethics of case study in educational research and evaluation. In R.G. Burgess (ed.), *The Ethics of Educational Research*, pp. 114–40. Lewes, Falmer Press.

Sivanandan, A. (1983) Challenging racism: strategies for the 1980s. *Race and Class*, 26, 38–43.

Sivanandan, A. (1985) RAT and the degradation of the black struggle. *Race and Class*, 36, 1–33.

Smith, D. and Tomlinson, S. (1989) *The School Effect*. London, PSI/Heinemann.

Smolicz, J.J. (1981) Cultural pluralism and educational policy: in search of stable multiculturalism. *Australian Journal of Education*, 25, 121–45.

Solomos, J. (1988) *Race and Racism in Contemporary Britain*. London, Macmillan.

Stone, M. (1981) *The Education of the Black Child in Britain*. London, Fontana.

Straker-Welds, M. (ed.) (1984) *Education for a Multicultural Society*. London, Bell and Hyman.

Street-Porter, R. (1978) *Race, Children and Cities*. Milton Keynes, Open University Press.

Sutcliffe, J. (1989) Deprived city schools face budget cuts. *Times Educational Supplement*, 24 February, p. 1.

Tanna, K. (1985) Opening the black box. *Times Educational Supplement*, 20 September, p. 27.

Taylor, M. (1981) *Caught Between: A Review of Research into the Education of Pupils of West Indian Origin*. Windsor, NFER/Nelson.

Thatcher, M. (1987) Speech to annual Conservative Party Conference. Blackpool, 9 October.

Thomas, B. (1984) Principles of anti-racist education. *Currents*, 2, 20–4.

Tomlinson, S. (1981) *Educational Subnormality*. London, Routledge and Kegan Paul.

Tomlinson, S. (1983) *Ethnic Minorities in British Schools*. London, Heinemann.

Tomlinson, S. (1984) *Home and School in Multicultural Britain*. London, Batsford.

Tomlinson, S. (1990) *Multicultural Education in White Schools*. London, Batsford.

Townsend, H.E.R. and Brittan, E. (1972) *Organisation in Multiracial Schools*. Slough, NFER.

Troyna, B. (1982) The ideological and policy response to black pupils in British schools. In A. Hartnett (ed.), *The Social Sciences in Educational Studies*, pp. 127–43. London, Heinemann Educational Books.

Troyna, B. (1983) Multiracial education: just another brick in the wall? *New Community*, 10, 424–8.

Troyna, B. (1984a) Multicultural education: emancipation or containment? In L. Barton and S. Walker (eds). *Social Crisis and Educational Research*, pp. 75–92. Beckenham, Croom Helm.

Troyna, B. (1984b) Fact or artefact? The 'educational underachievement' of black pupils. *British Journal of Sociology of Education*, 5, 153–66.

Troyna, B. (1985) The great divide: policies and practices in multicultural education. *British Journal of Sociology of Education*, 6, 209–223.

Troyna, B. (1987) Beyond multiculturalism: towards the enactment of anti-racist education in policy, provision and pedagogy. *Oxford Review of Education*, 13, 307–20.

Troyna, B. (1988) Paradigm regained: a critique of 'cultural deficit' perspectives in contemporary educational research. *Comparative Education*, 24, 273–83.

Troyna, B. (1989) 'A new planet?' Tackling racial inequality in all-white schools and colleges. In G.K. Verma (ed.), *Education for All: A Landmark in Pluralism*, pp. 175–91. Lewes, Falmer Press.

Troyna, B. (1992) *'The Hub' and 'The Rim': How LMS Buckles Antiracist Education*. Paper presented to the National Governors and Managers Fair, International Convention Centre, Birmingham, 13 June.

Troyna, B. and Ball, W. (1985) *Views from the Chalk Face: School Responses to an LEA's Multicultural Education Policy*. Policy Papers on Ethnic Relations, Coventry, University of Warwick.

Troyna, B. and Carrington, B. (1990) *Education, Racism and Reform*. London, Routledge.

Troyna, B. and Farrow, S. (1991) Science for all? Antiracism, science and the primary school. In A. Peacock (ed.), *Science in Primary Schools: The Multicultural Dimension*, pp. 111–23. London, Macmillan.

Troyna, B. and Hatcher, R. (1991a) Racist incidents in schools: a framework for analysis. *Journal of Education Policy*, 6, 17–31.

References 149

Troyna, B. and Hatcher, R. (1991b) 'British schools for British citizens'? *Oxford Review of Education*, 17, 287–99.

Troyna, B. and Hatcher, R. (1992) *Racism in Children's Lives*. London, Routledge.

Troyna, B. and Selman, L. (1989) Surviving in the 'survivalist culture': antiracist strategies and practice in the new ERA. *Journal of Further and Higher Education*, 13, 22–36.

Troyna, B. and Selman, L. (1991) *Implementing Multicultural and Antiracist Education in Mainly White Colleges*. London, Further Education Unit.

Troyna, B. and Williams, J. (1986) *Racism, Education and the State*. Beckenham, Croom Helm.

Turner, J. (ed.) (1987) *Rediscovering the Social Group*. Oxford, Blackwell.

van Dijk, T. (1987) *Communicating Racism: Ethnic Prejudice in Thought and Talk*. Newbury Park, Sage.

van Dijk, T. (1991) *Racism and the Press*. London, Routledge.

Verma, G.K. (ed.) (1989) *Education for All: A Landmark in Pluralism*. Lewes, Falmer Press.

Vincent, C. (1992) Tolerating intolerance: parental choice and relations in the UK – the Cleveland case. *Journal of Education Policy*, 7, 429–33.

Waddington, D., Jones, K. and Critcher, C. (1989) *Flashpoints: Studies in Public Disorder*. London, Routledge.

Watson, S. (ed.) (1990) *Playing the State: Australian Feminist Interventions*. Sydney, Allen and Unwin.

Weeks, A. (1982) The conservative curriculum. *Times Educational Supplement*, 21 May, p. 23.

Wellman, D. (1977) *Portraits of White Racism*. Cambridge, Cambridge University Press.

Wenger, G.C. (1987) Establishing a dialogue. In G.C. Wenger (ed.), *The Research Relationship*, pp. 198–219. London, Allen and Unwin.

Whitty, G. (1985) *Sociology and School Knowledge*. London, Methuen.

Whyte, J. (1986) *Girls into Science and Technology: The Story of a Project*. London, Routledge and Kegan Paul.

Willey, R. (1984) *Race, Equality and Schools*. London, Methuen.

Williams, J. (1981) Race and schooling: some recent contributions. *British Journal of Sociology of Education*, 2, 221–7.

Williams, J. (1985) Redefining institutional racism. *Ethnic and Racial Studies*, 8, 323–48.

Williams, J. (1986) Education and race: the racialisation of class inequalities? *British Journal of Sociology of Education*, 7, 135–54.

Wilson, S. (1979) Explorations of the usefulness of case study evaluations. *Evaluation Quarterly*, 3, 4–16.

Wolpe, A.M. (1988) *Within School Walls: The Role of Discipline, Sexuality and The Curriculum*. London, Routledge.

Wright, C. (1987) Black Students – White Pupils. In B. Troyna (ed.), *Racial Inequality in Education*, pp. 109–26. London, Tavistock/Routledge.

Wright, C. (1991) Comments in reply to the article by P. Foster. *British Educational Research Journal*, 16, 351–5.

Yeomans, A. (1983) Collaborative groupwork in primary and secondary schools: Britain and USA. *Durham and Newcastle Research Review*, 10, 95–105.

Young, K. and Connelly, N. (1981) *Policy and Practice in the Multi-racial City*. London, Policy Studies Institute.

Name Index

Quicke, J., 73

Rampton, A., 63–5
Ranson, S., 72, 75
Rattansi, A., 119, 125–6, 135
Reeves, F., 13, 17, 25, 28-9, 64, 66
Reicher, S., 59, 101, 102
Rex, J., 24, 64, 66, 108, 111
Reynolds, K., 43
Richardson, R., 34, 76
Roberts, K., 66
Robson, M., 132, 134
Rutherford, J., 28
Rutter, M., 67

Saggar, S., 32
Said, E., 8, 17
Sealey, A., 133
Select Committee on Race Relations
 and Immigration, 63
Selman, L., 121, 133, 134, 135
Sharron, H., 75
Shor, I., 16, 17
Short, G., 27, 82, 119, 121, 122, 134
Sihera, E., 98
Sikora, J., 76
Simons, H., 45
Sivanandan, A., 32, 125
Smith, D.J., 95–8, 101–2
Smolicz, J.J., 69
Solomos, J., 32, 63
Stone, M., 107
Strauss, A.L., 120–1
Street-Porter, R., 23
Swann, Lord, 7, 17, 60, 65–70, 109, 114

Tanna, K., 66
Taylor, M., 109
Thomas, B., 26
Tomlinson, S., 50, 63, 95–8, 101-2, 111
Troyna, B., 5, 6, 9, 14, 16, 17, 23, 24, 26–7, 28, 29, 30, 35, 39, 47, 64, 65, 66, 73, 75, 76, 78, 79, 83, 84, 91, 92, 97, 107, 109, 113, 120, 121, 123, 125, 128, 136
Turner, J., 102

van Dijk, T., 28, 128
Verma, G., 60, 62
Vincent, C., 78

Waddington, D., 128
Walker, J., 14, 17
Watson, S., 21
Weeks, A., 84
Wellman, D., 33
Wenger, G.C., 22
Whitty, G., 90
Whyte, J., 115
Williams, J., 5, 17, 30, 79, 83, 92, 109, 123, 125, 127
Wilson, S., 45
Winant, H., 11, 17
Wolpe, A.M., 125
Woods, P., 125
Wright, C., 109

Yeomans, A., 116
Young, K., 31

Subject Index

'cultural stranger' role, 107
cultural understanding, 47, 48
    in Manchester, 54–9

deracialization, discursive, 28–30
DES (Department of Education and
    Science), 24, 25, 72, 76, 77, 113–15
discursive deracialization, 28–30
dispersal policies ('bussing'), 24, 46, 55,
    103
Doing Good by Doing Little (Kirp), 27

Education Act (1944), 24, 52, 72, 75
Education for All (Swann Report), 7, 60,
    61–71, 95, 109, 114, 115
Education, Racism and Reform (Troyna and
    Carrington), 16
Education Reform Act (1988), 24, 35,
    43, 45, 46, 60, 62, 71–5, 78–9, 117
*Education in Schools: A Consultative
    Document* (DES), 25
emancipatory knowledge, 105
Empire Strikes Back, The (CCCS), 107
equal opportunities, 24, 25, 39, 47, 81
    and teaching, 91–2
equality
    and education policy, 39–40
    and multiculturalism, 5
equiphobia, 45, 117, 118
ESL (English as a second language), 24,
    46, 48
ethical dilemmas, in research, 104–16

fair procedures, 39
friendship groups, in schools, and
    ethnicity, 101–2

GIST (Girls into Science and
    Technology) project, 91, 115
government, and local politics, 34–5
grant-maintained schools (GMS), 73,
    76–7
groups, dominant and subordinate, 10,
    11–12

ideologies
    common-sense, 128, 136
    elaborated, 128
ILEA (Inner London Education
    Authority), 21, 30, 43, 46, 47

and benovelent multiculturalism, 48–
    54
and institutional racism, 123
*Implementing Multicultural and Antiracist
    Education in Mainly White Colleges*,
    121
individualism, cult of, in teaching, 90–1,
    92
individuals, and racial prejudice, 6–9, 12
inferential racism, 9
Institute of Race Relations (IRR), 106
institutional racism, 9–12, 30, 34, 40,
    123, 125
    and racialization, 13
    and whole-school policies, 82–4, 92
integration, 23, 24
Introduction to Race Relations (Troyna and
    Cashmore), 119

Just Schools (Kirp), 27
justice, and education policy, 38–9

Labour Party, 32, 45, 96
Language for Life, A (DES), 25, 80
language provision, in schools, 53, 68–9,
    80
LEAs (local education authorities), 21,
    33
    and antiracist education, 131
    and the Education Reform Act
        (1988), 72, 73–5, 77–8
    policy statements, 36
    as 'sites of struggle', 21, 35, 46
Liverpool, 32
local management of schools (LMS), 73,
    77, 78, 79
local politics, 21, 32–3, 34–5, 46–7
London Boroughs, plans for
    antiracist/multiethnic education, 44

Manchester, 30, 43, 46, 47, 76, 78
    cultural understanding in, 54–9
    Murder in the Playground report, 117–
        18
monoculturalism, 22, 23–4, 25, 28, 30,
    71
    and the Education Reform Act
        (1988), 60
    in the ILEA, 49
Multi-ethnic Education (ILEA), 52–3